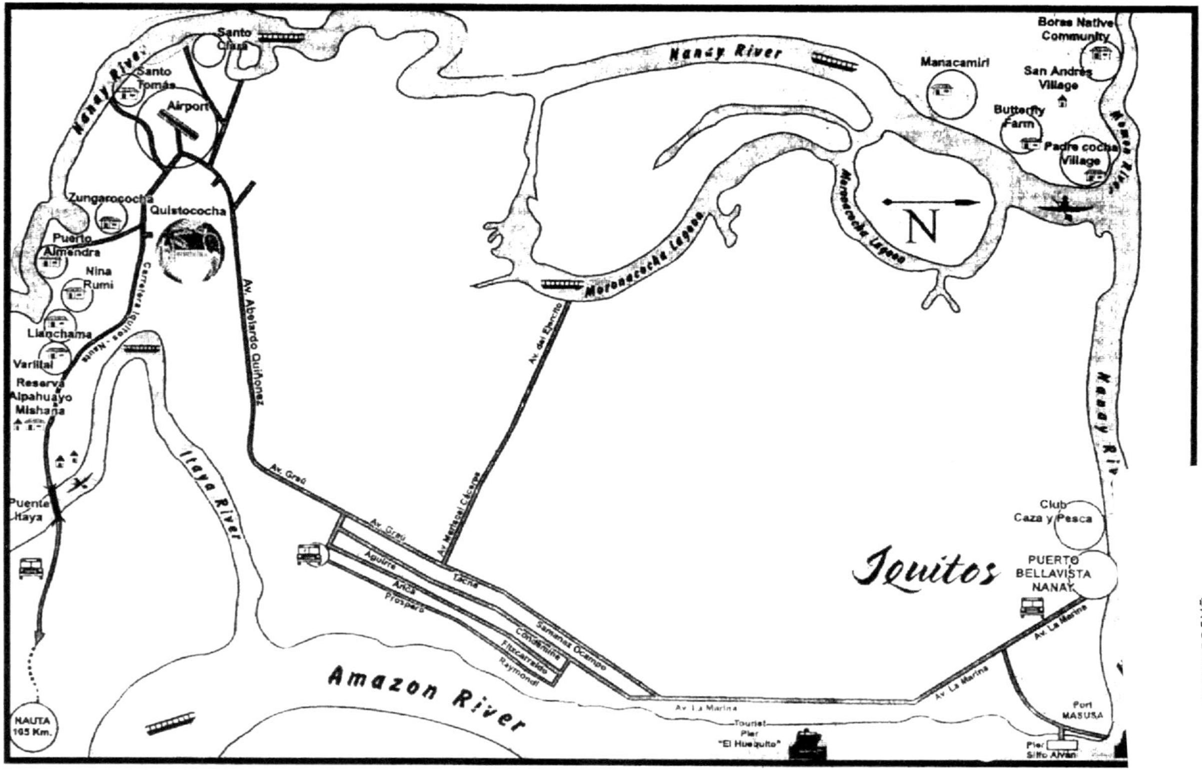

Map of villages, ports and rivers around Iquitos

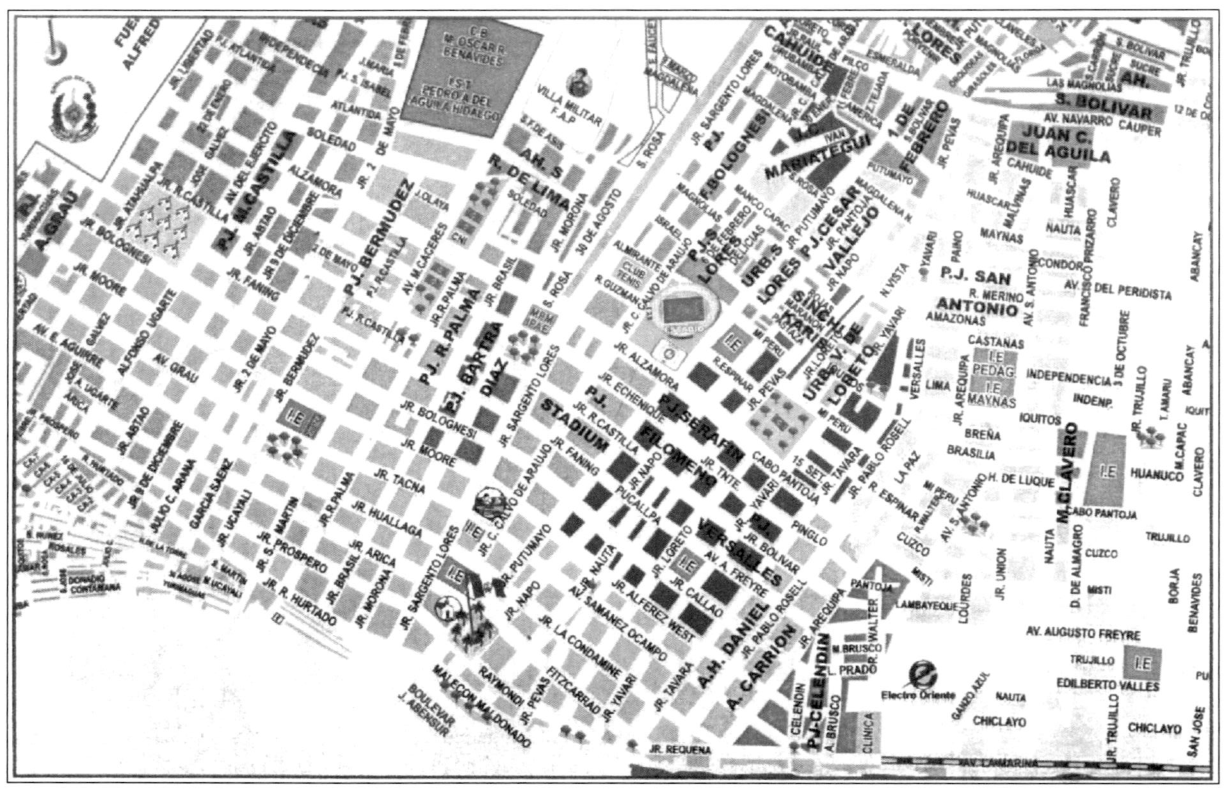

Street Map – Iquitos Centre

"Dawn on the Amazon"

Iquitos today – Plaza de Armas (kind courtesy César A. Vega)

Brigantine Próspero – historically reached Iquitos in 1864 on its maiden voyage (and gave its name to the main city thoroughfare)

IQUITOS

GATEWAY TO AMAZONIA

(The Alternative Travel Guide)

John Lane

John Lane

October 2014
(Fifth Edition)

John Lane
London

For Bella, without whom this book would never have happened.

Iquitos - Gateway to Amazonia (The Alternative Travel Guide)

First Published : June 2001
Second Edition : May 2006
Third Edition : February 2010
Fourth Edition : July 2012
Fifth Edition : October 2014

Published by John Lane (www.johnlanebooks.com) in collaboration with Bella Lane

A CIP catalogue record for this title is available from the British Library

ISBN 978-0-9566622-0-0

Printed and bound in Great Britain by
Witley Press, Hunstanton, Norfolk.
www.witleypress.co.uk

***Cover Picture**: Last of the Iquitos railway steam locomotives (All current photography by **Bella Lane**, except where indicated)*

Contents

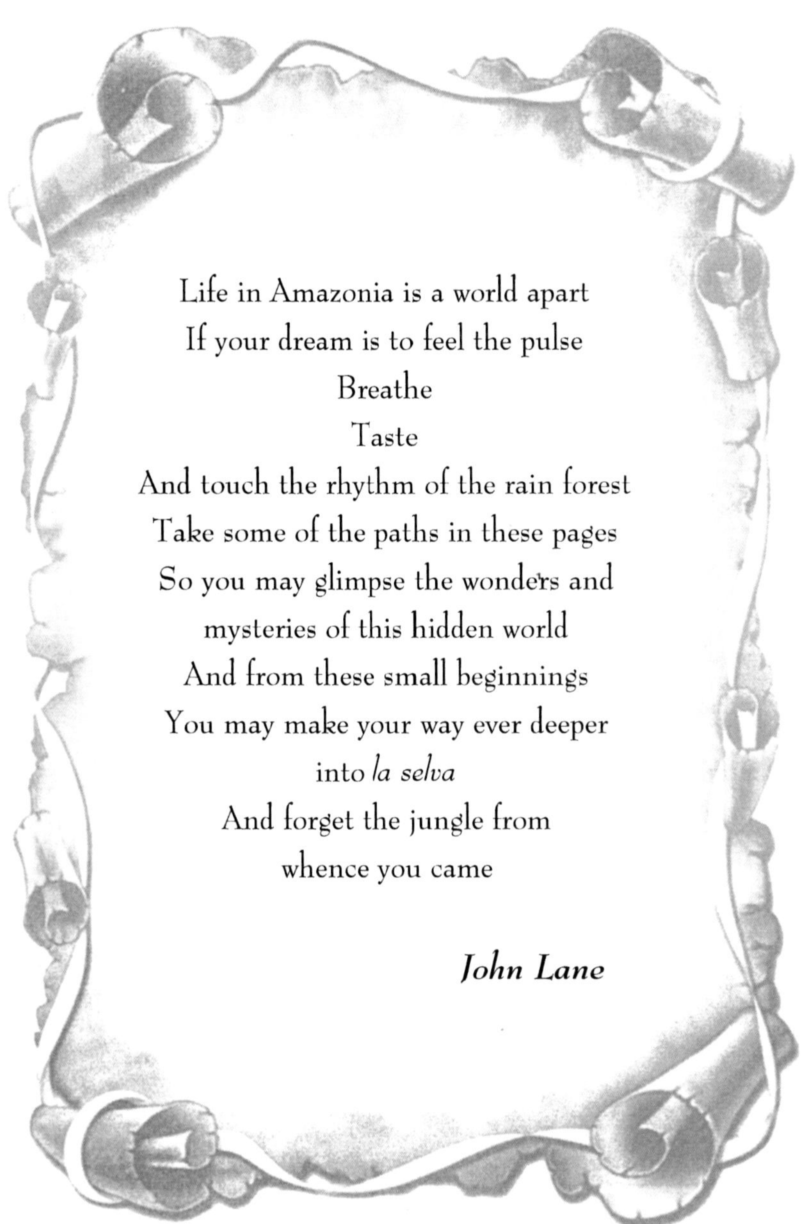

Life in Amazonia is a world apart
If your dream is to feel the pulse
Breathe
Taste
And touch the rhythm of the rain forest
Take some of the paths in these pages
So you may glimpse the wonders and
mysteries of this hidden world
And from these small beginnings
You may make your way ever deeper
into *la selva*
And forget the jungle from
whence you came

John Lane

Life in Amazonia

Requena River Front

Section I
Getting Orientated

"If not now, when?"

The Region of Loreto - Amazonia

The Department of Loreto in north-eastern Perú covers nearly 30% of the national territory, and has a recorded population (2012) of 1,000,100 (one million and one hundred) – in the First Edition of this book the 2001 estimated population of the region was half a million. The estimated overall population of Perú has now surpassed 30 million, with well over one third of this figure concentrated in the capital city of Lima, resulting in markedly differing population densities across the country. The Department of Loreto contains the following Provinces: Maynas (capital – Iquitos); Alto Amazonas (capital – Yurimaguas); Loreto (capital – Nauta); Requena (capital – Requena); Ucayali (capital – Contamana); Ramón Castilla (capital – Ramón Castilla). To which list must now (2005) be added the Province of Datem del Marañon (formerly part of Alto Amazonas), capital San Lorenzo.

The word 'Loreto' (loosely meaning 'wild laurel wood') is sometimes said to have no clear etymological derivation; however, if we go to the Latin, and hence *lauretum/laureta*, the rest is simple. Whatever, the name was brought to Amazonia from Italy by the intrepid Jesuit missionaries of the Seventeenth and Eighteenth Centuries, in particular by *Padre* Samuel Fritz who worked from 1686 to 1723 'among the Indians of the Amazon forests' and who died here in 1730 at the age of eighty. Father Fritz (originally from Bohemia, Czechoslovakia), who founded the *reduccion* or settlement of Loreto in the north east of the region, was not only an ardent proselytiser but also an eminent and indefatigable cartographer of international repute. Confusingly, 'his' Loreto is now in Colombia.[1]

---

[1] *El santuario Mariano de Loreto/La Santa Casa* (The Sanctuary of the Virgin Mary) is one of the most important in Italy (see also *La Virgen de Loreto*). In the thirteenth century the house in Nazareth where Mary received word of her impending birth of Jesus was miraculously transported by angels to Loreto in Italy overlooking the Adriatic Sea when threatened with destruction by the Moorish invasion of the Holy Land.

As a final historical aside, the 1896 Insurrection in Loreto had as its declared aim the founding of an autonomous federal state. However, the uprising (which extended as far as the townships of Moyobamba and Yurimaguas) was swiftly put down by the President of the day, Nicholás de Piérola, who despatched troops from Lima by way of Huánuco to Pozuzo, and thence via the rivers Pichis, Perené and Ucayali to the Amazon. Nonetheless, one outcome of the rebellion was the transfer of the official capital of Loreto from Moyobamba to Iquitos, thus further consolidating its position as the political and economic centre of the region.

Notwithstanding the advent of GPS, **maps** are still invaluable for tracing the rivers through Loreto and beyond, together with locating towns in the general region. Street vendors may well pass by with the answer to your needs, but otherwise *Librería Bazar Almafra* (*Jr.* Arica 321) has an excellent map of Loreto, and a comprehensive Iquitos street map. If you are visiting one of the jungle lodges, you will find that many of the *albergue* brochures contain useful town and river maps, and most of the lodge offices contain helpful large scale charts of the area. Plus, of course, the Internet …

Iquitos and Immediate Environs

To supplement the maps in this book, street maps of Iquitos and of the closely adjacent rivers (Amazon, Itaya, Momón and Nanay) are also available free from the Tourist Office and Iperú (see below). For serious orientation and an overview of the slightly complicated local river pattern, a large scale map measuring 115cm x 77cm can be bought for S/.15.00 from the *Centro Artesanal* at 572 Próspero. If all else fails, there is a map of the centre of the city of Iquitos in the *Telefónica* directory.

Nuts & Bolts

The Iquitos Tourist Office was formerly centrally situated in the Plaza de Armas at 236 Napo (and hoping to return when long-term refurbishment/rebuilding is completed); then they moved to the corner of Loreto/Raymondi, and now they are back on Jirón Napo, this time just up from the river, first block, No.161 next to Ari's Burgers, telephone/fax (065) 236144/260251, (e-mail: iperuiquitos@promperu.gob.pe), open 0830 – 1930, seven days a week . There is also a sub-office at Iquitos Airport which is staffed to cover incoming flights.

Iquitos Tourist Week is now celebrated in September (various dates have been tried over the years); the Feast of Saint John the Baptist on 24th June

prompts a week long fiesta with bands, dancing and local cuisine in the eponymous district of San Juan (a few kilometres from the city centre). The annual anniversary of the Founding of the City (5th January) is also the occasion for parades, concerts and other events, whilst Noche Buena and el Año Nuevo are marked in the ultra-effervescent and uninhibited style of the region.

Las Fiestas Patrias

The principal language of Perú is Spanish (*Castellano*); the second official language of the country is Quechua, the mother tongue of the Incas. In the Amazon rain forest many separate and distinct languages are spoken (originally purportedly in excess of 300), some still unwritten and now 'endangered', i.e. less than 5,000 speakers. The number of surviving languages across the Amazon Basin is probably around 70 nowadays.

The currency of Perú is Nuevos Soles, which replaced the Inti in 1991 (100 centimos to one Nuevo Sol, or S/.1.00). As ever, exchange rates fluctuate; to get the latest US dollar and pound sterling official rates, buy a newspaper (e.g. El Comercio) or visit www.xe.com or www.oanda.com.

To change the distances given in kilometres in this booklet to miles, multiply by 5 and divide by 8. Conversely, for changing miles to kilometres, multiply by 8 and divide by 5. Hectares to acres? Multiply by 2.47. Acres to hectares? Divide by 0.4047.

The office of Iperú (*Información y Asistencia al Turista* – Tourism Information and Assistance) is integrated with the Tourist Office now at *Jirón* Napo No.161, and in the Airport, telephone numbers (065)236144/260251. The 24hr helpline for travellers with any problems encountered regarding tourist services in Perú is (01)-574 8000. See also www.peru.travel; email: iperuiquitos@promperu.gob.pe

The present **British Honorary Consul** in Iquitos is Mr Joseph Plumb (San José Street #113 Second Floor, Punchana – Monday to Friday 0800-0930 and 1700-1830 (E-mail: joseph.plumb@fconet.fco.gov.uk) (telephone: 065-253364/cel:997517127). There is also an **American Citizens Services Representative** (US Warden of Iquitos) – see local newspapers for details.

The **Iquitos Times** and the **Amazon News** (normally produced monthly – available free in most hotels and hostels) are both good sources of information for visitors on local happenings, events, services and activities.

It is a *sine qua non* that nowadays almost all the organisations, tour operators, hotels, lodges and so forth mentioned herein have dedicated websites. The majority of these are listed in the text in parenthesis, but should this not be the case, *Google* or somesuch will assuredly do the necessary.

Belén market scenes

Section II
Familiarisation

"There is only one perfect road,
And that road is ahead of you,
Always ahead of you."

Iquitos – Profile

The so-called 'jungle-city' of Iquitos lies on Latitude 3 degrees 45 minutes South of the Equator, Longitude 73 degrees 14 minutes East of the Greenwich meridian, in the centre of the department of Loreto, Perú. The time zone is GMT -6. The height above sea level is variously given as being 104 metres, 122.4 metres and 130 metres; perhaps it is simplest to settle for an altitude of 'little more than 300 feet', which is easy to remember and is not very high considering that Iquitos is 3,084 km (1,928 miles) from the Atlantic Ocean (which gives an average gradient of 3.25cms per km, thus accounting for the meandering nature of the river Amazon). Iquitos is 1,859 km from Lima.

Along the eastern side to the north eastern point of the city is the river Amazon (Iquitos being on the left bank); from the southern side of Iquitos runs the river Nanay, curving round along the western extremity to link with the Amazon on the northern side. To the south east of the city is the river Itaya which runs into the Amazon on the eastern side. Consequently Iquitos is almost, but not quite, an island. There are happily (as yet) no bridges across any of these extensive stretches of water[2], in spite of talk of spanning the Nanay to link the townships of Indiana and Mazan with the city by road (the latter being on the river Napo, and thus facilitating the route through to Ecuador). Some would also have us believe that the 'island city' is 'floating', and that one day it may well sink from sight. This is unlikely to happen during your visit.

Ethnically the Loretano inhabitants of Iquitos (current population estimated to be in excess of 400,000 and fast approaching half a million – Perú's sixth largest city) are principally descendants of the former

---

[2] Nor indeed are there any bridges over the Amazon for its entire length

communities (tribes) of the Amazon rain forest[3] and in many cases, mixed (mestizo) descendants of the Spanish settlers of the colonial era. On account of their environment it has been said that the dwellers of the forest are a people who are 'serene, profound and contemplative.'

There is as yet no overland road route to Iquitos (thank goodness, as it would surely destroy the unique character of the city) – although there are speculative, ill-founded plans to address this (commercially attractive; ecologically disastrous). At present, the nearest you can get by road from Lima is Pucallpa (a long way to the south), after which you must take to the river Ucayali for between two and five days. In fact, access to Iquitos is generally via the rivers, principally the Amazon, or by air (one and a half hours from Lima; 50 minutes from Tarapoto; one hour from Pucallpa, all on scheduled services – *Lan Perú, Star Perú, Peruvian Airlines* etc – or by irregular float planes e.g. *Alas al Oriente, alasoriente@hotmail.com* on *Calle* Requena 349 or *North American Float Plane Services* at Napo 253, tel.221028). Interesting to recall that just one hundred years ago it was written: 'The river port of Iquitos is from 30 to 40 days journey from Lima under existing means of travel'.

Apart from being the administrative centre of Loreto, Iquitos serves as the Departmental entrepôt for the import of practically all the consumer goods and machinery on sale in the region, and for the export of timber down river through Brazil. Iquitos is the launch pad not only for most regional tourism but also for much of the oil exploration being conducted in Amazonia. The first oil well in South America was drilled as long ago as 1863 at Zorritos (Tumbes), Perú. Ironically, and by chance, it was one of the former rubber magnates of Loreto who came across traces of oil near Contamana (river Ucayali, downstream from Pucallpa) in 1917, the resultant confirmatory analysis leading to the first search for oil in the Amazon basin during the years 1922 to 1930.

Petroperú was formed some 45 years ago, on 24th July 1969; the first successful drilling at Trompeteros (river Corrientes, NW of the province) was achieved on 16th November 1971, leading to the establishment of other wells.

---

[3] Who themselves – according to some theories – are of Asiatic origin, having travelled from Siberia and beyond at a time very long ago, before the bridgehead through Alaska was broken by the Bering Strait

Construction of the Petroperú refinery 14kms from the city dates from October 1980. It opened 2 years later, replacing the original and then obsolete 1955 refinery and currently processing some 7,000 barrels daily to fulfil the needs of the region, with a capacity of 10,500 barrels (one barrel = 35 Imperial gallons or 42 US gallons). A crude-oil duct runs from the well-heads, such as those of Pavayacu, Capirona and Trompeteros, across the Andes to Bayovar on the coast of Piura (*Punta Aguja*), totalling more than 1,300kms of pipeline. The epic story of oil exploration and extraction in the Amazon Basin is as yet still in its opening chapters (see **Section VII** for further details).

Loreto is contiguous with Ecuador to the north west, Columbia to the north east and Brazil to the south east. Iquitos is the Amazon base of the Peruvian Navy, whose illustrious and fascinating history in Amazonia is recounted later in **Section VII**; there are also bases here for Land and Air forces, plus a US counter-narcotics presence. The Armed Forces of the Republic have been central to the defence and development of the region since Independence, getting on for 200 years ago (28th July 1821).

Geographical Digression

Before the prehistoric cataclysm that formed the Peruvian Andes, geological studies indicate that the majority of the rivers of the South American continent flowed westward into the Pacific Ocean. Since that time, and the arrival of the vast dividing mountain range, two currents were formed, one westward of short fast-flowing rivers, the other eastward to drain the vast lake that is now referred to as the Amazon basin. It was the latter flow that became the immense fluvial web that we know today, with the mighty Amazon being the main artery, fed by an estimated 1,400 tributaries. Resorting to a somewhat algebraic form of expression (and without tying too many knots and resultant tangles), the principal network of major rivers that conjointly form the Amazon from its source beyond Cusco may perhaps be portrayed thus: Urubamba (+ Yavero + Camisea + Picha) + Tambo (+ Ene + Apurimac) = Ucayali; Ucayali (+ Pachitea) + Marañon (+ Pastaza + Huallaga + Tigre) = Amazon. QED.

It is said that the volume of water in the river Amazon is greater than that of the next eight largest rivers in the world combined, and is three times the flow of all the rivers in the USA, so that more than one hundred miles into the Atlantic Ocean off the Amazon delta the water is still fresh, rather than salty. Indigenous native villagers with diverse customs are thought to have inhabited the river banks of the region and the deep forest since 20,000BC (and only

"Discovery of the Amazon by Francisco de Orellana 1542" – municipal mural by César Calvo de Araujo

"Foundation of Iquitos Town with the arrival of Navy ships 1864" – a second Araujo mural in sore need of restoration (and sadly two of the original four ships have been painted out)

now, with the innate stupidity and greed of modern mankind, is it being proposed to dam the river Amazon – witness the nine billion dollar Belo Monte hydro-electricity project in Brazil which will flood an area of 506 square kilometres, displace between 50 and 60 thousand indigenous people, and which will cause untold gross and lasting environmental damage to the greatest and most majestic river on the planet).[4]

A Brief History of Iquitos

Until 2010, on the north eastern side of the Plaza de Armas in Iquitos stood an imposing yellow building marked *Municipalidad de Maynas, Iquitos*, which up to the late 1990's was home to all the municipal administrative offices (now re-located in the Plaza Sargento Lores). Now, a new building is supposedly earmarked to re-house the highly helpful Iperú and Tourist Offices. Previously on the ground floor was an under-visited (and under-maintained) exhibition (alternating with various art displays) of old sepia photographs of Iquitos as it was 100 years ago (now re-hung in the 'new' Municipal Library at *Parque Zonal* and well worth seeing), and on the first floor was the Museum of Natural Science.

On the second floor, in the finely proportioned chandelier-hung *grand salon* (which became sadly derelict and ended in terminal decay), were two huge murals executed by **César Calvo de Araujo**. One painting depicted 'The discovery of the Amazon River by the Spanish Conqueror Francisco de Orellana 1542' and the other was entitled 'Foundation of Iquitos Town with the arrival of Navy ships sent from Lima by Marshal Ramón Castilla in 1864'. The valuable murals, peeling badly through lack of care and now precariously reinforced, were removed more or less intact in 2010 with the assistance of a German company – a remarkable feat of civil engineering – to rest on a bespoke welded metal support frame some six metres high in a purpose-built store shed *almacen* at *Parque Zonal* for eventual restoration and relocation of the resultant massive slabs of masonry, which surely weigh some ten tons apiece. Pending that happy day, they are photographed, reproduced and uniquely preserved for posterity herein. Together, these two pictures neatly encapsulate the origins of Iquitos from the European perspective. And if you

---

[4] For greater understanding of the havoc wrought by such schemes (and incidentally, the negative role played by the World Bank), read 'Kalabagh Dam – Weapon of Mass Destruction' by Arundati Roy, Farooq Sulehria and Aziz Narejo, published January 2006 by Jeddojuhd, Lahore

now visit the Municipal Library you will solve the conundrum of how the 'Navy ships' supposedly found their way from Lima on the Pacific *costa* over the towering barrier of the Andes to the Amazon – see also Section VII herein: Peruvian Navy.[5]

Reverting to the 'discovery' of the Amazon, the expedition instigated by *Conquistador* Francisco Pizarro (retired pig farmer, and first Governor of colonial Perú following the defeat of the Incas at Cajamarca in 1532) to explore the fabled region then referred to as *El Dorado* (and which became the Department of Loreto in 1861), set out from Cusco under the command of his brother Gonzalo Pizarro in 1539. In the process of travelling through Ayacucho, Jauja, Huánuco, Lima, Trujillo and onwards through Piura to Quito (*sic*, capital of Ecuador) and then east following the navigable portion of the river Napo, the 200 Spanish explorers and 3,000 indigenous supporters encountered many hardships, suffering hunger and sickness, prompting Gonzalo Pizarro to send a small party ahead in search of food and succour. This group led by **Francisco de Orellana**, and assisted by friendly natives, came to the River Amazon on 12th February 1542, the spot being marked today by the town of that name at the junction of the two rivers, the Napo and the Amazon (see **Section V**). Prevented (regrettably) from returning to the main body of the expedition by the adverse current, Francisco de Orellana subsequently continued downstream all the way to the Atlantic Ocean.

Three hundred and nine years later, on 23rd October 1851, the Peruvian Brazilian Agreement was signed (Perú having achieved Independence from Spain in 1821) determining the free navigation of the Great Amazon River to the sea (the Friendship, Trade and Navigation Treaty). This Declaration in turn prompted President Ramón Castilla to 'create the Military Political Department of Loreto' on 7th January 1861 and to order 'the construction of four steam ships, a dockyard and a navy *factorage* from England to be installed at some point of the Amazon river.' The exact 'point' on the Amazon was at that moment uncertain, with Tamshiyacu, Nauta and Francisco de Orellana all being considered. However, the strategic position of Iquitos was deemed to be superior and on 5th January 1864 the steam ships of the Peruvian Navy duly started to arrive at Iquitos Village. First came the 'Morona' and 'Pastaza' of

---

[5] Interestingly Araujo's painting only contains two ships; originally there were four, but two were unfortunately obliterated in process of an ill-conducted 'restoration' that went awry a few years ago. This explains the empty expanse of river now present in the picture ...

Examples of the 'azulejos' tiles from Portugal to be found in Iquitos decorating buildings of the rubber boom epoch

A "draga" (dredger) which scours and sifts the river bed in the search for gold, often unlicensed and illegal – yet another way of destroying the eco-system of the region

500 and 300 tons, and then two smaller steam boats of 50 tons, the 'Napo' and the 'Putumayo' (as recorded in the previously mentioned Municipal mural by César Calvo de Araujo), to be followed soon afterwards by the floating dock and the machinery for the factory. Today, Alzamora Street commemorates the name of the senior Captain of that naval expedition (which amazingly voyaged all the way across the Atlantic from Deptford on the river Thames), as does the plaque marking the site of the former naval factory on Malecón Tarapacá.

[Folklore has it in some quarters that the procurement of these – and previous – naval vessels for the Peruvian Navy from shipyards in Great Britain accustomed to building warships for the Royal Navy for centuries, saw the introduction of the ***hammock*** *to the rain forest. This in turn is said to have led to its subsequent very rapid and widespread adoption throughout the region and beyond. However, this whimsical hypothesis, plausible enough in itself, is belied by the existence of fibre hammocks (for example, made from Chambira palm) that are held to pre-date these events. There again, with the shelf life of a 'natural' hammock crafted from forest vines being measured at most in tens rather than hundreds of years, the conflicting evidence is at best inconclusive ...]*

However, between the salient dates of 1542 and 1864, proselytising Jesuit and Franciscan missionaries were active in forming the Iquito natives into groups or *reducciones*. The *reduccion* named Santa Bárbara de Iquitos was on the bank of what is now called the Nanay river, formerly inhabited by the Napeanos – and called **San Pablo de los Napeanos** – but later named Iquitos Village due to the preponderance of Iquito. The date often given for the founding of this riverside Jesuit settlement is 1757, although more properly it should be attributed to Jesuit *Padre* Pablo Maroni in May of 1729, with the first population census recording 81 people in 1808, rising to 200 in 1840. Since that time the pace of expansion accelerated, so that on 9th November 1897 Iquitos became the capital of the department of Loreto, during the Presidency of Nicolás de Piérola, partly in consequence of the Loretan Insurrection of 1896 (mentioned in Section I), but also as a result of the exceptional commercial development and the population explosion flowing from the rubber boom (see under).

[Entymological snippet contributed by Sr.Usiel of Aqua Expeditions: 'When the first "Westerners" came to Iquitos they not only threatened the traditional way of life of the indigenous people but also brought with them an

assortment of previously unknown diseases. As in other parts of Perú, the locals had no inheritance of immunity and were particularly vulnerable; the newcomers were therefore synonymous with sickness and many of the Iquito tribe moved away further up river. They named their new settlement "Nan-nay", meaning "sadness" in the Iquito tongue, and hence nowadays we have el río Nanay.']

The year 1905 saw the introduction of the first electric lights in Iquitos and in 1912 a wireless telegraphy link with Lima was inaugurated. These innovations were soon to be followed by the first paved roads and the introduction of piped water supplies and main drainage. All this practically in the lifetime, if not within the memory, of the city's current oldest inhabitants. As for the phenomenon of the rubber boom, at its height between 1880 and 1912 (a span of hardly more than 30 years), its effect on Iquitos merits separate attention.

The Rubber Boom

Awareness of the existence of 'elastic rubber' (*caucho, jebe, balata, gutapercha)* is as old as the discovery of the Americas (was it by Christopher Columbus in 1492 or by the Chinese in 1421?): the Aztecs and the Mayan Indians played games using rubber balls and traces of *caucho* have been found in the cloths used by the Incas. In 1870, at about the time that the French scientist and Amazon traveller Carlos de la Condamine was sending the first *jebe* (latex) samples back to Europe, the population of Iquitos was perhaps 1,500. Meanwhile on the other side of the globe in the decade of the 1870's, ever-increasing industrialisation in Europe and advancing technology, including commercialisation of Mr Goodyear's 'invention' of the process of vulcanisation (the addition of white lead and sulphur to the latex - discovered in the USA in 1839, patented in Britain by Hanncock in 1843) and the later development of Mr Dunlop's pneumatic tyre, created an unprecedented demand for *cauchuc*, obtainable from the rubber trees of the rain forest.

As ever, entrepreneurs were quick to move and, according to some accounts, by the 1880's Iquitos had over 20,000 inhabitants, although more conservative estimates cite only half this number. Foremost amongst whom were the legendary 'rubber barons,' aptly named on account of their fantastic wealth which led to all manner of extravagances (such as supposedly sending the weekly wash to be laundered in Europe to avoid contamination of the fine linens of the households by the muddy river water)[6] and other more flagrant and lurid excesses, even including for a brief period of two years the printing of their own private currency, a few examples of the notes still surviving over a century later and much sought after by collectors.

The downside to these three decades of opulence and the legacy of fine houses constructed almost exclusively of materials shipped in from the other side of the Atlantic[7], was the brutal exploitation of the forest Indians who, as a result of their local knowledge and skills, became both the locators and tappers of the *jebe* rubber trees ("the wood that weeps") in conditions of abject slavery. Indeed, great fortunes are rarely amassed without exploitation of one kind or another, and those accruing from the rubber boom were no exception, as vividly reported by W.E. Hardenberg at the time in '*Putumayo – The Devil's Paradise*'(1912), and also graphically later related by Richard Collier in his book *'The River that God Forgot'* (1968). It is conservatively estimated that up to a quarter of a million indigenous people lost their lives/were killed during the 'boom' era. In 1911 a commission of enquiry initiated by the British Foreign Office concluded that in the territory of Putumayo alone over the preceding five years the population of forest Indians (principally Huitotos, Boras, Andokes and Ocainas) had fallen from 50,000 to 8,000.

Behind the scenes, the end of the era was in sight almost before it had begun. In 1876 an unlikely expatriate Englishman named Henry Alexander Wickham, self-proclaimed pioneer living on the Amazon at Santarem, was commissioned by the British Government (via Sir Clements Markham, President of the Royal Geographical Society, and formerly an officer in the Royal Navy) to procure 70,000 seeds of the wild Brazilian rubber tree (at the time rubber of varying quality was being harvested with mixed success from around 100 different trees and plants). This was duly done, and the clandestinely obtained seeds of *Hevea braziliensis* were propagated at the Royal Botanical Gardens in Kew, London, under the aegis of the Director,

---

6 One of the more curious manifestations of the time was a clamour for 'English Toffees'; the obsession spread to the rest of Peru, and to some extent persists even to this day.

7 Italian marble; wrought ironwork for balustrades, gates and staircases from industrial Victorian England; Portuguese hand-painted decorative azulejos tiles.

Dr Joseph Hooker. Fewer than 3,000 grew but it was enough and the plants were sent to South East Asia where they flourished, surpassing the output of the previously cultivated indigenous Assam rubber tree, *Ficus elastica*. Such was the impact of the coup that Wickham was knighted in 1920 for 'services rendered to the plantation industry'.

The abuses of the rubber boom

Thus the Amazon bubble burst with sudden finality 37 years after Wickham's heist, when in consequence the next generation of global entrepreneurs (the noteworthy British explorer Markham again took the initiative in this context) created orderly rubber plantations in the British colony of Malaya (now part of Malaysia), successfully producing plentiful latex more economically and more competitively than the ad hoc arrangements prevailing in the Amazon rain forest. In 1902 a kilo of *caucho* fetched *Intis Soles* 2.00; by 1911 the price had risen to S/.6.00; by mid-1914 top grade Amazon rubber had fallen to less than one sol per kilo (two shillings and ninepence a pound), and by 1932 the market price of a kilo had collapsed to S/.0.45. The short-lived bonanza was well and truly over, with 1913 marking the year when the majority of the 'barons' hastily sold up as best they could and abandoned Iquitos (and Manaus) as quickly as they had arrived. Many families were bankrupted by the crisis, which was nothing short of disastrous, and suicides were not uncommon, the lavish properties and attendant luxury goods previously imported from Europe being auctioned daily at giveaway prices. The population of Iquitos fell dramatically almost overnight, although the 1940 census shows that by that time the city had recovered to over 30,000 inhabitants.

The opulence of that period, which was for some a 'golden era' (and which, as indicated, extended as far as Manaus in Brazil), is unlikely ever to be repeated, although revenues from oil, other mineral deposits and tourism undoubtedly have the potential to bring economic prosperity to the region and its people. In turn, that prosperity, properly husbanded and applied, could provide the necessary resources to safeguard the rich natural and historical inheritance of Loreto.

The rubber boom has left an indelible mark on the city of Iquitos and in the coming pages the legacy of that epoch will be encountered many times. In 1961 the City Hall of Maynas formed a Commission to resolve the vexed question of the date of the founding of the settlement. The year was finally agreed as being **1864** and President Fernando Belaúnde promulgated Law N.14702 in 1963 declaring the official date for the founding of Iquitos as the First Fluvial Port to be **5th January 1864.** This date is now celebrated annually with civic parades and festivities as the Iquitos Anniversary, the 150th Anniversary on 5th January 2014 having been a particularly vibrant occasion with huge crowds thronging the Malecon for the firework display, music and other events and historic re-enactments.

Iquitos Today

Colour, bustle and an over-abundance of *motocarros*[8], the raucous 3-wheeled motor taxis: these are the first impressions of Iquitos. Families riding on motor bikes, four or even five to a machine, ladies sitting precariously side-saddle, feet dangling inches from the tarmac. Crash helmets have yet to find their way to Iquitos; the Loretanos are waiting for the introduction of air-

---

[8] Some 25,000 – and counting; described by one newcomer as: 'candy-coloured motorcycle-pulled carriages'. When crossing the road at night, beware the vogue for putting red lights on the front of these vehicles, as well as at the rear.

conditioned safety helmets, even hard hats packed with dry ice or helmets that you can charge in the fridge during the night and then use in cool comfort during the day (patent pending).

Competing with the ubiquitous *motocarros* (check your insurance before using and know that the tariff for most in-town journeys should be no more than between S/.1.50 and S/.2.50; however, recently an unofficial 'minimum fare' of S/.2.00 seems to have crept in, so be sure agree the price before boarding, tips not expected) are the brightly coloured Toytown truncated antique-looking *autobuses* (the modern chassis for these originate in Korea and Japan, the body work and wooden panelled interiors were made locally in various workshops, many dating from circa 1960). The buses are somewhat slower than the *motocarros* but easier on the nerves with a standard tariff (currently) of one *sol* (S/.1.00 plus a bit on holidays). The colours of the buses relate both to the different operating companies and to the destinations, but for the absent-minded and un-informed they (usually) display a route indicator board alongside the driver, and you can always ask the *cobrador* (conductor) for confirmation. There are few formal bus-stops: picking up and setting down depend on the needs of the passengers (except when there are police at the road-side; then you may expect to travel one block more than you intended). With all this traffic intent on playing dodgem cars, the roads of Iquitos are inclined to be slightly frenetic (and sadly but seemingly inevitably, traffic jams have at last reached the city – previously unheard of), but in general life in the city and environs is tranquil and unhurried, even sleepy.

The Casonas of the Caucheros

At first superficial glance, Iquitos appears to be architecturally undistinguished but those making time to look beyond the buildings of the last 30 or 40 years to identify the former grand houses of the *caucheros* (the rubber barons) will be well rewarded (eg see Malecón Tarapacá below). In fact, given sufficient time you should be able to find no less than 80 (some claim as many as 120) of these bye gone mansions, all marked with a hopeful preservation plaque reading '*Patrimonio de la Nación.*'

To get started you could visit the following:

***Casa* Cohen** (401-437 Próspero): a building of one floor built in 1905 and decorated with pilasters ending in Corinthian capitals that support the cornices and friezes. The façade is faced with glazed tiles (*azulejos* from Portugal or Spain) of different colours. The sheer size of this residence illustrates the extent of the personal fortunes that were amassed during the rubber boom. The building now houses 'Los Portales' supermarket and a number of other shops. Opposite Cohen's House, at **402-418 Próspero**, is another heritage edifice with filigree ironwork from England and faced with fine tiles, until recently the Evangelical College and now for sale. On the third corner of Morona with Próspero (**No.383)** is another heritage house for the collection.

***Casa* Pinasco** (129-169 Próspero, in the centre of the south eastern side of the Plaza de Armas, next to *Casa de Fierro*): built in the first decade of the 20th century at the peak of the rubber boom by the Pinasco family who came from Italy. The façade of this grandiose building is in the English neo-classical style (see 1910 photograph reproduced herein). Nowadays it is home to a fast food outlet and to **Giornatta**, where an exotic range of ice creams is on sale with all the flavours of the fruits of the forest – and more.

***Casa* Morey** (413-429 Raymondi/200-234 Loreto): Previously the private University of Iquitos; closed and abandoned for three years, now fully restored as a bijou hotel and very much a heritage gem (see *Plaza Ramón Castilla*), with several notable period pictures and fascinating artefacts on display. Architecturally, two floors with a balcony of forged iron, the façade with flat pilasters, built in the first decade of the 20th Century with materials imported from Europe by the Morey family, including the *azulejos* glazed tiles, the friezes and the neo-classical elements.

[The pre-eminent founding father of the Morey dynasty was the legendary Adolfo Morey Arias, whose father came from the Balearics and his mother from Ecuador, who was born in 1862 and brought up in Chachapoyas. After service in the War of the Pacific against Chile, having enlisted in 1879 at the age of 17 years, he moved first to Tarapoto where he farmed without great success, and then to Yurimaguas where he traded in tobacco and straw hats. On arrival in Iquitos around 1900 he started a trading house and steamship company – Adolfo Morey and Sons – providing a regular service for cargo and passengers to Yurimaguas, and also for external trade to Belém on the Amazon delta through Manaus. With a flotilla of vessels ('Arias', 'Morey', 'Adolfo', 'Iquitos', 'Yurimaguas', 'Estefita') constructed in shipyards in England, Germany and France this network swiftly expanded to ply all the navigable rivers of the Peruvian forest region and to serve all the river ports therein.

Prosperity continued unabated until the fall in the price of the rubber latex and the onset of the First World War in 1914. Undeterred, Sr. Morey quickly re-shaped his business, conceiving the idea of providing a steamship service between Iquitos and Lima via Belém, utilising the Panama Canal to reach Callao. He inaugurated this venture personally in 1918 onboard the 'Yurimaguas' of 200 tons, voyaging across the Caribbean to reach the Pacific Ocean and thence proceeding due south, a journey of some two months. An indefatigable pioneer of river navigation, Sr. Morey also travelled to Europe and the USA; in 1929 he added three more passenger vessels to his fleet and in 1930 was decorated with the award of the Peruvian Order of the Sun in official recognition of his endeavours. He died in 1943 whilst actually on the wheel of one his ships (appropriately the 'Morey') at Belém at the age of 81 and was buried in that city. In 1952 his remains were repatriated from Brazil and now rest in the family tomb in the Iquitos cemetery.

*As a final footnote, the steam vessel 'Estefita', which is mentioned above and was one of the original Morey & Sons flotilla, worked on the rivers Napo and Putumayo. In 1911 she accompanied the Peruvian naval gunboat 'America' to take part in the dramatic action in la Pedrera against the Colombians on 10th, 11th and 12th July of that year, ferrying troops and munitions in support of the successful operation (see under **Plaza Clavero** for details). Still in service 40 years later, she sank just off the port of Iquitos on 11th November 1951.]*

Returning to the subject of the great mansions of those who made their transient fortunes during the rubber boom, buildings of similar provenance can be found throughout the centre of the city, and with practice and familiarity it becomes increasingly easy to spot them (although beware of imposters). For example:

141-149 Sargento Lores. Formerly Barcia's House, now the local taxation office, distinguished by its arches and balconies and the façade of beautiful glazed tiles in 'Art Nouveau' style with figures in white, violet, green and orange.

263 Nauta. The Union Amazonica Lodge, neighbouring the Hotel Marañon. An imposing columned building in classical style with the four Doric supporting pillars on the ground floor being repeated on the second. The doors and windows are surmounted and supported by mouldings and pilasters. Built as a place of worship and inaugurated on 5th January 1908, there was reputedly 'a large pelota court in front' (although it is difficult to establish this fanciful observation from the roadside). The architect was **Comandante Romulo Enrique Espinar**, responsible for the first plan for the layout of the city of Iquitos.

234-252 Próspero. Just down from the Plaza de Armas; the ground floors of these two buildings have been mutilated but the upper storeys retain all the familiar architectural hallmarks of the era of the *caucheros.* Across the street is another rich seam of architecture: **237-243** with pale blue *azulejos* tiles, Ionic columns surmounted by 'Corinthian,' marked 'Manuel Santillán 1902' high under the eaves; **247-251** with its mix of balconies and wrought iron balustrades (not so long ago it housed the well-named Manguare Internet *cabina);* **253-259** with its particularly fine tiles.

272 Próspero. Styled as the 'Stock Market' in the records. Built in 1906, the first owners being Mr Manuel Yrujo and Santos Company. (Note that this building and the next two detailed are adjacent and conveniently close to the Plaza de Armas).

278-286 Próspero. One floor of five doors and six pilasters. Currently Bank Wiese Sudameris, the first owner was Sr. Tomas Ramirez.

288-298 Próspero. One floor, doors and windows with the original bars of forged iron, the façade presents pilasters with Corinthian tops. Sr. Santiago L. García Saenz was the first owner and like many other worthies of the day, he also has a street named after him. In spite of the 'heritage' plaque, part of the front of the building has been altered and destroyed (the municipal guardians of the heritage of Iquitos need to wake up to these on-going acts of vandalism).

Próspero is a continuing architectural (and historical) treasure trove, for example: **516-528** marked '1900 – L.F. Morey & Sons,' (the 'R' has dropped off but never mind – this was *Louis Felipe Morey Arias*, born 1854 in Tarapoto and elder brother of *Adolfo* – see above – one of the greatest entrepreneurs of his day whose numerous businesses netted millions of *soles*); the building was formerly a grand residence and trading centre in the manner of the times, with especially fine English ironwork, and surmounted by stone balustrades but now in sad decline.(By the way, on the corner here is the spot to buy your new sun hat or cap, to replace the one you absent-mindedly left in the *lancha*). **589-516** is not only a heritage building but it provides a reminder that Próspero was previously *Jirón* Lima (the plaque on 201 Próspero – now the Reniec offices – records that this re-naming was done on 8th October 1975 at the prompting of the Peruvian Navy, to "return the historic name of Próspero to the principal street of the City," the Jersey-built brigantine 'Próspero' being one of the first ships to arrive in Iquitos, towed by the

Morona in January 1864 – see the rare illustration reproduced on page 4, and also the boxed text in Section VII for more fascinating details on the good ship Próspero); **601-615** – wrought iron filigree balustrades and Corinthian columns on yet another imposing building. And so on (and indeed, whilst you happen to be dissecting Próspero, why not study the intersection with *Calle* Brasil to see if you can identify the hotel wherein Hugo Chavez, late President of Venezuela, took refuge for three months in 1992 following a failed coup attempt in his native country; amongst the fugitive group at that time also happened to be one Nicolás Maduro, the current President of Venezuela).

260-268 Malecón Tarapacá. A beautifully proportioned house of two floors with four doors on the ground floor, ending in arches. The first floor has four rectangular spans on the windows which are decorated with Corinthian capitals. Traditional glazed tiles of the time, and balustrades of forged iron, probably from England. Until fairly recently this fine building, epitome of the period, was the Consulate of Colombia (now to be found at *calle Calvo de Araujo* # 431)[9]; the current occupant is the well-presented **Amazon Bistro.**

302-308 Malecón Tarapacá. Formerly *Casa* Hernández, now the local Peruvian Air Force Command. A handsome building of two floors decorated with a curved and projecting balcony; the customary elegant balustrades are of forged iron from England. There are high flat pilasters with Corinthian capitals on the extravagant glazed tile façade.

170-180 Sargento Lores. Archetypal 'boom' building: two floors, covered with *azulejo* glazed tiles of geometric design; balconies of forged iron with thick supporting cornices. Original owner was Sr. Manuel Rocha; now it is the elegant **Maloca Restaurant**.

200-212 Napo. The so-called 'House of Clay' (read on). Originally the house of **Carlos Fermín Fitzcarrald**, styled as '*Rey del caucho'* and one of the earliest pioneers in the exportation of *caucho* and one of the most controversial and flamboyant of the 'barons.' He was drowned at the age of 36 in 1897 when his new steam boat, the *Adolfito',* fresh from England 'sank in a whirlpool on the river Urubamba and he was trapped asleep in his cabin.' Another account says that 'one of the links on the chain connecting the wheel to the rudder parted, steering was lost and the craft was swept on to a large

[9] Renowned Loretano polymath: see later under **cathedral, Plaza de Armas**

rock which holed the hull. Fitzcarrald, a strong swimmer, tried unsuccessfully in the darkness to save his business partner, **Vaca Diez**, and both perished. When the bodies were recovered days later they were still locked in each other's arms.' Fitzcarrald's former residence is a rare example of a surviving 'adobe' house (clay – principal soil of the Amazon Basin). It has a central arched courtyard and the balcony is wooden with imitation balustrades; in general the style is more reminiscent of the Andes rather than the *selva*. It is recorded that 'the roofs (sic) are made of rustic wood,' although today the roof is unfortunately of rusty corrugated iron. Indications are that the house was built prior to the height of the excesses of the 'boom' when practically all building materials were imported from the other side of the Atlantic, regardless of cost.

Raymondi/Nauta. This junction, with the huge Colegio Fernando Lores (1908) on one corner (recently re-painted in startling green), a fine house of two storeys dated 1936 opposite and another heritage building on the third corner (plaque removed) is the beginning of a rich seam of architectural treasures in Raymondi, including **257-265**, **272** and **276.** (The fame of heroic **Sergeant Fernando Lores** – whose bust is in the Public Library, in the courtyard of the College and on the main square at Tamshiyacu, not to mention Plaza Sargento Lores and the street named after him – is covered separately under *Plazas*).

More History …

Additionally, there are many other legacies and reminders of the past to be found in Iquitos, all covered in more detail later on – the statues and memorials in the plazas and parks constitute a history lesson in themselves. The intriguing story of the ***Casa de Fierro*** is summarised herein under *Plaza de Armas*; in the former *Casa de Gobierno* (now the *Prefectura Loreto)* in Malecón Tarapacá are both ***el Museo Amazónico*** and ***la Biblioteca Amazónica***. The Municipal Museum, natural history treasure trove, and the Municipal Library (both regrettably moved from the *Plaza de Armas*) have already been mentioned. Even the line of 'scribes' sitting with their old-fashioned typewriters in *calle* Putumayo are an element of the city history, waiting in the shade to prepare letters, *denuncias* and documents for those in need (their numbers have halved, and halved again in the last ten years, colourful casualties of computerisation).

"Asi es la Selva"

Sadly, genuine primary forest is a rarity nowadays

… And more on the Present

Coming back to the present, the **shops** in Iquitos lack little and new ones, *a la moda,* are opening all the time (usual trading hours approximately 0730-1300 and 1500-1945 except Sundays). For reading material, two recommended **bookshops** are SBS at Nauta 248, and Tamara on Próspero 268-270[10]. Radiating from Próspero there are any number of **photographic studios** well-equipped with the latest digital technological variants (note well that taking pictures of airports, military bases, police stations and high tension pylons is forbidden). Should need arise, then for professional photography Jesús Panduro (cel: 940383736) could well be your man. Moving on, a good sprinkling of **laundrettes** can be found, such as (for example) *Lavandería* Imperial at Putumayo 150, where you can study three fascinating sepia photographs of 'old' Iquitos dated 1890, 1910 and 1915 whilst your wash is in the tumbler.[11] For a complete **laundry and pressing** service, *Lavanderia* Express at Ricardo Palma 451 is the place (Sra. Graciela) (0800-2100).

On the subject of personal organisation, the latest address for the **Iquitos Immigration Office** (which is given to frequent moves) is Av. Cáceres *cuadra* 18 (tel: 235371, open 0800 to 1200 Monday to Friday). **Haircut**? Styling? For men, look no further than *Dos Mil* (Sr. Leonardo S. Torres Lozano), *Calle* Bermudez 463 (Plaza 28 de Julio). Ladies may proceed to *el Centro de Bellaza*, **Marivel Spa**, Ricardo Palma 487 (tel: 224104; cel: 965-615585; RPM *429872) for all their needs and just about everything in pursuit of beauty and perfection. Or to ***Spa Liz***, Morona 582 (tel: 505654; cel: 965650143) for the full works. Putumayo *Cdra 13* (by the Stadium) is the place where 'informal' alfresco barbers abound. And finally, for high quality bespoke hand-crafted leather shoes or sandals, ***Zapatería Universal*** at Jr.Próspero No.656 is not to be missed.

Restaurants (see Section III), bars, discotheques and travel agents abound in Iquitos. Likewise, there is a range of **fitness centres** (*gimnasíos*); two of the most recently opened (2006/7) and 'state of the art' are *jully spa* at 779

---

[10] Sorry – Tamara has gone, disappeared from the face of the earth! Nothing is forever.

[11] Sra. Victoria Wong Ramirez de Ferreira (*gerente*) has now moved into resplendent new premises at Jr.Nauta No.125 (i.e. the next block – telf: 65-231768). The old photos are still displayed, and also note that one of the best collections of historic snaps of Iquitos is in the Conference Room on the panoramic 6th floor of the hotel Dorado Plaza.

Sargento Lores and *Zona Fitness Club* at 229 Sargento Lores. Both provide a comprehensive range of activities; the choice is yours, do not delay. Or, if you want to buy some weights and bars for yourself, Jesus Gonzales in ***La Casa del Deportista*** has the answer (*Calle* Ricardo Palma 426, tel:065-225447/Cel.985666055).

The one **cinema** (fondly remembered, just off Plaza *28 de Julio*, on the corner of *Jr*.Huallaga) which closed several years ago has now re-opened on Arica (258 – just off the Main Square) with four *salas* and almost the very latest films. Another relatively recent venture to look out for is the **Iquitos Symphony Orchestra**: Director: Sr.Fernando Cordova (Cel.998587609), Vice Director: Sr.Daniel Manrique (Cel.953967867).

The Iquitos Symphony Orchestra – long may it flourish

Cable Vision/*Cable San Juan* and **Cable Movistar**/*Cable Magico* are available locally, giving around 90 television channels. There is a plethora of FM **local radio stations**, amongst which are Radio Loreto, Radio *Caribeña,* Radio Stereo 10, Radio Astoria, Radio 'A' (*del Amor*), and *La Voz de la Selva.* Radio *Nacional* is on 101.30 with broadcasts of classical music to be found on weekday evenings between 2100 and 2200, if you are fortunate. Radio *Ritmo Romántica* is on 93.10. However, it is the throbbing **market places** and the **river embarkation points** which are the true heart of life in Iquitos and again, these are dealt with separately in Sections III & IV.

There is no shortage of **Internet** *cabinas* in the city (e.g. famed *El Cyber,* formerly on *Plaza de Armas* but now moved just around the corner to Jr.Putumayo 374 as *Cyber Super Internet* and claiming to be open 365 days a year, 24hrs a day); if travelling with a laptop, surges in the local electricity supply make use of a stabiliser highly advisable; power cuts are not infrequent. If staying long enough to make it worthwhile, you can buy one (an *estabilizador)* for US$40.00 from Argot (Morona 272). The local **power supply** is 220 volts.

Outgoing international **telephone calls** are easily made from Iquitos, e.g. from Napo 349 Call Center and many similar facilities (00 prior to country code). Ringing in to Iquitos from abroad, access the international facility, then dial 51 (Perú country code), 65 (Iquitos city code) followed by the six digit local number. If you are in Perú but outside Iquitos, just use 065. Be aware that in-bound international calls to Telefónica mobiles (cellulars) in Perú not only result in a bill for the caller, as might be expected, but also a charge for the innocent recipient of the call. For Directory Enquiries dial 103.

After all that, you may decide to send news home using pen and ink. Post cards can be bought almost anywhere. To mail them you need to go to the **Post Office** (*Serpost*) on Arica 4/Morona (open 0730-1945 Monday to Friday, 0730-1845 Saturdays, closed – on occasions – for lunch 1300-1345; supposedly open Sundays and Fiestas 0900-1300). Expect to pay S/.3.80 for a letter to Europe, S/.3.50 to USA. If your friends at home like to receive exotic stamps from distant parts, take care not to receive an impersonal plonk from the franking machine at the counter. Best to buy some of the colourful and decorative Peruvian stamps as a separate transaction and stick them on yourself (although, sadly, shared experience in recent years is that because of the attractiveness of the stamps, more than half of items sent never make it to their destination).

Security. Iquitos can be as 'safe' or 'unsafe' as most cities of the third millennium. Herewith a reminder of the basic, oft-repeated (and oft-neglected) rules. At night, common sense should help you to avoid being in the wrong place at the wrong time – venture into 'dark and hidden places' and you will assuredly pay the price – as others have done before you.

During daylight, stay alert, particularly in the market places. If you have a smart camera, avoid waving it around more than necessary. If you have a nice watch or handbag, leave them in the hotel safe, together with the bulk of your money. Carry a photocopy of your passport rather than the original. If you are in close proximity with other people in transport or in the street, particularly if you are being jostled, and you have anything which is of value to you (e.g. your wallet), best to keep your hand on it. If you have a fashionable pair of Gucci shades and you like to wear them on top of your head (for reasons best known to yourself), don't be surprised if a hand comes through the open window of your microbus and borrows them. Bags and daysacks of canvas etc are susceptible to razor and knife slits; opening zip pockets on back packs is light work for the light-fingered – make it a front pack if you are standing in a queue. Politely resist the kind suggestion of the helpful passer-by who offers to assist you with your luggage. And if you insist on wearing a money bag on the outside of your clothes around your waist, remember that (quite aside from sartorial considerations) it announces to the world: "In this little pouch, here is treasure!" Finally, always count your change carefully (that's not to imply that short-changing is endemic, it's just an arithmetical thing) and invariably check the authenticity of all bank notes, particularly the larger denominations (don't have any qualms about this routine, holding notes up to the light for scrutiny is a national custom and no offence is meant or taken)[12].

The Central Police Station in Iquitos is located at Morona 120 (telephone 231123) – not to be confused with the Regional Police HQ at 147 Brasil (to be found, as it happens, next door to the former town jail building, still emblazoned as such although in fact it is now situated out at San Huan).

[12] However, having done this, it is as well to know what you are looking for ... e.g. on the left hand side of the face of a 'good' note there will be a watermark reproduction of the portrait that is displayed on the right; the features of this right hand picture will feel slightly elevated when lightly rubbed between forefinger and thumb; under the watermark you will see a rectangle at the bottom of the note, coloured half-and-half in the note's denominational colours – hold the note flat at eye level and the appropriate number of *soles* will appear in the box as if by magic (sadly this feature is no longer present in more recent notes). If you sniff a sound note, you will immediately recognise the distinctive odour of the genuine article, and finally, if you squeeze a suspect bill into a ball, a true note will stay 'scrunched' – a dud will unfurl.

The old Iquitos prison on Brasil Cdra 1

Other local police stations are listed in the Directory. The emergency telephone number for Police assistance is 231131; to summon immediate mobile police presence ring 241000/241001. The Fire Brigade (*Los Bomberos* – an all-volunteer force in Perú) are on telephone 267555. District Fire Stations are in the Directory (historically Iquitos has suffered much from periodic large-scale conflagrations which consumed whole areas of the city in the past – e.g. 1865 & 1872). The Tourist Police are based at Sargento Lores 834 (and are no longer normally present at the Airport); their new telephone number is: 980122202/mobile 965-935932.

Finance. There is no requirement to carry a mountain of money in Iquitos; long gone are the days of travellers' cheques and other such financial adventures. The city has 24hr ATM **cashpoints** (*cajeros automáticos),* giving local currency or US Dollars in return for Visa, Mastercard, Visa Electron, Maestro, Delta, Access, Travel Money Cards, etc. Just for starters, Crediexpress and the Banco Continental machines are both at the Plaza de Armas end of Próspero (Nos.228 and 343 respectively) and there is another cashpoint just across the square. The number of **banks** is too numerous to mention, although on occasions the wait in the queue can be pretty long. All hotels accept plastic, as do restaurants and shops. **Money changers** are at the top end of Próspero, concentrated at the intersection with Morona; to be avoided in the dark, never get distracted by third parties, engage one on one, check all notes, take your time, count and re-count. Best advice is to stick to banks, hotels and authorised money exchange offices.

Health. Notwithstanding your immunisation precautions in advance of travelling, and your anti-malaria prophylactics, you might perhaps require treatment for minor sickness or in the event of an accident. Construction of the first hospital in Iquitos started in 1903; nowadays medically the city is served by **two public hospitals** with Emergency Departments open 24hrs a day, namely, the *Hospital Regional de Loreto* (Av. 28 de Julio *cuadra* 10, Punchana – tel.252004/252733) and the *Hospital de Apoyo* (Cornejo Portugal 1710 – tel. 264715). For an **Ambulance ring 251882 or 264710** respectively. Amongst the 24hr health facilities accepting private patients (see also Yellow Pages) are the *Clínica Adventista Ana Stahl* (Av. La Marina 285; telephone 252535/252518) and the *Hospital Militar Santa Rosa* (Cornejo Portugal 1648; telephone 264771).

In general, the **local water** supply is not used for drinking by visitors without being boiled first; bottled water is readily and cheaply available. *Agua de Mesa* in 20 litre containers (*un bedon*) will be delivered by Aquaselva at short notice (telephone: 224012). If you need a **dentist**, take your pick from the Yellow Pages …

Plaza de Armas

The centre of the Plaza was 'remodelled' in 1998 and is a lively place in which to sit and enjoy the morning newspaper or to stroll in the cool of the evening. It boasts a spectacular variable fountain which plays on undetermined occasions; at 1900 on most Sunday nights, and on Fiestas, the local Armed Forces or Police bands do the same, weather permitting. Every Sunday morning (usually starting at 0900) there is a grand military and civic parade in the Plaza at which the National and Departmental Flags are raised formally, followed by a march past[13]. At 'sunset' (fixed at 1800) the Flags are

[13] As an aperitif, the unsung, largely unseen hero of these events is Sr.Francisco Yumbato, who unfailingly appears from nowhere soon after dawn to shin hazardously high up the three flagpoles to put the requisite halliards and flags in place, regardless of the prevailing weather and heedless to the risks.

Plaza de Armas circa 1910 – remarkably the little railway ran for a further three decades (note Casa Pinasco behind)

The Iron House is clearly identifiable, but the chapel on the left gave way to the Cathedral on the other side of the Plaza in 1911

lowered to the sound of the bugle, during which time it is customary for pedestrians in the Plaza to stand to attention. Visitors should respect the solemnity of these occasions, which are a reminder that Iquitos is not only a frontier outpost with regard to the forest but also in the context of the national boundaries of Perú, and that not only in the past but also in more recent times there have been armed incursions, disputes and declarations of hostilities.

Around the time of *Las Fiestas Patrias* (27th and 28th July), life in the Plaza is particularly active. There is an annual book and artefacts fair for a fortnight, and in the evenings there is an extensive programme of cultural activities with the emphasis on music and dancing. The collection of shady trees in the square, perhaps 20 to 50 years old (some of the older specimens having been removed during *remodelacion*), will be even more impressive in another 30 years. However, these trees provide a good cross section of those to be found generally in Iquitos and arboreal recognition talents can be honed by seeking out the following: *mamey, aguaje, tulipa africana, castaña, parinari* and coconut palm (to restore confidence). To check your compass, stand in the centre of the Plaza with your back to the corner housing the *Casa de Fierro* and the corner of the square that you are facing is pretty much due north, with the cathedral corner on your left being west.

The central Obelisk Memorial in the Plaza was inaugurated on 31st December 1908 and commemorates the 173 Loretanos who lost their lives in *La Guerra de Pacífico,* the disastrous war against Chile 1879-1883[14]. The bas-relief engravings on either side of the memorial record one land and one sea battle from that war, the latter sometimes being erroneously considered to the Abtao combat, although as this was an engagement by combined units of the Peruvian and Chilean naval squadrons against Spanish warships in 1866, this is highly unlikely. More possibly it is a record of the events of 21st May 1879 off the harbour of Iquique, where Admiral Grau in *Huáscar* rammed and sank the wooden Chilean corvette *Esmeralda* (less helpfully, Grau's escort, the handy frigate *Independencia*, was subsequently lost on the rocks further down the coast pursuing the Chilean gunboat *Covadonga*), but it is not possible to be more specific. Just for the record, the names of the three ships represented

[14] Which Peru entered to assist neighbouring Bolivia, honouring a mutual defence Treaty obligation, but found herself conducting hostilities alone following the fall of Tacna and the storming of the port of Arica by the Chileans in June 1880, whereupon the Bolivian troops 'quietly disbanded and returned to La Paz and the interior'.

are inscribed as *Yuacolda, Iancoue* and *Indipendencia* (sic), which only serves to mystify rather than illuminate.

Hearsay has it that the two bronze engravings were commissioned in Italy and that somewhere along the line the instructions became confused and the word *Chilenos* became converted into *Chinos*. Certainly the depiction of the opposing soldiers in the obelisk picture, particularly with regard to the strange conical hats, lends substance to the anecdote. Whilst on the subject of folklore and apocryphal stories, at the foot of the memorial is a life size statue of a wounded soldier in cast metal. Legend has it that one day during cleaning operations the heavy statue slipped off its ledge, revealing Rodin's unmistakeable signature on the underside.

There is also a second monument, put in place a century after (i.e. 27th July 1964) the memorable day that the first Navy ships, the *Morona, Pastaza* (towing the brig *Próspero*), *Napo* and *Putumayo,* arrived in Iquitos in 1864. Additionally, this monument confirms the precise geographical co-ordinates of the city and the distance of Iquitos from the Atlantic Ocean (1928 land miles) – plus a height above sea level of 122.4 metres (coincidentally providing a nice mix of Imperial and Metric measurements).

Starting from the southern corner of the Plaza and rotating clockwise 360 degrees through the points of the compass, several fine buildings surviving from the halcyon days of the rubber boom of a century ago can be seen, including the former residence (the '**House of Clay**' – now 'Mibanco') of the famed and filmed (Werner Herzog 1982 – 'Fitzcarraldo' – starring Klaus Kinski) *cauchero* Fermín Fitzcarrald (the surname being a distortion of 'Fitzgerald' arising from local pronunciation difficulties). The Iquitos **passenger railway** used to run across the south eastern side of the Plaza in front of the *Casa de Fierro* and *Casa* Pinasco (*vide* illustrative photo, circa 1910), whilst on the site now occupied by the Hotel El Dorado Plaza formerly stood the **city theatre**, *El Teatro Alhambra,* which flourished from about 1910. It was completely destroyed by fire on 27th January 1931, the blaze also gutting the adjacent Town Hall. It was re-built in 1943 but again reduced to ashes in 1954, a sad cultural loss to the city (but read on – there is hope).

The Catholic **cathedral** on the south west side of the square (*La Iglesia Matriz* – The Mother Church), with its handsome Swiss clock, eccentric Roman numeral IIII (replicated on the church clock face in Yurimaguas, somewhat remarkably) and quietly euphonious Toytown chimes (when working), dates from 1911, replacing a chapel dating from 1832 that previously stood almost in the centre (about where the fountain is now) of what was in those times often known as *Plaza Matriz.* The new cathedral was finally blessed and inaugurated on 16th March 1919, although the graceful tower, with its icing sugar and wedding cake connotations, was not completed until 1924, a further 5 years later (the clock being installed in 1925).

In 1945 extensive renovation and expansion were set in hand, being completed in 1948. Work included the installation of the 18 fine **stained glass windows**, made in Lima using ancient techniques perfected in Europe and showing images of different Augustine saints. Under each window used to be recorded the name of the donating family; hopefully this information will be restored before the records are lost. The **three murals** (triptych) on the south west wall of the cathedral above the high altar depict 'the propagation of the faith' in the *selva* and are the work of the acclaimed Loretano *yurimaguino* artist, poet, narrator and composer **César Calvo de Araujo** who died in 1970 (and who painted the two aforementioned – but now stored – historical murals in the demolished Municipal Building). The nine oil paintings on the ceiling of the cathedral are the work of a team of artists: Ayda Young (6 paintings), Víctor Morey, Américo Pinasco (cf Pinasco's House) and Padre Edilberto Valles. The theme of these pictures is the life of the Virgin Mary.

Diametrically opposite the cathedral, just off the square up Raymondi to the east, is a towering derelict mildewed concrete eye-sore (ineffectually painted sky blue) of 11 floors (in contravention of planning controls) topped with radio aerials (and now also home to a variety of sprouting shrubs and small trees – and ingenious squatters) visible for miles around. This building started life in the early 1980s as a projected hotel but encountered sinking structural and financial difficulties getting on for three decades ago and has been a dilemma for the municipality ever since. The latest (ongoing) plan is to remove the top three floors to reduce weight and to bring the structure back to life. Meanwhile, should you chance to get lost, it is a useful landmark and homing beacon, especially if you are using the old version of the map given in the Telefónica Yellow Pages. The map is fine, but the accompanying 'compass rose' needs to be rotated approximately 135 degrees clockwise to correct the printing error (now adjusted and corrected in the 2006 re-print).

As already explained, in the same yellow building that should have housed the Tourist Office was formerly the Municipal natural history museum (no charge, open 0700-2000 week days and Saturdays) where, after an hour or so of (possibly) solitary contemplation you would have been much better informed on the history, tribes, animals, reptiles and fish of the region and even the various types of wood to be found in the forest. Some of the exhibits are quite old now, and the extent of the display was unfortunately slowly suffering erosion and attrition, the demise of the stuffed animals being accelerated by their random inclusion in the annual Plaza de Armas nativity tableau, which does them a power of no good. Demolition of the building was completed in January 2011; now it is a case of 'watch this space' – on 5th January 2012 the Mayor formally announced that from 'the ruins of the old municipal palace would rise the new municipal theatre …'.

On the other side of the square is the Banco de Credito, situated in a well-restored primrose and white *cauchero* mansion; by contrast, adjacent to the bank is the hugely uninspiring Centro Social International which disgracefully replaced another fine heritage building (which should have been protected) not so many years ago.

The Casa de Fierro

Finally, the Plaza de Armas is home to the ***Casa de Fierro,*** or strictly speaking, half of it. The pioneering concept of this design by **Gustave Eiffel** was intended to serve as a pre-fabricated portable home for officials working overseas in the French and British colonies in Africa (rather overlooking the fact that, with its metal construction, it serves as a most effective oven in hot climates), and the 'Iron House' was originally unveiled at the Paris Exhibition of 1878 (with panels supposedly having been made in England at the Sheffield foundries). The design was subsequently displayed at an International Exhibition in Brussels, where it was bought by French industrial *cauchero* **Julius H. Toots** who was visiting Europe at the time. An alternative version of the story relates that the structure was bought direct from the Paris Universal Exposition in 1889. Whatever, Toots arranged its transport to Iquitos in a Bolivian ship where it arrived in 1890. Toots (great name) then re-assessed the considerable size of the structure that he had come to own, divided it into two halves and offered them for sale to the other *caucheros* of the day (some late night accounts talk of a 'third' Iron House, but they cannot be substantiated).

One half was then bought by the Brazilian Vaca Diaz, business partner of Fermín Fitzcarrald, for projected use as his headquarters in Madre de Dios. His ambitious plan was to move it via the Rivers Ucayali, Urubamba and Mishagua by way of the 'Forgotten Isthmus' linking the rivers. This route was first explored by the ill-fated **Faustino Maldonado** in 1861 (he drowned soon afterwards in the rapids of the Mamoré River but is remembered in the name of Puerto Maldonado, founded in 1902) and then re-discovered by Fitzcarrald 33 years later. However, owing to the low level of water prevailing in the rivers at the time and other difficulties such as communications and the scale of the operation, his dream never came to fruition. Instead, this portion of the *Casa de Fierro* was put on the Malecón Tarapacá at the end of Putumayo where now stands the rundown albeit freshly painted *Real* Hotel (circa 1960, formerly *Hotel de Turistas).* It was then acquired by businessman Francisco Borges but never served as anything more constructive than 'an object of admiration' and consequently suffered badly from neglect and the elements. So much so that in about 1920 it was dismantled, much of it being disposed of as junk metal. However, the main frame was embodied in the construction of the Central covered market (Sargento Lores 5/Moore 3), together with a newly purchased iron structure imported from Germany. There it remains identifiable to the eye of the keen and perceptive observer to this very day, coincidentally and by a serendipitous chain of events making it first cousin to another of Eiffel's creations, the iron fish market on the left bank of the River Guadalquiver in Seville, Andalucia, *el puerto de las Indias.*

The other half of the *Casa de Fierro* was re-assembled on the southern corner of the Plaza de Armas at Putumayo/Próspero, where it still stands as a testament to the height of the extravagances of the rubber boom, and where its ongoing history is still in process of being written. Firstly Spanish *cauchero* Anselmo del Aguila converted it to his mansion and then, at the end of the époque, it was sold to become *El Abanico Restaurant* (i.e. The Fan, owned by Spaniard Julio Queija). The next transformation was into a sweet factory and confectioner's shop named *La Patita* ('Little Duck' under the ownership of Chinaman Mentol Chu). When Chu died, one Juan Velasco del Aguila (coincidentally) converted it to a commercial centre, only for it to be sold yet again to become the 'Fortes House' grocery store. When the proprietor (Jose Fortes DaCasa) died the building was inherited by his son. The shop was closed to be succeeded by a miscellany of diverse emporia on the ground floor, whilst the upstairs of the building was used as the *Club Social de Iquitos* until 1985.

A period of decline and deterioration followed but the **Iron House** (still in the hands of the Fortes family) was subsequently and eventually restored to become once again a living monument to an opulent past, so that from 1998 until 2005 the upper floor and balcony served as the Restaurant Regal (and, as it happened, the British Consulate) under the management of Mr Philip Duffy.

This prime site again fell vacant, and for two years the second floor became a store for pharmaceuticals, until April 2007 when it re-opened as *The Amazon Café & Restaurant* (Cleve & Paula Durden), a venue that in its turn closed at the end of 2010. As of 2014 the new occupants are awaited with interest – and impatience … meantime, what should be a centrally sited heritage gem has become a rusting eyesore.

Plaza de Armas (Concluding)

The Plaza de Armas locale contains a number of other cafés and restaurants open from early in the morning to late at night, none more popular than **Ari's Burgers** and the multi-faceted, 24-hour much-visited vibrant **Yellow Rose of Texas** at 180 Putumayo ('just 50 feet off the Square' – go to www.yellowroseoftexasiquitos to see the full extent of the ever-expanding facilities).

Aside from the ubiquitous monthly Iquitos Times (Putumayo 163) and bi-lingual Amazon News (Putumayo 174), local and national newspapers and magazines (though not in English) can be bought on occasions on the pavement under the *Casa de Fierro*, or alternatively in the shadow of the House of Clay (Prospéro-Plaza-Raimondi intersection). *El Comercio,* elegantly written and S/.3.00, comes up from Lima in the late afternoon (S/.5.00 on Sundays); for a more pungent political read and world headlines try *Liberación,* on sale around 2 p.m. for S/.1.50 and spend the other 50 Centimos on *La Región*, champion of all that is green, to learn the latest on illegal felling and extraction of timber from the forest, river contamination and other local news of human successes, frailties and failings – in inverse order.

Tourists in the square will be offered many services, ranging from a shoeshine by Marcello or Herbert and a tee-shirt from Anterro, to the purchase of a *mata mata,* a prehistoric-looking river tortoise with a triangular head and a disagreeable smell. Best to stick to the shoeshine and tee-shirts, or seek out the wide-ranging advice of resident *guia* Robinson ("Anything you need to know you may ask me freely."). In conclusion, the Plaza **bull ring**, reputedly remembered by some of the city's elders, has long since disappeared under the foundations of the 'old' Municipal building (itself now vanished), bull-fighting not being an activity of *la selva* but a *cauchero* importation from the coast and the mountains.

Other Plazas and Parks

In addition to the Plaza de Armas, Iquitos has several other Plazas of note, not only as pleasantly shady parks and squares in which to relax but also of much historical interest for their statues and monuments.

Plaza 28 de Julio. The Independence Day Park (Bermúdez/Aguirre) formed in 1939. Long ago it was an Iquito farm, later the area became the original city cemetery (a branch line or 'spur' extension along San Martin Street was added to the city railroad specifically to accommodate demand for transportation of the earthly/heavenly remains of citizens to their final resting place). After that, the cemetery became a football pitch, liable to unexpected subsidence. The Plaza is a substantially large square, much favoured for gatherings and meetings, although not by **Pope John Paul II** when historically he visited Iquitos Airport on 5th February 1985. Nor indeed by **HRH Prince Andrew**, who (according to the Editor of the Times of Iquitos) memorably declined to descend from his aircraft during a refuelling stop, thereby causing much dismay and disappointment amongst the pre-arranged line of worthy dignitaries assembled and waiting expectantly on the tarmac (and who was apparently fallaciously famously reported in a local paper to have been sighted fleetingly onboard wearing a Davy Crockett fox-fur hat for the non-occasion, as inadvertently erroneously advised by his mother). Returning to reality, on 13th August 2012 a special plaque was unveiled in the Plaza to record the UNESCO nomination of the Amazon River and associated rain forest as one of the seven natural wonders of the world – theoretically a great boost for tourism.

The tall central obelisk in the square is topped by a heroic female warrior with sword and shield and flowing robes (possibly María Andrea Parado de Bellido, shot by the Royalists at Ayacucho in 1822, or perhaps Brigida Silva de Ochoa, another brave patriot during the struggle for Independence). The monument itself commemorates the Treaty of Rio de Janeiro of 29th January 1942, depicting the then President of the Republic, Dr Manuel Prado, 'director of the defence of our sovereign territory'. This Protocol marked the end of the war with Ecuador which started in 1941 over the disputed border delineation, a continuing dispute that has resulted in periodic tension and skirmishes since that time, culminating in another brief war in 1995 and a further debatable agreement in 1998, which has perhaps resolved matters for the time being.

In passing, observe that the green 10 *Nuevos Soles* note in your wallet also commemorates one of the Peruvian Air Force heroes of the 1941–42 war with

Ecuador, **José Abelardo Quiñones Gonzáles**, who gave his life on 23rd July 1941 attacking Ecuadorian artillery positions at the age of 27; the road out to Iquitos airport is named in his memory.

Returning to the Plaza 28 de Julio, with its mature *Parinari* fruit trees that are perhaps 60 years old (some recently cut down and not yet replaced – who makes these decisions?), between the four **fountains** scattered in the square and away from the picturesque **dovecotes** and the decorative **bandstand** of stone and wood (*una glorieta* given to the Municipality by the Chinese colony of Iquitos on 24th March 1948) are two other commemorative plinths.

On one, marked as a gift of 'La Nacion Argentina' to the people of Iquitos in August 1983, is a bust of the **Argentinean General José Francisco de San Martín** (1778-1850), brilliant military strategist and foremost southern leader in the struggle against colonial Spain. After successfully liberating Chile in 1818 he entered Lima on 12th July 1821 as *Protector of Perú*, declaring the independence of the country on 28th July 1821. Shortly afterwards he withdrew from politics and public life and retired to exile in France. A bust of famed **Venezuelan General Simón Bolívar** (*El Liberator*, 1783-1830) surmounts the other plinth, who through his victories over the Spanish was instigator of 'freedom' not only in what became independent Venezuela but also in the territories that were delineated as Bolivia (named in his honour), Colombia, Ecuador and Perú (and who, as it happens, lived just behind what is now Selfridges in Oxford Street, London in 1810). To this day Bolívar remains a legendary symbol of hope for countless millions in South America seeking relief from poverty, notwithstanding the fact that his detractors claim he was, if not a failure, only 'half a success', in that although he achieved liberation from Spanish rule he failed to put anything permanent in its place – as evidenced by the turbulent history of the continent over the subsequent two hundred years.

The final relic in this Plaza is a narrow-gauge, wood-fired, 4-wheeled piston **steam engine** (as depicted on the front cover) made a century ago in the Petit Bourg Decauville workshops in France and named *Locomotora 'Moronacocha'*. It was this diminutive engine (one of four) that entered service in Iquitos in 1905 at the height of the rubber boom to pull the four carriages of the passenger and freight train that formerly ran across the Plaza de Armas in front of Pinasco's House (as in the photograph). From there it trundled down into Raymondi, left at where the busy **Booth Line**[15] wharf used to be (opened in 1904), then into the length of Loreto. Finally it made its way out to Moronacocha to collect timber 'for construction in booming Iquitos, or for fuel in the new electrical plant on Yavari street' – with a slight diversion to swing past the city sports stadium. The railway, operated by the Booth Company of London, England (quieter and more ecologically-friendly than the current plague of *motorcarros*), functioned for almost 35 years until the start of the Second World War in 1939. At its height there were four lines – one to the docks, the loop line along the Malecon, the cemetery line, and the Moronacocha plus stadium route.

The busy Booth Line wharf, circa 1910, 'where boxes of sterling notes were commonplace amidst the freight on the jetty'

[15] Booth Line: The pre-eminent and dominant trans-Atlantic steamship company of the time in the region. Founded in Liverpool by brothers Alfred and Charles Booth in 1866 to service Brazilian ports, and in 1897 opening a direct link to Iquitos through Manaus. This was subsequently replicated from New York, totalling a peak of 26 vessels in service. Seven ships were sunk by U-boats on the Atlantic route in the Great War, and a further five were torpedoed in the Second World War, leaving but four Booth Line ships remaining. This number dwindled to two in 1992 when, after 126 years the Booth Steamship Company was no more.

Plaza Grau. This is located in the middle of *Avenida* Grau, once one of the most elegant thoroughfares of Iquitos with its central reservation of mature *Mamey* trees and palms under-planted with flame-red *canna* lilies. Previously the Plaza equalled in size that of Plaza 28 de Julio but buildings have progressively encroached and reduced the area to little more than a postage stamp. Nonetheless, enclosed by traditional navy blue and white posts with chain rails (forever in need of a re-paint), there still stands the bust of **Admiral Miguel Grau Seminario,** national hero, born in Piura (where you can visit his house) in 1834, killed in action 1879 and known as '*El Caballero de los mares*' (The Gentleman of the Seas) on account of his custom of invariably rescuing the survivors of the enemy ships that he sank.

As every Peruvian schoolchild knows, it was Admiral Grau who, after an uncertain naval career which included one expulsion and another spell in prison, found undying fame in command of the monitor ***Huascar***[16] (single turret, two 10-inch Armstrong guns, 4-5 inch armour plating) during the Pacific War (1879 – 1883) against Chile. For the first 5 months he inspired the nation with his gallant exploits, capturing or destroying no less than 17 Chilean vessels, and in this initial phase of the war preventing the invasion of Peru from seaward. But finally 'the *Huascar* became his tomb' at the age of 45 (along with all his officers and most of the ship's company) when the previously invulnerable ship was cornered in the Bay of Mejillones off Punta Angamos by the refitted Chilean ironclads *Almirante Cochrane* and *Blanco Encalada* (both 3,560 tons, 9 inch armour plating, six 12-inch Armstrong guns firing Palliser armour piercing shells, built in Hull 1875), plus two iron corvettes (*Chacabuco* and *O'Higgins*), the schooner *Codavonga* and several other units, 325 miles south of Arica, on 8th October 1879, which day is still celebrated nationally as Navy Day and as '*el dia de Combate de Angamos*'. The outcome of the one-sided engagement was inevitable, and thereafter 'the Chileans dominated the sea and were free to land their troops wherever they wished'.

The Iquitos monument, which depicts the embattled and outgunned *Huascar,* was erected in 1936. The second-in-command of the encircled ship, Elías Aguirre, is also commemorated locally, Aguirre Street running parallel to Grau Avenue. (Contrary to popular belief, *Huascar* was not sunk in this

---

[16] Huáscar – a 16th century Inca Chieftan who was the *Sapa Inca* of the Inca Empire, namely the Great Inca and ruler of the Kingdom of Cusco.

action; she was recovered by the Chileans, repaired and returned to active service - including the bombardment of Callao in 1880 - ending her days as a submarine depot and training ship. Having been built and launched in the Laird Brothers' Shipyard in Birkenhead, Great Britain, in 1865 (1,130 tons, 10 knots), the venerable vessel is still afloat, immaculately preserved as a museum and as 'a symbol of brotherhood between Chile and Peru', open to the public in the Chilean naval base of Talcahuano, some 300 miles south of Valparaiso/Santiago. For the majority of Peruvians this is a sadly distant shrine, although the pilgrimage can be undertaken without difficulty from Santiago, either by air to Concepcíon or by train to Chillán).

The Peruvian Navy monitor 'Huascar', captured at the Battle of Angamos, 8th October 1879 and now a museum ship in Chile

[There is one further irresistible digression on the subject of this superbly constructed heavily-armoured fighting vessel which deservedly occupies such a celebrated and iconic position in the naval history of Peru. Somewhat ironically, it was the Huascar that featured in only the second recorded instance of a sea battle between ships of the Royal Navy and Peru (the first

maritime confrontation being The Hidalgo Incident[17] *in 1830 – more of a skirmish than a battle), namely the Pacocha incident of 22nd May 1877 (so-called from the Bay of Pacocha where it took place). Briefly, the Government of that time under President Mariano Prado lost control of the Huascar which was commandeered by a maverick rebel group of sailors under 'reformist' Nicholás de Piérola (who himself later became President), and subsequent events led to a retaliatory engagement with the larger but technically vastly inferior and older cruiser HMS SHAH (without the benefit of armour-plating), and the out-dated wooden corvette HMS AMETHYST (with muzzle-loading, trunnion mounted guns). Aside from the political aspects of this inconclusive tactical skirmish (although no doubt dramatic enough for the participants, with several British sailors injured and one Peruvian killed), it was the first time that the Royal Navy had fired their recently-acquired Whitehead self-propelled torpedoes in anger. The rules of engagement required prior Admiralty approval for employment of this newly-invented weapon; however, on the day and frustrated but the lack of damage inflicted on the elusive and well-protected Huascar, and the failure to capture her, the British Commander at the scene, Rear Admiral Algernon de Horsey proceeded anyway, given that communication of the time was far from instantaneous. In the event, the torpedoes missed their target, and taking advantage of territorial shoal waters Huascar slipped away after dark – only to be re-taken by Government forces just two days later. The inconclusive outcome of the naval engagement provoked much controversy at the time on the British side, and with one digression leading to another, it may be mentioned that the name Pacocha was subsequently used for a Peruvian naval submarine, which unfortunately collided on the surface with a Japanese fishing boat on 26th August 1988, killing eight crew members. The remaining 22 men onboard the submarine survived when an officer succeeded in shutting a watertight door against the overwhelming force of the inrushing water in an act officially recognised as being humanly impossible and consequently deemed to have been a miracle.]*[18]

---

[17] A complex chain of events involving the seizure of the bullion cargo of the British-owned brigantine Hidalgo by the Peruvian port authorities at Callao, and culminating in a Royal Navy prize crew from HM Ships *Sapphire* and *Tribune* taking possession of the Peruvian sloop-of-war *Libertad* – exacerbated by the fact that the Peruvian vice-president, General La Fuente, happened to be on board at the time.

[18] I am greatly indebted to author-historians Paul Goulder and Serena Cant for enticing me down these fascinating and meandering paths.

Plaza Francisco Bolognesi. This triangular park of undulating grass and trees, bordered by Moore, Leticia and Av. Abelardo Quiñones contains no less than one full-size statue (of **Coronel Francisco Bolognesi Cervantes**, 1816-1880, *'Héroe legendario del Morro de Arica'*), and six other busts of Peruvian heroes (in cheerful contravention of the obscure Peruvian regulation which decrees 'one park, one memorial; one square, one statue'). Plaza Grau is on the way, so it is convenient to visit the two squares together.

Bolognesi joined the Army in 1853 when war with Bolivia seemed imminent; he then took part in the victorious campaign against Ecuador in 1859-60. When Chile declared war against Perú (and Bolivia) in 1879[19], Coronel Bolognesi served with distinction in the battles of San Francisco and Tarapacá (cf Malecón Tarapacá below) in November of that year. Next, when the Peruvian defences of Tacna were re-organised in April 1880, Bolognesi became the commander of forces at Arica, where, just two months later on 7th June 1880 he died with many other Peruvians fighting vastly superior Chilean forces and defending his position – and the Flag – 'to the final cartridge'. In graphic paintings of the action, the gallant Colonel is invariably depicted heroically mounted on a rearing white charger, the national standard in hand; one hundred and thirty one years later ***'El Día de la Bandera'*** is still celebrated in Peru on 7th June annually.

Walking clockwise round the park, the other six memorials are as follows:

Don Ramón Castilla *(Patrono de Caballería del Ejército Peruano)* – 6th August 1884. Patron of Calvary for the Peruvian armed forces (covered in more detail below).

José Olaya *'héroe del Perú.'* The plaque has been removed from the plinth but briefly the story of José Silverio Olaya Balandra (1782-1823), humble fisherman of the Bay of Chorrillos (Lima) is as follows. In 1823 when Royalists (*'los realistas')* were occupying the city of Lima, Olaya became the link between *'los patriotas'* in Lima and those in the port of Callao. On being captured Olaya was tortured, given 200 lashes, had his finger nails extracted and was hung by the thumbs but refused to co-operate with the enemy saying

---

[19] The cause of the conflict was a long-running dispute between Chile and Bolivia over the boundary of the Bolivian Atacama province. The outcome of hostilities was that Bolivia lost Atacame province in its entirety (and the port of Antofagasta), whilst Peru lost Tarapacá province (and the port of Arica) in perpetuity, both provinces being endowed with great mineral wealth.

'if I had a thousand lives, I would give all of them for my country' (*Si mil vidas tuviera gustoso las daría por la Patria)*. Patron of the Communications Branch of the Peruvian armed forces. (Unsurprisingly, there is another fine, life-size statue in memory of José Olaya in Lima on the Chorrillos esplanade, facing across the bay to Callao).

General Pedro Muñiz Sevilla (1st September 1884). Patron of the Administration Services of the Peruvian armed forces (but beyond that, his other claims to distinction have remained elusive).

Mariscal Andrés Avelino Cáceres, '*Campaña de la Breña 1882.'* Born 1833, died at the age of 90 in 1923, was twice elected President of Perú. Professional soldier, veteran of the battle of ***'Dos de Mayo'*** (2nd May 1866), the successful defence of Callao by Peruvian, Chilean and Columbian allied forces against attack by a Spanish invasion fleet that had earlier threatened Valparaiso in an endeavour to regain the lost colonies of South America. Later, during the war against Chile 1879-1883 he fought the invaders the length and breadth of Perú, from Tarapacá to the Mantaro valley, earning the title 'the Wizard of the Andes.' His lifetime achievements deserve a separate book to themselves, but for the moment we must be content that at least his name is commemorated in ***Avenida Maríscal Caceres*** which leads away from *Plaza 28th Julio*, and which is of particular interest for the central reservation memorials thereon to fallen heroes of Peru engaged in a succession of colourfully named battles and engagements that are now largely forgotten (e.g. *Combatientes del Caquetá 1911; Putumayo 1933; Gueppi 1933; Angusilla 1933; Yabuyanos 1933; Trocha Gueppi, Pantoja; Defensores del Río Napo 1903; Torres Causana 1904; Roca Fuerte 1941*).

Coronel José Joaquín Inclan – 9th December 1883 '*Patrono de la 5a División de Servicios del Ejército Peruano'*. Hero of the *Dos de Mayo* defence of Callao in 1866 and Patron of Artillery for the Peruvian armed forces.

Almirante T.C. Pedro Ruíz Gallo – 24th Abril 1884 *'Patrono del Arma de Ingeniería'.* Patron of the Engineers, Peruvian armed forces. Amongst many talents, he was an exceptionally skilled clockmaker. His most outstanding piece, 'resembling the clock of the Cathedral of Alsace, eleven feet high and six in its widest part, being a mechanical marvel of the time,' which marked not only the hour but the date, the month, the phases of the moon and the state of the tides, and even various historical events, was in 1871 installed in readiness for the Park Plaza Industrial Exhibition in Lima. Subsequently it was allegedly removed from Lima to Chile by the invaders during the War of the Pacific, but this account is strenuously refuted by Peru's neighbours, who claim that the monumental piece was dismantled and packed away by Peruvian workers ahead of the occupation in 1883, suggesting that the clock is even now in the private possession of 'a prominent aristocratic family' in Peru. Who knows? In any event, this magnificent and unique creation is to this day mysteriously and tantalisingly nowhere to be found, north or south of the border. As for the maker, he was unluckily killed in an explosion caused by a careless assistant whilst arming torpedoes in 1882 (this year being in slight disagreement with the one recorded on Gallo's memorial in the Plaza).

Ask any of the small boys playing football in the shade of the *palmeras, castañas* and *parinaris* for more information on the history of the national heroes commemorated in Plaza Bolognesi and they will gaze at the statues unknowingly, never having noticed them before except as handy goalposts. On your way back to the centre of town, stop off at *Shambo,* 1048 Av. Grau for a *chupete* (local specie of fruit ice cream on a stick) of *copoazú, ungurahui, aguaje, mango, coco, camu-camu, uvos* or *lúcuma* (there is a second *Shambo* shop on the corner of Huallaga/Morona – and others, in case of addiction).

Plaza Sargento Lores. Located at Morona and Castilla, and site of the new Municipal Offices. The Plaza is spacious, grass and palms, and has been renovated since the municipal move. The central statue is of *Loretano* **Sergeant Fernando Lores Tenazoa** ('Hero of Gueppi') in combat, serving with *La Marina de Guerra*. He enrolled in the Peruvian Forces in 1933 at the time of the conflict with Colombia over the disputed border town of Leticia and was sent with other reinforcements to the garrison of Gueppi 'where in action with the enemy he was mortally wounded and died on 27th April 1933'. But here, somewhat less prosaically, is a more graphic account of events, with a slightly different date, culled and translated from other records:

'*On 26th March 1933 Colombia launched a ferocious attack on the Peruvian Garrison of Gueppi situated in Alto Putumayo, aided by German military advisers and using 700 men backed by artillery, two gunboats and eleven dive bombers. The garrison numbered a mere 185 men, without aerial or naval support; nonetheless, they vowed to fight to the end. Sergeant Lores was outstanding amongst the valiant defenders, dodging the incoming fire of the gunboats, the bullets and the bombs, running from hiding place to hiding place firing as he went to give an enhanced impression of the number of defensive machine gun posts. By ten in the morning the bloody struggle was at its height. Harried from the air, the Peruvian relieving force was unable to advance and it was at this moment that Sergeant Lores fell, gravely wounded but maintaining fire on the enemy to his ultimate breath. One hundred Peruvians died in that heroic resistance, only two men were taken prisoner. It was the 26th of March 1933. According to the military surgeon who tried to save him, before expiring Sergeant Lores cried "Viva el Perú, carajo! Muera Colombia!" And with that, he died.*'

Fernando Lores was a former pupil at the eponymous College on the corner of Nauta and Raymondi, which was re-named in his honour.

Plaza Ramón Castilla. Overlooking the rivers, two blocks from the Plaza de Armas on the corner of Raymondi with Loreto, also known as *La Plaza del Amor*, with its subdued lighting and romantic setting. Planted with red hibiscus (*cucarda)* and slender palms and a pleasant spot to relax at the end of the day. The central statue is of **President Ramón Castilla** (1799-1867) gazing eastwards across the waters of the Amazon, a fitting tribute to the distinguished general and far-sighted statesman whose vision and decree of 1861 determined not only the future of Iquitos but also the previously fast-eroding boundaries of Loreto. He served four terms as President of the Republic (a total of 15 years) and died whilst on active service campaigning for re-election.

Adjacent to the statue of President Castilla is an enormous cannon, allegedly naval, possibly nearly two tons in weight and dating from the early nineteenth century. It is emblazoned with the Peruvian heraldic symbols of a llama, a tree and the horn of plenty, but beyond that (if there ever was a commemorative plaque, it has long gone) there are no clues to its provenance, and residents around the square are unable to shed light on where it came from, or how it got there …

[Stop press: Now known to be a Spanish 'Sentinela' cannon, dating from around 1815 and used for coastal defence. Not so long ago it was discovered buried in the former British cemetery in Callao and was excavated and recovered in 2002. Unfortunately (a euphemism, if ever there was), in process of restoration the associated magnificent Spanish Royal Shield on the cannon was erroneously reduced to molten metal and destroyed. In lieu, and by way of a substitute decoration the Peruvian heraldic escutcheon was added (as observed and remarked above). In 2007 the cannon was moved to Iquitos by means of a military aircraft, and installed in the Plaza for posterity – and the subsequent puzzlement of all. My thanks to historian Sr.Gonzalo Maguiña,

prime mover in these happenings and formerly resident in Iquitos, for these revelations].

Beneath the Plaza is a busy embarkation point, nowadays used mainly by launches from the various river lodges, but formerly this is where the picturesque cargo steamer docks were situated during the epoch of the rubber boom and thereafter. At the corner of the square are two more heritage buildings, 201 Loreto and 206-234 Loreto. The latter historical monument is particularly grand in construction and size, with carved stone balustrades, Corinthian columns, Regency style mouldings and carved friezes. It is monographed 'LVF' (as an aid to those researching the great families of the period) and dated 1913, the year when the price of *caucho* was at its highest. In fact, this building was previously part of the Morey empire and was built by Luis Morey, owner of many steamships of the epoch, as mentioned separately. After some years of neglect, restoration of the dilapidated edifice to a high standard has recently (2011) been completed, and the 'new' owners, **AmazonEco** (see their website), are justifiably proud of having converted the historic heritage mansion into an ideally situated elegant 14 room boutique hotel (**Casa Morey**) furnished and decorated with many interesting artefacts and pictures of the period, with extremely spacious accommodation, a bijou courtyard pool, fine views over the water and an ambience of a bygone era (www.lacasamorey.com).

Before leaving the Plaza, note *La Taberna del Cauchero* sushi bar in *La Posada del Cauchero*, creation of chef Diego innovatively blending Amazon culinary delights with Japanese. *La Posada* itself is full of historic photos and information, well worth browsing. Finally, from *Plaza Ramon Castilla* there is a wooden elevated scenic walkway (permanently on the point of restoration) that leads somewhat perilously through to *Plaza Clavero.*

Plaza Clavero. Just before Raymondi becomes Requena en route to the Av. de la Marina lies Plaza Clavero (dating from 1952) with its hibiscus shrubs, park benches, chains and anchors and blue and white naval theme overlooking the wide and deceptively tranquil waters of the Amazon. Also looking out across the river is the bust of **Lieutenant (First Grade) José Manuel Sixto Clavero Muga**, inspired commander of the Peruvian gunboat 'América' at the time of the triumphant action in *la Pedrera* against the Colombians on 12th July 1911 (see Section VII for a full account of this dramatic engagement, under *The Peruvian Navy in the Amazon Basin*). Sadly, he succumbed to yellow fever just one month later after returning to the safety of Iquitos, dying on 11th August 1911 in the house that is today No.349 in Sargento Lores.

During Tourist Week, and on other highdays and holidays, the Navy used to tow the veteran warship '**América**' (history and specifications in Section VII) out into the river and anchor her off the Plaza under the gaze of her former gallant Captain (and incidentally, not far from the spot where the *Pedrera* munitions and troop transport vessel 'Estefita' sank just over 60 years ago), dressed overall with bunting during the day and floodlit by night a century after that historic combat. Nowadays the ship is open to the public annually on Navy Day (8th October, anniversary of the Battle of Angamos - see above, *Plaza Grau*); the bullet holes and battle scars in the superstructure plating of the gunboat are still in evidence, and in 2010 she was repainted to restore her original authentic delivery white livery with black-topped yellow funnels, in lieu of the coat of 'battleship grey' which had been applied at some later stage in her long life. The ship is normally berthed at the Naval Base, and may be visited on written application by prior appointment (see page 143 for details). A fascinating conducted formal tour is given, and the old photographs and relevant artefacts are not to be missed. Other heroes of the *Pedrera* action, such as Cabo Pantoja, Pablo Rossell and Teniente Pinglo are all recorded in Iquitos street names.

Plaza Quiñones. The very latest 'square' in Iquitos, and a spaciously handsome one at that, opened and inaugurated by President Humala himself in March 2013, located at Km.5 on the airport road (appropriately *Avenida Quiñones*). Four fine fountains demarcate the *plaza*, with gallant aviator José Abelardo Quiñones Gonzáles and his doomed aircraft being the central portrayal (see page 43 for more on this national hero, and even go to the museum in the house where he lived in Pimentel, on the coast near Chiclayo).

Waterfront homes

Puerto de Belén – "La Venecia Loretana"

National Day, July 2001: BAP América anchored off Iquitos City accompanied by BAP Amazon (built in the USA in 1934 by Electric Bolt Co, now General Dynamics, and still in service more than three quarters of a century later). In those days BAP América was painted 'battleship grey'; now she is back to her original authentic colour, namely, white.

Malecón Tarapacá

This is the river-front 'promenade' of Iquitos, the name Tarapacá being in wistful memory of Peruvian territory way to the south of the country annexed by Chile after the Pacific War. The boulevard was at the height of its splendour in the early 1900's but from the dramatic end of the rubber boom in 1913 until 1960 it entered a period of progressive and un-maintained decline, during which time the ever-changing course of the river Amazon (which in those days ran directly in towards the shore – from where is now the southern end of Iquitos Island – before turning at right angles towards Nanay) inexorably ate away the foundations. The result was that much of the terrace collapsed into the mud, and additionally an entire street was lost (*Calle Francisco de Orellana* is no longer with us). Moreover, and strictly speaking, it is now the river Itaya that flows beyond the boulevard, and the confluence with the Amazon (marked by the meeting of the black waters and the brown waters respectively), does not occur until Bellavista Nanay is reached (and where the dolphins play).

Renovation commenced in 1994, the re-construction and re-design being completed in July 2001, including new lights, flower-beds and palms, creative fountains, a bathing pink dolphin and other decorative 'works of art'. Aptly and upliftingly, the translation of the inscription on the plaque in the shadow of the commanding statue of **Simón Bolívar** looking across the majestic expanse of the Amazon reads: "From this shore we see the horizon of new hope … let us walk together".

By night, Malecón Tarapacá is thronged with people, activity and colour, with the tranquil moon reflecting on the water in the background. Now the promenade has indeed regained much of its former glory (although the pavement is in places once again in process of dire upheaval and subsidence; this time less so as a result of the forces of nature, and apparently rather more attributable to faulty foundations).

Malecón Tarapacá is justifiably a popular spot, and there are many bars and restaurants, not least being the *Fitzcarraldo*. However, the **following short walk** of 20 to 30 minutes is best undertaken in the first half of the morning or towards the end of the afternoon (to avoid the heat of the day). Start by taking a *motocarro* to the junction of San Martín with R. Hurtado (named in memory of Major Ramírez Hurtado, Second-in-Command of the 9th Infantry Battalion, who died of fever early in the last century travelling from the frontier lands of Caquetá to Iquitos). Having paid the fare, put the river on your right hand and prepare to return on foot to the Malecón Tarapacá 'boulevard'. But before setting off, pause to admire the fine examples of *cauchero* houses at 101 San Martín and 702-718 R. Hurtado on your left. Stroll on and admire Nos.686-676, 672-664 and 650, all sanguinely marked for preservation with the blue lettered plaque '*patrimonio de la nación.*' And if that treasure trove was not enough, now note Nos.622 and 614, and then 584-572 where Hurtado becomes Tarapacá.

Taking a rest for a moment from these grand houses, turn to the river and to your right, looking across the greenery of the papaya, banana and *zapote,* enjoy the vista of the picturesque traditional frond-roofed houses *(Irapay* and *Yarina)* of Belén running down to the river Amazon, unchanged from the view enjoyed from the *cauchero* balconies a century previously. A view that is still fringed by the same delicate lilac flowers of the ubiquitous floating aquatic plant of the Amazon basin, *las huamas* (may also be sighted in the tropical hothouse at Kew Gardens, London), favourite food of the endangered *charapa* water tortoise (hence the endearment *charapitas* – cf Section IX).

Walk on for more history. On your left, note the red brick chimney rising from the side of the pavement. '1864 – *Fundación de la Factoría Naval*' says the plaque (SIMAI – *Servicio Industrial de la Marina Iquitos*)(Peruvian officialdom is addicted to obscure acronyms), the date tying-in neatly with the decree of President Ramón Castilla and the stored picture formerly in the Municipal Museum of the Navy ships arriving in Iquitos. Advance down the road a short way and whilst admiring the architecture of No.512, now the home of *El Comando de la Movilización del Ejército Peruano,* ask the sentries what the factory used to make. Bricks? Cannon? Sloops of war for the defence of the river? In fact, the workshops were manned by craftsmen contracted from England and skilled artisans from the Port of Callao (Lima) who carried out 'repairs to naval motors and engines, and made spare parts, milling machines and agricultural tools'. The original factory was damaged in an uncontainable conflagration that destroyed much of the town on National Day in 1865, caused by ill-sited celebratory fireworks. It suffered yet another fire in 1872 and it was not fully repaired until 1880. Today nothing remains of the carpentry and reverberating metal workshops or the foundry. Only the chimney survives as a prompt for the imagination.

Time for a slight diversion. Deviate left into Brazil, where there are more, yet more architectural treasures: foremost is No.138, opposite are 145, 156 (dated 1919), 158, 162 up to 174. Look along the handsome façade of the houses, try the restaurants for some light refreshment and then return to Malecón Tarapacá to savour Nos.466-422, faced in the fashion of the day with tiles from Portugal. Now look left down Morona, shaded by majestic trees planted perhaps a century earlier, before registering the first of the boulevard statues (albeit now sadly in process of disintegration). This is a lifesize 'faux bronze' in memory of **Balbina Dora Soto Correa**, complete with rifle; '*Heroina del Pueblo – Defensora del Suelo Patria – El Pueblo te Honra*' [no translation necessary], born Caballococha 30.8.26, died Iquitos 09.01.01'. The inscription (lamentably) tells us nothing further ... too young (surely?) to have participated in the 1941 conflict with Ecuador, we are left to wonder how and where and when Señora Balbina achieved fame and glory. (*In fact, she was an orphan, and did indeed succeed in enlisting in the Peruvian armed forces at the age of 15 – after initially being rejected on account of her age – to fight against the Ecuadoreans in the war of 1941*).

The second statue you will encounter is of **Orlando Casanova Heler** (1943-1997), not a household name worldwide, but renowned in Iquitos as a favourite children's writer ('*Por haber dado vox a los hijos del bosque para deleite de los niños Amazonicas*'). Unfortunately, and once again, half of this statue is missing (blown away, apparently); hopefully the remainder will last for a little longer to commemorate the distinguished author.

The next fine building of note in Malecón Tarapacá is the restored *Casa de Gobierno* (started in 1863 and completed in 1902), now the ***Prefectura Loreto*** and the ***Museo Amazónico,*** inaugurated in 1996. Best not to break your walk at this moment, but make a note to return to enjoy the Museum and the exceptional interior of the building, the cool courtyard, the artefacts, the pictures, and most of all, the unique and irreplaceable collection (fast dwindling) of bronze-painted fibreglass statues by **Felipe Lettersten,** made from actual body-casts (moulds) of indigenous people of the various tribes of the region (the artist sadly died of a heart attack in his late forties, hardly more than a decade ago). The museum is currently open 0900-1300 and 1600-1800 Monday to Friday, 0900-1300 Saturdays; over the past decade the number of exhibits has been much reduced, but it is still well recommended, particularly if your visit coincides with one of the periodic special exhibitions (entrance is now free), not least to admire the wonderful mahogany carved furniture, doors, ceilings and panelling.

La Sala de Lectura – Prefectura Loreto, Malecón Tarapacá

At the far end of this same building (No.354) is the admirably presented ***Biblioteca Amazónica***, created in 1972 under the auspices of the *Centro de Estudios Teológicos de la Amazonía.* It was formerly open 0845-1200 and 1500-2000, Mondays to Fridays where for a monthly subscription of S/.6.00 (annual carnet fee S/.10.00) in gracious surroundings you could access the extensive collection of books and records relating to all aspects of the region (the first 3 days used to be free for visitors, but sadly no more, according to the receptionist; never mind). Nowadays this researcher's treasure trove is markedly less accessible, with a much reduced and uncertain opening non-schedule, which is a pity. Incidentally, the ***Prefectura*** building has recently become home for the new Iquitos **ballet school**, whose first public performance was staged in January 2013 as part of the Iquitos Anniversary cultural programme.

Now, here's another distraction to be set aside for a rainy day. Number 332 on the Malecón houses Dr Richard Bodmer's *Exhibición permanente de Culturas Indígenas Amazónicas,* open eight to eight seven days a week, a handful of *soles* to enter. Diverse, colourful and fascinating indigenous artefacts from the Amazon Basin on two floors; not to be missed.

For a change of scenery, now gaze riverwards to absorb the 180 degree panoramic view of the river Itaya to the right, the Amazon in front and to the left. All this in scarcely more than a few hundred yards. Two more collector's houses on your left and time for another diversion, this time into Sargento Lores. On your left you will find what must be the best preserved run of architecture in the city: 75 metres of Iquitos as it was at the height of its former glory. The final building is now occupied (mundanely) by the local Tax Office and just before that is *Grupo Aéreo 42* (mentioned separately in Section V). In the historic building opposite (190) is Restaurant Maloca (also mentioned separately, see Section III). Note also Nos.170-180: now you are well on the way to having sighted at least half of the 'rubber boom' houses, and there are more to be found further down Sargento Lores after crossing Próspero. But resist the temptation and return to Malecón Tarapacá where our route lies, and where there are more prizes to be collected.

The first gem is on the corner of the boulevard and Putumayo. '1908-1912' says the date on this magnificently ornate structure, formerly the Malecón Palace Hotel (200-208 Malecón Tarapacá), now the *Comandancia del Ejército* and HQ for the area Armed Forces. The building, built at the behest of rubber baron Otoniel Vela, has three floors and is decorated with forged iron and arabesques in the cornices with baroque and neo-classical styles. The façade is covered with particularly resplendent *azulejos,* the glazed tiles shipped in from Spain and Portugal, whilst inside is to be found abundant Italian marble and fine carpentry of the highest quality. *Padre* Joaquín García Sánchez, celebrated historian of *Amazonía*, considers that this edifice represents the ultimate expression of the 'architectural language' of the era, inspired by the art nouveau movement.

After this excitement, the Hotel Reál on the former site of one half of the *Casa de Fierro* (now removed to the Central Market) comes as more than something of a disappointment, fresh coat of paint notwithstanding (apart from the occasional macaws in the foyer), and it is kindest to hurry on without comment, enjoying the far-horizon view on our right of the confluence of the black waters of the river Itaya with the lighter, dun-coloured waters of the Amazon as we go – and noting the existence of the '***Centro Artesanal Anaconda***' (also due for renovation) for a possible criffle-cruffle visit later.

Cross the intersection with Napo (at which point hereon the promenade becomes Malecón Maldonado) and continue along the front to the Nauta intersection, glancing down the road to see our old friend the *Colegio* Fernando Lores. Your river front stroll is almost at an end now, and it just remains to enjoy the not-so-finely restored Seminary of St Augustín (note the shadow of the rich decorations over the windows which have been blithely obliterated) with its wide façade of two floors, decorated with a cornice that supports balustrades. In 1903 the Seminary was the house of a local family, becoming a primary school in 1935 and a secondary school in 1952 before being rebuilt by the sage Augustinians for its present role, thereby providing theological students with an inspiring and elevating vista of the mighty Amazon. And as a final observation, note that the bell in the Seminary campanile was (according to local historian Sr.Gonzalo Maguiña) cast in the erstwhile naval factory and is indeed apparently (he says) marked on the rim to that very effect. Down below the windows of the Seminary are thatched floating houses with a bevy of boats and small craft, and right at the very end of the promenade is a river-view restaurant for a well-earned cooling *refresco* after your cerebral walk. *Bravo!*

Handicraft Shopping

There is no shortage of shops in Iquitos where you can buy souvenir tee-shirts and other mementos of your visit to Amazonia. For example, Yagua blowpipes and bows and arrows (which will be confiscated at the Airport in Lima if you attempt to carry them as 'hand baggage'), Bora necklaces and bracelets, masks made of *topa* wood, replica romantically painted paddles, bags of *chambira* palm, *shicra* (palm) hunting pouches, typical tribal costumes ('grass skirts'), musical instruments *(wiros* and *zampoñas)*, wood carvings of *palo sangre* (a dark reddish wood with a handsome grain), carved parrots, red and black *huairuro* seeds as 'happy journey' charms, curtains and lampshades made from *pashaco* seeds and the scales of *paiche,* statuesque replica toucans and macaws, unique and colourful *arpillera* (South American/Peruvian appliqué) depictions of rain forest scenes hand-worked by stitch-artists Patricia & Jorge Cardenas on sale in the Explorama lodges. Something for everyone. Except don't encourage or support the sale of stuffed animals, feather adornments, reptile and cat skins, stuffed birds or glass cases of butterflies. Or even shrunken heads. In any case, the export of protected plant and animal species, dead or alive, is prohibited.

Some of the handicraft shops specialise in a variety of fortifying and medicinal concoctions such as *Chuchuhuasi, Uña de Gato, Siete y Veintiun Raices, Witochado, Pachuli, Abuta, Rompe Calzón, Hembra Tumba,*

Levántate Lázaro, Parado-Largo-Muerto, and so forth. Some of them – for example *Uña de Gato* – possess recognised and proven (if not totally understood) health benefits. Aphrodisiacal properties are claimed for many of the potions (as is implicit in the names) but, unlike the man who ate half a dozen oysters for dinner and then returned to the restaurant the following morning to complain that only five of them worked, don't expect too much. In moderation, none of the drinks should do you any harm; in the former Regal Restaurant bar there used to be a scientific analysis of *Siete Raíces* on display, and a tribute to its protective powers against all the ills of the jungle.

If you have time, a visit to *El Centro Artesanal* at San Juan on the left hand side of Av. Abelardo Quiñones (the Airport Road, use the frequent buses for one *sol*, or up to S/. 4.00 by *motocarro* from the centre of town) is well worth it, not only for the competitive prices but also for the concentrated range of items on offer. Whilst you are travelling in that direction, take the opportunity to visit the *Instituto de Investigaciones de la Amazonía Peruana (iiap)* at Km 2.5 open 0800 to 2000 weekdays and 0800 to 1200 Saturdays. This centre has excellent displays and pictorial presentations on a wide variety of rain forest natural history topics, ranging from fruits and orchids, butterflies and bats, reptiles and fish (and surprisingly, even shoes made from fish skins), to insects and edible snails, and is a recommended precursor to the jungle trip which you are planning.

In continuation of this theme, a right turn at the Varsovia *grifo*, 4.6kms from the Plaza de Armas (just before the Honda and Caterpillar concessions), and right again after 50 metres will bring you to the little-known one hectare site of CIRNA-UNAP (*Centro de Investigaciones de Recursos Naturales*) and LIPNAA-UNAP (!) (*Laboratorio de Investigaciones de Productos Naturales Antiparasitarios de la Amazonia*) where *Ing.*Leonor Arevalo Encinas may give you an illuminating tour of the botanical garden, including a giant Ayahuasca vine. *Universidad Nacional de la Amazonía Peruana* (UNAP) also have another botanical garden at Zungarococha which is open to visitors during daylight hours.

Iquitos Football Stadium and Iquitos General Cemetery

Strange bedfellows and not automatically on the customary tourist trail, but they both deserve a mention (and a visit) so here they are. The 'new' **Football Stadium** (*Estadio Max Augustin* – adjacent to the Iquitos Tennis Club and the old runway), was completed late in 2005 with a seating capacity of 17,500 and the latest in synthetic turf to World Cup standards ('may be used for 15 hours a day for 15 years before requiring maintenance'). It has replaced the former wooden stands and nostalgic muddy grass of the previous venue and was funded by the Regional Government of Loreto through revenue accrued from the oil of the Amazon basin. Ultra modern, this is a gem not to be missed by *aficionados* of the so-called 'beautiful game', particularly as typically entrance is S/.5.00 in the covered west stand, S/.3.00 in the east stand (also under cover), and S/.1.00 at either end – first class football for 25 pence, and a highly colourful evening guaranteed, games promulgated in *La Región*. Rumour has it that – amongst other notables – Ronaldo himself has graced the turf here; given time and sufficient repetition the fantasy will surely become fact. And one concluding nugget that is indeed a fact: the *pista atletico* around the pitch opens daily as an early morning mecca for joggers, entrance S/.1.00.

Turning to the **Cemetery** (*Cementerio 'San Miguel Arcangel', Calle Alfonso Ugarte*), this was inaugurated in 1902, having moved from what is now the *Plaza 28 de Julio* (as mentioned), although some of the graves pre-date this. Such as that for Carlos F. Fiscarrald (sic), *Fallecido 9.7.1897*, 'Remembered by his friend and companion Cardozo'. As in all cemeteries, herein lies a treasure trove of history, fertile ground for conjecture and intriguing investigation. One of the largest and most ornate mausoleums is *Mausoleo "Morey"* (cf *Casa* Morey under 'Iquitos Today'), equalled only by that of the Tomas Bartra family. In the centre of the cemetery is a cenotaph remembering some of the 'fallen heroes of Loreto' (*La Patria a los Heroes Caidos en Loreto*) – most of the names thereon featuring eleswhere in this Guide. Nearby is the vault of Carmen Rosa Canduro dated 12.11.89, combatant in the 1941 conflict against Ecuador who accompanied her husband to war and took up arms after he was killed. And of course, the last resting place of *Teniente* Clavero is here.

These are but graveyard *apéritifs*; with the help of the knowledgeable *Capillan* in the gatehouse office there is much more to be unearthed and garnered hereabouts, not least concerning those who allegedly fled to South America from Berlin in 1945. In any event, space is at a premium these days, and in lieu the ***Jardínes del Edén*** at Km 9 on the road to Nauta has become the latter day tranquil and beautifully tended resting place of choice for those called by Higher Authority.

Climate

Basically the weather is very warm, usually hot, humid (average 84%) and delightfully rainy throughout the year. There are fine days and fresh days and wet days, often all three on the same day. One moment you can be under blue skies dotted with cotton-wool cumulus; the next moment if can be pouring with dramatic intensity. Hence the knowing local expression: 'this is *sol de lluvia'* to indicate that the sun may be shining now but just wait and see. Moral: never leave your washing unattended on the line. From *Los Chinos* (Belén market) you can still buy a collapsible (i.e. folding) umbrella for 5 *Nuevos Soles* (about one pound sterling, one US dollar and 60 cents), which has to be the best value for money either side of the equator. Or you can invest in a 'poncho' for not much more and exchange the experience of being soaked in the rain to that of being soaked in perspiration.

Generally temperatures range through the nineties (Fahrenheit) during the day down into the seventies at night (say 38° down to 22° Centigrade). On occasions the temperature slides above and below the normal range; coats and even mufflers have been sighted in the Plaza de Armas, but not often. Visitors should come to Iquitos prepared to feel hot; the more you manage without using the air conditioning, the quicker you will acclimatize. *La Selva* is normally notably windless in comparison with Europe or North America (hence the absence of sailing craft, let alone windsurfers on the rivers), although it is blessed with welcome zephyrs and sporadic soft breezes from time to time. However, some meteorological depressions are accompanied by strong winds (*ventarones* – 'big winds') which wreak havoc on the corrugated iron and thatched roofs (*las calaminas y las ojas*) of the local houses. Also, the forest trees are inclined to be vulnerable on these occasions, the anchorage provided by their roots being generally rather shallow (hence the preponderance of trees – such as the Lupuna – sporting extensive above-ground architectural buttress-like support growths, or *alas* wings).

The division of the year into seasons tends to be slightly academic; however, the supposedly 'dry' season from April/May to October (November to March being the rainy season) is considered to be 'summer,' even though it is technically the southern hemisphere winter. To compound the confusion, in Amazonia the days and nights (i.e. duration of light and darkness) are of about equal length but the difference in temperature is marked. This causes many forest dwellers to consider night-time to be winter-time. Coming back to the coats and mufflers, the months June to September produce the occasional phenomenon of an *ola de friaje,* in other words a wave of southern polar air over the region, which may last perhaps four or five days. Day temperatures 10 degrees below normal and night temperatures around 6 degrees under the norm are accompanied by continuous grey skies and drizzle. Local hearsay has it that the *Fiesta de San Juan* (24th June) will invariably be the occasion for such an uncharacteristic (and unhealthy) visitation. Reverting to the subject of hypothetical rainy and dry seasons, many consider it more relevant to divide the year according to whether the river waters are high (i.e. broadly and generally December through to May) or low (i.e. the remaining months of the year). Notably, the extreme floods of April/May 2012 caused unprecedented economic hardship and disruption in the region. A 'wake up call' indeed say the climate change realists, not without good reason.

Recommended Reading

A Very Peruvian Practice ('Travels with La Señora') by John Lane (Published by John Murray, Albermarle Street, London); best seller – hardback 2003, paper back 2004. ISBN 0-7195-6209-0. See www.johnlanebooks.com or Amazon Books.

La Doctora by Linnea Smith MD ('The Journal of an American Doctor practising medicine on the Amazon') ISBN 1-57025-140-1 Pfeifer-Hamilton, Duluth, Minnesota 1999

Amazon Magic *(The Life Story of Ayahuasquero and Shaman)* – Don Agustín Rivas Vásquez, ISBN 0-9674-255-0-6

Así es la Selva – *Avencio Villarejo* ISBN 84 98295 46 8 (Centro de Estudios Teológicos de la Amazonía, Putumayo 355, Iquitos, Perú)

Bosques de la Paz – Walter H.Wust & Alejandro Balaguer, ISBN 9972-52-022-6

El Linaje de los Orígenes (La historia desconocida de los Iquito) – Percy Vilchez Vela (Previously obtainable from bookshop Tamara, price S/.25 …)

Memorias de un Misionero (La aventura de un agustino en la Selva) – Avencio Villarejo, ISBN: 9972-40-132-4 (Centro de Estudios Teológicos de la Amazonía, Putumayo 355, Iquitos)

Panorama Histórico de la Amazonía Peruana *(Municipalidad Provincial de Maynas) – Humberto Morey Alejo y Gabel Daniel Sotil García* (Obtainable from the Municipal Offices in Iquitos, Plaza Sargento Lores, price S/.30.00)

The Amazon: Past, Present and Future – Alain Gheerbrant, ISBN 0 500 30005 4 (Published by Thames and Hudson/New Horizon)

Liberators: South America's Savage Wars of Freedom 1810-30 – Robert Harvey (John Murray, 2000) ISBN 1-84119-623-1)

The River that God Forgot – Richard Collier (Collins 1968)

The Putumayo*: *The Devil's Paradise – W.E. Hardenburg (First published December 1912)(Latterly re-issued by the Ulan Press)

Homeward Blows the Wind – John Lane (johnlanebooks 2014) ISBN 978-0-9566622-7-9

Suggested Viewing

"Fitzcarraldo" – New World Pictures (Werner Herzog)(Klaus Kinski) 1982

"The Wrath of God" – Aguirre 1972

"Burden of Dreams" – 1982 (ISBN 0-933621-05-01) (Home Video – Deluxe Series)

River scene: Henry VIII bound for Pucallpa and another boat from the Tapiche river converge on cargo pontoon 'Sinchi Roca' at Requena, late afternoon

The magnificent former Malecón Palace Hotel, built 1908-12, now occupied by the Armed Forces. Designed in Barcelona by architect Vinals, disciple of Gaudi. In the foreground (comparing unfavourably) is the more recent Hotel Reál

The old Alhambra Theatre – burnt to the ground in 1954 and where now stands Hotel El Dorado Plaza. Also shown is the now demolished Municipal Building, and the surviving 'House of Clay' (Fitzcarraldo's House)

Section III
Eating Out

"He who is fastest is first."

Culinary Specialities

The typical foods of the region are many and are not to be missed, either in restaurants or from street stalls. The health risks associated with the latter are generally lower than those involved in riding in a *motocarro.* In former times the rules for world travellers were succinct: 'Peel it, boil it or leave it.' These days this advice can be tempered with personal discretion; however, still think twice before eating raw, unpeeled vegetables, salads and fruit. That said, here are just a few of the specialities and wayside offerings available.

Anticuchos. Skewered bull's heart (or cow); in other words, kebabs. Historically, has to have been an 'importation' from *la sierra* or *la costa.*

Barquillos. Fan-shaped sweet wafers, highly popular with children (50 *centimos* for 5)

Biscocho. Sweetened bread, special to Iquitos.

Caldo de Gallina. Fortifying chicken broth (Andean importation).

Cecina. Smoked, dried and salted pork meat.

Cebiche. One of the culinary highlights to be found in Perú, on *la costa* as well as in *la selva.* Raw fish (e.g. *paiche, corvina, dorado)* marinaded in lemon juice, with chopped onions, other vegetables such as orange sweet potato, maize, *yuca* (Adam's needle, cassava or manioc).

Chancaca. Dark brown, fudge-like *dulce* (sweet) prepared from sugar cane, boiled and then set. Excellent energy source when travelling, and also added to *chicha de maíz* to spice things up (see under *Frutas y Refrescos)*

Chilcano. Culinary preparation of clear fish soup using coriander, onions and garlic (eg *Chilcano de Sabalo, Carachama, Gamitana*).

Chonta. The heart of the palm tree; used in most salads with a variety of other ingredients. Palm-heart salad with fish is a typical meal of Holy Week.

Chupetes. Iced-lollies, of all varieties.

Churros. Éclair-shaped, sweet, sugar-coated, finger-sized 'pastry' made from eggs and flour. Available from street vendors throughout Iquitos – and

Perú (origin: Lima). Excellent. Very popular (and economic).

Cocada. Grated coconut mixed with hot *jarabe* (sugar and water 'syrup') and allowed to cool. Delicious (50 centimos for a little bag).

Empanada. Indicating 'stuffed' (in a culinary sense), e.g. ***Empanada de Yuca***.

Inchicapi. Peanut and chicken soup with corn flour, garlic, onion, *culantro* (coriander), salt, *yuca*.

Inchicucho. Corn flour and ground peanut with chilli.

Juanes. Ingredients: cooked rice, chicken, egg, olives. Seasoned and wrapped in *bijao/vijau* leaves.

Maíz Morado. Purple maize is a mutation of common 'sweet corn' dating back thousands of years and is unique to Peru in terms of colour and taste. Amongst the many claimed merits and beneficial outcomes are anti-ageing properties, improved circulation and heart conditioning, treatment of cancer and lowering of high blood pressure; it is also a diuretic.

Mazamorra of Gamitana. A rasped plantain (green banana) thick soup with *gamitana* fish (*mazamorra*: anything broken into small bits and pieces).

Mazamorra Morada. Literally 'violet or mulberry-coloured mash or pulp'. In this instance flour of purple maize is mixed with honey and sugar – a favourite concoction in Perú – and to the resultant paste pieces of chopped apple and/or dried plum are added to complete the *postre.* Readily available from street vendors as well as in restaurants.

Mingado. 'Like rice pudding, but without sophistication; when the larder is empty in the home, mother cooks *mingado* in the morning using freshly husked rice from the *chacra* with any sugar and milk that may be available (probably not, and probably without). Boiled for half an hour, then everyone dips in until it is finished, especially on cold and rainy days.' Sustaining and simple, but hardly to everyone's taste, especially when served unsweetened.

Pan de Cerveza. Bread with dark ale incorporated.

Pango de Sabalo. A style of cooking salted preserved fish solely in water with green bananas (hence *pango de ...* whatever kind of salted fish is to hand).

Panqueques. Yes, pancakes (flour, milk, eggs – as ever was), served with forest honey or *manjar* 'chocolate cream' (from Cajamarca).

Parihuela. A thick soup, the primary ingredient of which is fish from the sea (rather than river fish). Hence it owes more to *la costa* than *la selva*, but the dish/description may be encountered anywhere in Peru these days.

Patacones. Savoury banana slices (or roundels), first fried and then flattened into shape.

Patarashca. A method of cooking fish seasoned with *culantro* (coriander), garlic, onions, Amazon sweet chillies (*aji dulce*), and salt & pepper, in which it is enveloped in *bijao* leaves and steamed over charcoal (*carbon*).

Picadillo de Paiche. Cooked and crumbled *paiche* combined with regional vegetables.

Pícarones. Best described as fried doughnut rings, served hot with natural sugar-based syrup. Perú-wide, but originated in Lima, and popular as a *postre* in the winter months.

Plátano Ingüiri. Boiled green bananas. The same green bananas can be fried or grilled.

Ponche. Whipped white of eggs and sugar; nothing else (*masato* – fermented *yuca*-based liquor – may be added to taste, even coffee). A stimulating breakfast favourite.

Sarapatera/Zarapatera. Soup of turtle/tortoise meat, garlic and onion prepared over charcoal in the tortoise shell and served with cooked plantain.

Tacacho. Roasted plaintain (green banana), mushed and kneaded with fried pork meat (*cecina)* and served hot.

Tamalitos. Diminutive form of *Tamales* which contain *maíz,* peanuts, chicken or other meat and olives wrapped in *bijau* leaves. It is difficult for visitors to differentiate between *tamalitos* and *juanes;* the latter contain rice, the former contain ground sweet corn.

Timbuche. A concentrated soup of any fish (cf ***Chilcano*** – indigenous term for this manner of preparing and presenting fish).

Turrones de Mani. Peanut-based sticky pastries. Sustaining when travelling.

Restaurants

The variety and number of restaurants in Iquitos offering *'platos típicos'* is seemingly endless (and ever-changing) and may good fortune attend the efforts of he or she who attempts the almost impossible and Sisyphean task of cataloguing them all. Suffice to say that starting with those encircling the

Plaza de Armas, so long as you are able to walk 25 metres or so and have a few coins in your pocket, you will never go hungry in whatever district of the city you happen to be. Equally, you are unlikely to be disappointed, and that particularly includes *'los restaurants informales'*, the tables outside houses in the evening that are an extension of the family cuisine but ideal for an impromptu supper. In this respect, be sure to pay a visit to the cluster of quality stalls at ***Cancha el Ovalo,*** Yavari Cuadra 15 (specialists in *caldo de gallina regional* – amongst many other things).

The local liquor factory previously run by the **Gran Maloca** enterprise still produces liquers made from local fruits, such as mango, *cocona, mamey* and *carambola (Carambola Fuerte*). For formal dining, note the Ocucaje and Tacama white wines from Ica (south of Lima), a long way from Loreto, but still in Perú, land of abundance.

Breakfast with a difference can be taken from dawn onwards in ***Mercado Central*** (highly recommended – look out for *Sras.* Ana and Maria). Or you may visit ***Las Jugueras*** at the entrance to **Belén Market** (Calle 9 de Diciembre/Próspero): for example, one Nuevo Sol for two tumblers of blended fresh fruits (*jugo surtido)* and an avocado roll sandwich from *Jugerías La Gatita, Carmencita, Mishel, Carito,* and *Los Refrigerios Di Laura* and *Mary.*[20] However, if you feel more comfortable eating with a roof over your head, you can return to the Plaza de Armas for a traditional breakfast at **Ari's Burgers**[21] and the neighbouring hostelries, or try ***Ivalú Juguería*** (Sargento Lores 215) for your *jugo, tamales, juanes, pasteles, tortas* and other typical offerings. For your mid-morning coffee (or breakfast, or afternoon tea), and a rare slice of apple strudel, ***Maria's Café*** is the place (*Jr.* Nauta 292), where Maria herself is a direct descendant of the Morey family (*see earlier*).

For a quick lunch of *Cebiche de Dorado* (raw fish marinaded in lemon juice with onions, camote, *cancha* toasted maize, health-giving *yuyos* seaweed from the Pacific Ocean accompanied by a *cevada refresco* – see below), *Cebichería* '**Hay Que Rico**' at Ucayali 230 is hard to beat in return for S/.5.50 and whilst you are eating you can have your shorts adjusted or have a

---

[20] Sorry – inflation has taken its toll. Most probably one sol for one glass these days, and even the customary courtesy of a *yapita* top-up may not be forthcoming.

[21] By the by, Ari's Hotel opened in 2012, just down Próspero.

new dress run up just down the street at 'Elegance' (Ucayali 250). **Mar Adentro** seafood restaurant at Sargento Lores 766 also does a very generous *cebiche.* At **Restaurant 'Paulina'** (Tacna 591), S/.6.00 will get you a palm heart *(chonta)* salad followed by an alligator steak (white meat – *lagarto* – just enjoy it, don't think about what it was like when it was alive) from the menu of the day, or a choice of numerous other local dishes. Just off the Plaza at Fitzcarrald No.131 you will find a good menu at **Restaurant Huasai**, well presented and popular throughout the day, especially at lunchtime.

To overlook the river and *Puerto Belén*, go no further than the balcony of **Restaurant *La Pascana*** on Hurtado. To take to the river itself, you should be sure to visit the floating restaurant ***Al Frio y al Fuego*** with its unbeatable view (especially the lights at night) of the waterfront (and joined by the novelty of a floating swimming pool as of January 2009) for a memorable lunch or dinner (access to its private pontoon and ferry boats from Av. *La Marina* – reservations Jr.Pevas 252, tel: 224862/233119). If in spite of all the alternatives you are overcome with an irresistible hankering for roast chicken and chips, then visit ***El Pollón*** (*Pollería Restaurante,* Plaza de Armas, Próspero 151) or try *la pollería* **'Super Pollo'** in Plaza 28 de Julio (Aguirre/San Martín).

All of which just about brings us back to where we came in. Time to enjoy a delectable fresh fruit smoothie (made only with purified water, as is the ice) at the **Dawn on the Amazon Café** on the boulevard (Malecón Maldonado 185) and meditate. Indeed, now that you are comfortably seated, take the menu firmly in hand – it would be madness to leave without first sampling the incomparable local and international cuisine (with over 50 choices, and ranked No.1 restaurant in Iquitos by Trip Adviser for the past three years), and for peace of mind, know that the salads are only washed in purified water, not once but thrice. Indeed, as a further example of Bill and Marmelita's meticulous attention to detail, they have even sourced special fluoride-free salt from the Maras terraces, travelling personally to Cusco to that end. Now this alone is used in the restaurant and on the tables (in the custom made salt cellars), and in the absence of contrary evidence this is believed to be unique – certainly in Iquitos.

The colourful and busy riverfront boulevard at dusk

Regional Recipes

Following publication of the first edition of this booklet all those years ago, it was suggested that some recipes might be of interest in addition to details of regional culinary specialities. It was not easy to persuade local chefs to share the secrets of their success but here are a few ideas.

Tortilla Española. This dish is popular throughout Loreto (and of course, much further afield). It is included both because of its connection with colonial times and the fact that the primary ingredient, the potato, originated in Perú. The recipe was contributed by the *Chef de Alta Cocina* of the restaurant *La Casa de España* (Roma 190, San Isidro, Lima) during a visit to Iquitos.

Ingredients (4 persons): 6 white potatoes; 1 onion (white or red); 8 eggs; olive oil; salt.

Preparation. Peel and wash the potatoes then cut them into 'fine wheels'. Wash the onion and similarly cut it finely. Put an abundance of oil in the frying pan and when it is hot, fry the potato and onion together until golden.

Take them from the pan and cleanse from grease. Now beat the eggs in a bowl and add the fried potatoes and onion. Remove the oil from the frying pan and then pour in the egg, potato and onion mixture, applying slow heat. Give the *tortilla* a turn so that both sides cook nicely, decorate to taste and serve ready to eat.

Asado a la Parrilla. BBQ roast, basic recipe from *Un Restaurant Informal,* Río Mar. Popular throughout the region.

Ingredients (4 persons): 2kg of chops (wide-cut ribs), dressed and seasoned with salt for 5 minutes.

Preparation. Make a good fire with the charcoal or coals glowing brightly; put the roast on the grill and leave it to cook. When that side is nicely done, turn the chops and repeat the process. Easy. Relax, eat and enjoy.

Brocheta de Largato Fitz. 'Alligator Kebabs' donated by Liliana at the Fitzcarraldo Restaurant Bar.

Preparation. Load the skewers with squares of alligator, seasoned with lemon, vinegar, ginger, oregano (majorum), soy sauce, garlic salt and *ajino moto* (a powdered derivation from sugar cane). Alternate the pieces of alligator with cubes of pineapple, tinned or fresh. Fry everything. Mix a sauce consisting of an olive oil base, garlic, soy sauce, 2 teaspoons of pineapple juice, *ajino,* vinegar, salt, sugar and *chuño* (a form of potato flour). Decorate with *papaya* slices and *marrasquino* and serve with fried yucca. (Any missing ingredients – substitute with imagination).

Picadillo de Paiche. 'Paiche Hash' offered by *Ama de Casa* Patricia of Punchana.

Ingredients (2 persons): 1/4kg of dried and salted paiche fish; 5 *aji* ('sweet dwarf chilli') or one pepper; 2 medium sized onions; 1 'tooth' of garlic; a pinch of ground *guisador* or use *palillo* instead (apparently untranslatable: if not available, press on; no one is likely to notice); a teaspoon of oil. Salt and pepper to taste.

Preparation. 4 hours in advance, soak the paiche to get rid of the salt, changing the water as necessary. Then, when you are sure all the salt is out of the paiche, cook it for 8-12 minutes, drain and fry. But keep half a cup of the cooking water for later. 'Shred' or crumble the fish. Then, into a frying pan pour the oil, *palillo,* pepper, a pinch of salt and the garlic. Heat and leave it until golden. Add the onion, sweet chilli or pepper, fry lightly and finally add the cooked shredded paiche; cook well and turn frequently, adding the half cup of 'fish water' to the mixture as necessary to keep moist. Serve with *yuca* or potatoes; decorate with lettuce and slices of lemon.

Tacacho. Recipe kindly contributed by the former Iquitos Director of Tourism, Gerald W. Mayeaux (now of the Yellow Rose of Texas).

Ingredients: 4 green (peeled) bananas; ½ cup of pig fat (lard); 1 cup of pork 'chiclins' or 'scratchings' (chopped fried pork 'skin' – a mix of fat and meat); ¼ teaspoon of salt.

Preparation. Roast the bananas over the coals and then break into small pieces using a wooden mallet. Heat the lard until liquid and then pour the fat onto the crumbled bananas. Add in the salt and the heated pork pieces and knead the mixture into '*tacachos'* about the size of a 'soft ball' (says Gerald) (anything between a golf ball and a small tennis ball will do).

Chupe Peruana. Donated by *Srta*. Margot López from Santa Rita.

Ingredients (for 4): 16 prawns (approx); 12 pasta (approx); 4 new potatoes (approx); 1 small (200g) tin 'evaporated' milk; 4 small eggs; 100 grams green peas; 1 fish stock cube (e.g. Knorr); 1 pinch of toasted oregano; 1 fine garlic and salt to taste.

Preparation: 'In one pan put ¾ litre of hot water, salt, garlic, fish cube, new potatoes and the pasta and boil for five minutes. Then add the prawns and green peas and boil for three minutes more. Little by little add the egg whites like rain and boil for two minutes. To add the oregano, taste and pulverize with your hands and add the egg yokes and all the milk, boiling for 30 seconds. Then your *chupe* is ready! So, *!Buen Provecho!*'

Aguadito de Pollo. Contributed by Stitch Artist Pati of Calle Morona.

Ingredients (serves 4): 4 chicken thighs; 2 fistfuls of rice (soak for half an hour); 100 grms of green lentils; 100 grms of spinach; 1 bunch of coriander; 1 medium carrot; 1 little onion; '*¼ de un ají mirasol y 4 ají dulces'*; garlic; tumeric; *orégano*; laurel; *ajinomoto*; olive oil; salt and pepper to taste.

Preparation: 'Fry in oil the garlic, onion, pepper and tumeric. When the mixture is well cooked, add the chicken thighs until they are golden, then include the green lentils and the chopped carrot. Leave to simmer for some minutes, then add the spinach, coriander, and the *ají dulces y mirasol* (all put through the liquefier with a cup of water). When all these ingredients are in the saucepan, add the rice, laurel, *orégano, ajinomoto,* plus salt to taste. Let boil for 30 minutes until the rice is cooked, then serve with two pieces of *yuca* (manioc/cassava) and a *refresco de cocona.*'

Inchicapi Regional Gallina. Contributed verbally by 'Princesa' Ordóñez from the uncharted heart of *la selva* and translated from the original tribal dialect. Serves 12.

Ingredients: 1 hen (approx.3kg); 200 grms liquefied fresh peanuts; 200 grms corn flour plus a little cold water; 12 liquidised sweet seeded Amazonian peppers; 50grm liquidised coriander; 5 leaves laurel herb; half soup spoon oregano; 12 cloves garlic; 3 blended onions; salt & pepper, cumin seeds, *aji ajinomoto* seasoning.

Preparation: 'Cut the chicken into 12 pieces, add salt, pepper, cumin and garlic; let stand for one hour. In a large pot boil five litres of fresh water with the five laurel leaves and salt. When bubbling, add the chicken followed gently by all the 'soup' ingredients, whisking the whilst to prevent burning and preserving the creamy texture. Boil for half an hour. Finally add the liquidised coriander, and sit for five minutes. Served accompanied by 'chips' of cooked green plantain or cassava – or both.

Frutas y Refrescos

This is an introductory guide to some of the 'fruits of the forest', many of which are used to produce *refrescos* – cool fruit drinks laden with vitamins.

Aguaje – Fruit of the aguaje palm, ubiquitous, seemingly on sale year round. Resembles a small brown pine cone; is soaked in water and peeled to reveal the yellow flesh around a large seed. The *refresco* is known as *aguajina.* Highly popular, although consumption is reportedly prohibited in Brazil because 'the fruit contains 75% female hormones, leading to adverse consequences for males'. The regrettable practice of cutting down entire palms to harvest the fruit is now prohibited by law (as a substitute for common sense). Horticulturalists take note: only *Aguaje* that have seeded and grown naturally will bear fruit; it is said that raised and transplanted seedlings are either barren or will shed their harvest prematurely.

Almendra – A vine, with three seeds to each fruit, ready to eat.

Anona – Not dissimilar in appearance to the Chirimoya fruit to be found on sale in Lima, although brown rather than green and with soft, almost milky flesh. Described as a once-in-a-while not-to-be-missed-before-you-leave treat; certainly its consumption defies all known rules of etiquette and it is best eaten in the shower. Do not swallow the large black seeds as they may have dire consequences for your digestive system. The mother tree is vigorous and medium sized.

Caihua – A forest vine (with green leaves similarly shaped to those of Virginia Creeper) producing a large fruit somewhere between a cucumber and a green pepper, eaten as a vegetable. Not especially tasty on its own, but passable when stuffed (like a marrow), and when eaten as an accompaniment to rice and fish.

Carambola – Yellowy-green, medium sized fruit like a Chinese lantern. The tree is similar in size to an orange tree. *Carambola Fuerte* is a locally made liquer.

Camu Camu – Exclusive to *la selva,* the shrub likes low-lying areas adjacent to the water. The fruit is full of vitamins (one *camu camu* supposedly contains the Vit.C of 40 oranges or 10 lemons) and looks like a small plum. Extensively used for medicines, perfumes, liquors and *refrescos.* The export crop of the future. Every part of this shrub has its use, not only the fruit (which is additionally used in jams, syrups and even hair balms). The bark is used in the production of the restorative liquor '*Siete Raíces*', whilst the bark and the roots in conjunction make medicine to alleviate diarrhoea and rheumatism. The shredded leaves make a fusion with water with which to bathe the head against fever or to ingest to mollify 'internal fever' or migraine.

Caimito – Yellow fruit, size of an orange. Peeled to reveal white, almost transparent sweet flesh, eaten raw. Delicious, and much appreciated by the *paucar* birds as well as by *homo sapiens*, but rather messy as the peel contains an obdurately sticky resin that requires paraffin to remove. The parent tree is large and stately.

Casho – Also *caju* (cashew); red, size of a small pear. Bitter-sweet. It is of course the seed, the cashew nut curiously placed externally on the fruit, which is most sought after, although it has to be cooked or roasted before eating otherwise it is singularly caustic.

Cebada is a *refresco* made from grain (*trigo*), and although hardly a 'fruit of the forest' is included here as it is a frequently encountered accompaniment for *cebiche*. Served cold, although the process involves boiling in water (and is therefore 'safe' for *gringos*); ideal for hot days, certainly health giving and even (reputedly) 'good for the brain'.

Cereza – Wild cherry of the forest.

Chambira – A miniature coconut. Tedious to open but sold on the street ready-prepared.

Chapaja – Yet another mini-coconut palm, with great clusters of abundant hanging fruit, rated locally as '*deliciosos*' (eaten direct).

Chapo (chapito) – Made from the *capirona* yellow banana (one of over a hundred different kinds); stewed and eaten with milk – a staple family food.

Charichuela – diminutive fig-sized yellow fruit of the giant parent tree, used to make a *refresco* or alcoholic beverage.

Chicha de Maíz – *chicha* signifies a preparation conserved (and often fermented) for later consumption. In this case derived, as the name suggests, from sweet corn and lovingly prepared over a period of some weeks, with the addition of honey and 'forest herbs' (and *chancaca* – above). Popularly served at *mingas* – any community activity, such as the tidying of the *plaza* or re-roofing the *maloca.*

Chicha Morada – Made from purple maize, and included here for completeness; Andean in origin but spread widely throughout Péru. Non-alcoholic. Served cold but the preparation involves boiling the maize with cinnamon (*canela*), cloves, 'rich orange peel' and any other spices that may come to hand. Good for the brain (apparently) and a popular accompaniment for *cebiche.*

Cidra – The missing link between oranges and lemons. The leaves make an excellent cup of tea.

Coco – Coconuts are not indigenous to *la selva*, although nowadays they are certainly ubiquitous, having found their way through Pucallpa from *la costa* long ago, hence their inclusion here. The 'milk' (juice) taken naturally makes for a highly refreshing drink on a hot day.

Cocona – Roundish, plum-sized citrous fruit, native of *la selva alta*. Red and yellow skin with yellow flesh. Grows in bush form. Not only a choice *refresco*, rich in vitamin C and minerals, but also a healing agent for the skin, an anti-oxidant, good for controlling blood pressure and for 'cleaning and revitalising the head'. Culinary use is in the form of a cream mixed with *aji* (chilli); perfumes are amongst the cosmetics employing cocona. Global interest has led to commercialisation and exportation

Copoazú – large melon-sized fruit, used for *refrescos*, *chupetes* and ices.

Guaba – A legume rather than a fruit, the giant seed pods of this plant can be up to a metre in length. The edible part is the cotton-like pulp which surrounds the seeds (beware of little maggots!), the extraction of which passes the time on river trips.

Guayaba – Red and yellow fruit, tasting like an apple but slightly smaller. Can be eaten raw (the whole fruit is edible) and is much favoured for jam making.

Guanabana – Member of the *chirimoya* family (rich fruit of the coast, white flesh contained in a 'spikey' green covering), but sweeter and softer, used for *refrescos, chupetes* and ices or eaten directly. Prized for its health-giving properties, namely anti-carcinogenic, anti-ulcers, parasites and bacteria; respiratory and stress benefits, and the promotion of healing.

Huasaí – Edible, oily palm fruit used for palm wine and ice cream.

Huingo – Football-sized curiosity; grows on the slenderest of stems straight out of the bark of the parent – the Calabash Tree of South America. The gourd is useful as a container.

Humari – Something between an apple and a large plum in size; purply/black when ripe. The huge pip/seed stone within is surrounded by bright yellow flesh which may be spread on bread, hence *la mantequilla de la selva* – 'the butter of the forest'.

Huito – Size of a grapefruit, light brown, neither sweet nor sour, this citric fruit comes from a large tree of the forest. *Huitochado* is a drink prepared with *huito,* sugar and fermented cane juice. Can be used to make a black dye, applied to the skin as a renovator and repellent.

Limón – Forest-grown lemon.

Macambo – Size of an ostrich egg, greeny-yellow, ribbed. Cut like a melon and eat the pulp directly. The seeds can be extracted, peeled, then toasted over charcoal and eaten from skewers (popularly on sale at Bellavista Nanay). The tree is huge.

Mamey – Ubiquitous tree throughout the region, identified by its glossy dark green leaves and the carpet of purple blossom under the branches. Fruit like a scarlet apple, hidden from sight by the thick green foliage when on the tree; may be eaten fresh or, more adventurously, made into jam.

Mandarinas Silvestres – Mandarins, possibly originally introduced from *la selva alta,* but with a thick green skin, used for marmalades and cakes; also has insect repellent properties. Spectacularly, the juice squeezed from the skin can be ignited to produce a shower of sparks.

Mango – Commonly known fruit (as in Africa, SE Asia etc) with juicy yellow flesh. The fresh growing tips of the polished dark green foliage of the tree are tinted red, aiding identification and avoiding confusion with the

Mamey tree. The tastiest of all the mangos come from Tarapota – heart of *la selva alta.* Here in the rain forest the 'wild mango' variant (*sacha mango* – i.e. 'looks like a mango') is slightly larger, as is the internal seed, leaving just a thin layer of edible flesh, the consistency and flavour of which is not dissimilar to a Brazil nut. (Digression: it is said that the mothers of *los demonios* dwell in the dark depths of the branches of ancient mango trees in the heart of the forest …).

Maracúya – Passion fruit; the wild vine reaches high into the forest canopy.

Melón – As encountered in other parts of the world, although not as succulent; grown on the fertile alluvium exposed when the rivers are low. Water melon: *melon de agua* or *sandia.*

Palta – Avocado. Nowadays these are also flown up from Lima, and are double the price of the forest *palta.*

Papaya – Also known as *paw paw* in Asia. Frequently encountered large greeny-yellow fruit with bright orange flesh that grows from the slender trees with frond-like leaves that are found in everyone's smallholding (*chacra*). Much used in *jugos.* Consumption of cool cubes of *papaya* have been found to provide a modicum of amelioration for those unfortunates suffering from the extremely unpleasant effects of dengue fever.

Parinari – Fruit of the shady *parinari* tree. Two species: the large fruit is insipid; the small fruit has a good taste for *refrescos.*

Pijuayo – Green, orange, red palm fruit; eaten cooked, orange flesh. Makes excellent bait for fishing. Highly nutritional, rich in carbohydrates. Used for *refrescos* and sauces. Size of a small apple.

Piña – Pineapple. Grown commercially in the region; processing plant needed to facilitate preservation and export (vacancy: entrepreneur wanted). Aside from pineapple juice, the peel/skin of the pineapple (*cascara de piña*) is commonly boiled, and after straining and the addition of sugar, the resultant preparation (apart from being made into *chupetes*) is used as a favoured enriching base for other concoctions, such as *Chicha Morada* and *Mazamorra Morada.*

Pisco Sour – Slyly slipped in here for good measure; certainly a *refresco* of sorts, definitely nourishing and sustaining, and very much the property of Peru (in spite of neighbouring claims). The *pisco* spirit itself is 'white brandy', a distillation from *muscat* grapes (produced in the vineyards around

Ica in the south – a Spanish contribution). The recipe is: three parts pisco, 1 part lemon juice, sugar to taste (ideally in the form of *jarabe de goma* – literally 'rubber syrup': white cane sugar, water and gum Arabic (sic); a magic ingredient, much favoured by mixologists, and with a thousand ramifications), white of egg, ice. Blend and serve; add a pinch of cinnamon and a drop of angostura bitters to embellish.

Platanos – There are at least 120 varieties of banana. The large 'green' bananas are used for cooking; the finger-sized yellow bananas are the best for dessert. The huge 'hands' of bananas brought in by boat from the forest villages to *Puerto Productores* on Av. La Marina are as much as a man can carry.

Sacha-Inchi – Yes, a nut rather than a fruit, but brimming with goodness and not to be missed; grows in clusters on a vine. The name derives from two Quechua words: *sacha* = looks like; *inchi* = peanut. Now grown commercially for the Omega 3 content – lowers cholesterol, generally health-giving, quite the latest thing in salad oil.

Taperiba – Green fruit, yellow inside. Broadly similar to an apple when eaten, but sweeter, juicier and generally more exotic.

Toronja – Type of lemon, used for *cebiches* and *refrescos.*

Tumbo – More of a vegetable, hanging from the creepers of the *tumbo* plant, almost the size of a rugby ball, yellow in colour. Used for *refrescos* (and for promoting abortions).

Tutumo – See *Huingo,* the calabash gourd.

Umari – Egg-sized but with a large seed. However, the edible part is very nutritional.

Ungurahui – Another palm fruit, the natural oils of which are beneficial for the hair and skin. The fruit is used for *refrescos;* the oil is extracted for cosmetic use.

Uvilla – Also *ubilla.* Similar in appearance to a grape (*uvas rusticas),* hence *La Uva de la Selva.* Eaten directly, inconveniently large pips. Grows on a medium-sized tree rather than a vine.

Uvos – Another rustic cousin of the grape. Large tree, small fruit. ***Uvachado*** is an alcoholic drink prepared from *uvos,* forest honey and fermented cane-juice.

Vacavilla – A coffee-coloured, coffee-tasting *refresco* made from the black fruits of this member of the palm family.

Yarina – Another palm fruit, like little eggs, containing clear pulp tasting of coconut.

Zachamango – Large egg-shaped brown fruit growing on a sizeable tree. Eaten directly. (Yes – that word *sacha* again: 'looks like a mango').

Zapote – Greeny brown fruit, fist-sized, from a tall and slender tree, usually cultivated. Sweet, eaten directly (impossible to do this with dignity, but never mind); bright orange flesh. Delicate, highly-decorative yellow flowers.

Other 'drinks' that may be encountered

Masato: this is fermented liquor made from *yuca* ***(El Shibe)*** or *pijuayo* or *tumbo* fruit. (The same root vegetable *yuca* will be encountered in other parts of the world as 'manioc' or 'cassava'). ***Aguardiente*** is a dark green alcoholic derivative from sugar cane (*'el whisky de los nativos')*; another name for this fermented cane juice is ***Huarapo.*** A preparation of *cocona* fruit, sugar and *aguardiente* produces ***Coconachado*** *(el champaña de la selva)*. ***Chuchuhuasi*** is prepared from bark of the tree of the same name, marinaded in *aguardiente.* ***Chapo*** is a *jugo* (a mix in the blender) rather than a *refresco;* as already mentioned it is made from ripe *Capirona* bananas. ***Cahuana*** is an extremely bitter but fortifying preparation of *yuca* and the pulp of *aguaje.*

Raspadillas are not strictly drinks but fruit-flavoured multi-coloured crushed ice sold by roadside vendors from equally colourful carts, especially popular with children. Likewise ***Curichi*** and ***Marciano:*** flavoured ice sold in plastic bags (take care – preparation does not necessarily involve boiling the water). ***Hierba Luisa:*** this herb abounds in the forest, the leaves of which, fresh or dried, are used to produce a tea with both digestive and relaxing properties, served hot or cold (also an ingredient in *Inca Cola*). And whilst on the subject of fringe 'drinks', try a glass of **Ponche** for your breakfast when next in Belén Market or from *Mamá Conchita* in *Mercado Central* – a frothy white whipped-egg and sugar concoction, sometimes fortified with black malt beer or *masato*.

Visiting the Markets

There are three main 'general purpose' market-places in Iquitos: **Belén** (best entered at the junction of 9 de Diciembre with Ramírez Hurtado), **Modelo** (enter from the junction of Arequipa with Callao) and **Central**

(Sargento Lores and Moore)[22]. There is a fourth market – **Sachachorros** – situated between Av. Grau and *Cdra* 14 of Aguirre, principally for clothing and groceries (and a favourite and well recommended destination before New Year's Eve).

As mentioned separately, Central Market is housed in the 'other half' of the *Casa de Fierro* and in consequence is relatively small but with easy access and convenient for breakfast. Modelo has a greater area of stalls, half covered, half outside, but is more compact, slightly cleaner and the general scene is marginally less demented than Belén, which is a vast congested labyrinth of traders and buyers extending practically the length and breadth of Belén Town from Alfonso Ugarte to García Saenz. Prices between the three markets vary little, although frantic Belén just has the edge; the height of the rivers is really the deciding factor. When the water is highest (February to May), prices are high. When the waters recede, fish are plentiful because they are easier to catch, and more fertile alluvial land is available for growing produce locally.

The range of goods, fish, meat, fruit and vegetables on offer is nothing short of amazing, which makes a visit to the markets so compelling, particularly to Belén, starting with the famous shops and stalls of ***Los Chinos*** on the outskirts, selling practically everything at the lowest prices. Delving deeper into the market, each zone and alley in Belén has its speciality, be it footwear, watches, spectacles, dried frogs or the medicinal plants and aphrodisiacs of the forest exclusively on sale in *Pasaje* Don Paquito. These include the renowned and exotic enervating elixirs such as *7 Raíces, 21 Raíces, Tumba Hembra, Levántate Lazaro, Rompe Calzón, Para Para (*not to be confused with *Piri-Piri* which is a reed with an onion like bulb used as an antidote for snake bites), *Parado Listo Muerto, Uvachado* and other curative and medicinal root, bark, leaf and twig preparations – for example *Sangre de Grado, Uña de Gato* and *Chuchuhuasi,* plus persuasive *Pusanga* and other mementos of the Amazon. Near to Don Paquito is the section of the market devoted to the sale of locally produced tobacco, obtainable in all its forms, from leaves rolled to shape a giant baguette or finely cut, ready to make cigarettes known locally as *mapachos* (lit. 'disordered') or *espanta tunchis* ('drive away the demons!').

The rubbish and mud underfoot in the market is invariably indescribable,

---

[22] Once upon a time it was supposedly sited on the riverfront boulevard, but I have yet to put a date on this ...

but it is well worth the heat, sweat and toil. Especially if you can find your way to **Plaza Belén** (at the confluence of *calle* 5, *calle* 7 and *calle* Pénjamo) where sits the beautiful wrought iron **bandstand** which is on occasion attributed to Gustave Eiffel. This gem of eight columns on an octagonal base with balustrades of forged iron topped by a dome with decorative flowers and a cockerel weather vane with the cardinal points is much in need care and restoration, and when the river is high it is practically swamped by the stalls of traders displaced from the lower reaches of the market, so that if inclined, the visitor can play Bingo with maize grain in the rusty shadow of this masterpiece. Perhaps it is indeed the work of Gustave Eiffel. If so, the famous architect will be pleased to know that when the River Itaya falls, the Bandstand is reportedly put to good use at least once a month.

In fact, the ***glorieta*** was a gift to the city from the Chinese community of Iquitos in 1921 to mark the first 100 years of Peruvian Independence, although that need not necessarily exclude the hand of Eiffel from the work of art. Either way, and ninety years later, perhaps the resident Chinese community could be prevailed upon to brighten their kind gesture with a renovative coat of paint. The commemorative plaque on the base of the stand explains that Plaza Belén was not constructed until 1965, being officially opened on 28th July of that year. Consequently, what we may call the Chino-Gallic Bandstand was originally sited in the Plaza de Armas until 1963 (just across the road in front of *Casa Fitzcarrald,* as depicted in various old sepia photographs), when it was moved to Plaza Clavero and then on again to Belén in 1965. Whither next?

Classic oxbow lake formation

Manguaré drums – el río Yanamono

Fishing at Barrio Florido

Section IV
Short Excursions and Taking to the Rivers

"They can who think they can."

Quistococha

This National Tourist Park was first opened in 1979 and can be reached in less than half an hour from the centre of Iquitos; the name is a derivation, or rather, a distortion, of *Cristo Cocha*, meaning 'Lake of Christ'. It covers a site of some 369 hectares (more than 800 acres) of verdant forest, although currently only a small part of this is utilised for visitors and there are plans for expansion (some accounts record the total park area as being 400 hectares). The river Itaya borders Quistococha and there is a large lake for boating, fishing and swimming (from *Tunchi Playa* or 'Ghost Beach').

The legend concerning what is now the bathing lake in the park is rather confused, but in essence (and with scarcely any embellishment) it runs more or less as follows. Apparently, in days long gone, every time 'bad things' happened in the nearby villages, the island in the centre of the lake would move, which was not only amazing but alarming. Whereupon all the parrots in the vicinity would whirl around at top speed overhead, squawking frantically at what was undoubtedly an unusual occurrence, and simultaneously everyone in the villages was terrified and there was general depression. Eventually the local priest was called to perform mass to exorcise the evil spirits. As he gave the final blessing he threw a crucifix into the waters, at which moment the island gave a terminal shuddering heave of great intensity and a gigantic black snake appeared and swam off into the distance. The curious thing for the onlookers was that this monstrous snake was whistling as it went on its way, this being a known phenomenon amongst snakes, but one which is more often encountered when they are sleeping. All of which serves to half-explain the naming of the park and the beach.

So much for that. Around the zoo area the many kinds of fruit and other trees are marked with their names (*cumalas blancas, catahuas, renacos, marupas, paltas, aguajes, zapotes, umaris, pijuayos, pichohuayos, guabas* etc). In the zoo itself there is a good collection of the 'cats' of the jungle (ocelots, pumas, jaguars), along with *ronsocos* ('water pigs'), tapirs, giant otters, jungle rodents, alligators, and lots of different monkeys (including spider monkeys). The aviary houses colourful *huacamayos* (macaws), *Pihuichos* (little green parrots who sing before it rains), *pichicos*, and a solitary *Tuyuyo*, a Jaribu stork. In the reptile house you can see *mantonas* (boas), try a live anaconda for size round your neck and take a photograph for posterity. In the outdoor fish tanks are huge *paiche*, speciality of the Amazon, which could probably be your only opportunity to come face to face with this monster, other than as a slice of fish steak (from a fish farm) on your dinner plate. There are also *sabalos* and *boquichicos*. At the other end of the scale, in the aquarium are dozens of varieties of smaller fish, including lugubrious *bujurquis, macanas rayadas, shiripiras, pez cruz, bagres, carachamas, palometas* and the more widely known *piraña*, plus a separate compound for young alligators.

A visit to Quistococha is an excellent aperitif before staying in a jungle lodge or travelling on the rivers. A flying visit could be done in about an hour, but to do justice to the Park, allow at least 2 to 3 hours, particularly if you want to digest all the local legend information that is displayed on the entrance path, walk the jungle trail (don't forget your repellent) and have time for a *refresco* or to sample a *suri* palm-maggot by the artificial beach (*tunchi playa*) after swimming and enjoying the view from one of the two *maloca* round houses. To fish on the lake (56.5 hectares), arrive early (say 0700 when the park opens) for best results and to avoid the heat.

You can travel to Quistococha by *combi (collectivo* or *micro)* from the centre of Iquitos (departing irregularly throughout the day from the block bordered by Alfonso Ugarte, Próspero, José Gálvez and Arica, signposted *El Paradero omnibus y combi*) or in similar style from the corner of Bermúdez with Moore just off the Plaza *28 de Julio* (behind *Colegio San Agustín)* for S/.2.00, but a personal *motocarro* should be no more than S/.12.00 for two or three passengers (one way) and you may feel it worth paying the extra for the convenience. Most economically, you can use the 'new' bus service No.49 from *Av. Marina* down *Arica* through *Belén* (returning *Belén/Huallaga*); or pick up bus No.56 in Jr. Tacna[23] which also goes all the way for S/.1.00. Alternatively, you can take an *Aeropuerto* banana-coloured bus to the

---

[23] And whilst you're in Tacna, do have a look at No.193 – surely the oldest store in Iquitos, caught in a time-warp!

terminus and use a *motocarro* for the final kilometre or so. Same for the return journey (take your time in the park, you will find lots of eager *motocarros* waiting at the exit when you want to leave). The road is tarmac throughout, the distance south westwards down the Nauta *carretera* being just over 8 miles (13 kilometres).

During the week you will have the park practically to yourself; at weekends and on fiestas and holidays it is more crowded. On arrival you may be greeted by one or more small boys offering to show you round; in fact they can be excellent guides, full of information (and if Alfredo is on duty, you are in luck, especially if halfway round you are joined by Federico the tame monkey). Postscript: as mentioned, be sure to take your insect repellent.

One final thought: If you visit the Park on a night when the moon is full, with sufficient patience you may be fortunate enough to encounter *La Sirena*, The Siren of the Lagoon of Quistococha. For it is on these moonlit nights that a beautiful woman emerges from the water to sit at the edge of the lake, where, with immense sadness, she combs her long hair as it glistens in the moonbeams. Her name is Flor del Yavari, exiled to the lake by her father, a renowned and forbidding Yacuruna (a scaly denizen of the deep – see Section VII, Legendary Inhabitants of the Forest), who never forgave *La Sirena* for falling in love with a mortal. *Asi es.*

*[Having thus whetted your interest in the regional nature trail, you may also like to visit the **Manatee Conservation Centre**, now re-named El Centro de Rescate Amazónico to reflect wider activities, conveniently situated just short of Quistacocha on the opposite side of the Nauta road, 4.5kms past the Airport and open every day. Visitors may personally stroke and bottle feed the fascinating baby manatees, and there are also rescued river otters and monkeys to be seen; run by IIAP, the Peruvian Amazon Research Institute – very popular and rightly so, well recommended (entrance just S/.5.00). Then go the whole hog and take a 30 minute rápido downriver to the animal refuge **Fundo Neyser** (Centro de Custodia Temporal Neyser) this side of Indiana for some personal interaction with monkeys, snakes and birds, tying this excursion in with a visit to **Monkey Island** (page 98).]*

Manatee Conservation Centre: "Yo tambien quiero vivir!"

Bellavista Nanay

Formerly a separate village 3 kilometres to the north of Iquitos, Bellavista Nanay (which predictably lies on the banks of the River Nanay) is nowadays linked to the city by timber mills and other light industrial development along the length of the *Carretera de la Marina (Avenida La Marina),* much of it currently defunct, derelict and rusting. However, the riverside food-stall and restaurant market is full of interest and activity for a late afternoon or early evening visit, particularly at weekends, whether to eat or simply for amazement value. Try roasted *Macambo* seeds on a wooden skewer and *tacacho de plátano azado en carbón* (best described as barbequed banana balls mixed with flakes of pork and pig's fat – see Recipes). You can also enjoy *anticuchos de suris de aguaje,* but in that case it's probably best that you don't know that these are skewers of lightly toasted fat white giant maggots that are extracted from inside the trunk of fallen *aguaje* palms. Some people eat them raw. Perhaps sample roasted caiman hunks instead...

For a fistful of dollars (or considerably less, according to your negotiating skills), a private or group boat can be rented from Bellavista Nanay to visit the **Bora** or **Yagua** tribes (and to participate in the Anaconda dance and buy artefacts). Or you can go afloat simply to view and enjoy the general area, and to take photographs of the picturesque houses (see below: Iquitos Waterfront). Between late July and mid-November when the rivers are low – *el estiaje* – trips to the beaches are available. These seasonal sand bars get pretty crowded at weekend but with lots of movement and colour they can be fun and are highly popular.

For rather less (2 or 3 *Nuevos Soles)* visitors can take a ride across the River Nanay on one of the regular public passenger boats which run up river to **Padre Cocha** (15 minutes), situated at the entrance to the *Río Momón*, and down the Nanay into the Amazon to **Barrio Florido** (25 minutes). Both water trips are relaxing and interesting, providing a window onto local river life. The village of Padre Cocha gives access to the fascinating **Pilpintuwasi** (yes, more Quechwa) **Butterfly Farm** (open Tuesday to Sunday, 0900-1600, tel: 232665/cell: 965932999, www.amazonanimalorphanage.com – sound the *manguaré* drum to announce your arrival to the staff), which in addition to the beautiful butterflies has become a refuge for abandoned animals. These include a jaguar, ant-eaters (with tongues of 80cms in length), tapir and a variety of monkeys, including two orphaned howlers.

Barrio Florido has rather more local colour and the houses are of traditional wood, roofed with fronds as opposed to the *material noble* (in other words, concrete) of Padre Cocha. Moreover, the trip to Barrio Florido runs past the river base of the Peruvian Navy, including the beached remains of a river corvette, circa 1940, World War II vintage and probably procured from the USA, now being rapidly consumed by the invading forest. The village lies just short of the Petroperú refinery[24] and particulary when the water level is high, there is the chance to hire a *canoa* on an informal basis to do some fishing. After which a meal can be taken at the restaurant *Señor de Los Milagros* run by the *Club de Madres de Barrio Florido,* a typical offering for 2 *Nuevos Soles* being pork soup followed by pork with rice and *crema de pallares* (the favourite bean of the Incas) with a *refresco* of *chicha morada* (the dark red sweet corn), a menu which admittedly owes more to *la costa* or *la sierra* rather than *la selva.*

---

[24] Some way beyond the refinery, and before Indiana, **Sinchicuy** is located – a former US outpost engaged in the battle against drugs, and now manned by Peruvian officials with the same intent.

Also at Bellavista Nanay is the *Club Social Deportivo de Caza y Pesca* (founded 29th June 1976), just a 5 minute canoe ride offshore. A call to the Administrator on telephone 252039 will elicit entrance fee and subscription rates and details of facilities available to members (including boat and float plane moorings).

Iquitos Waterfront

For *aficiónados* of quaysides and all things nautical, provided that the river waters are high (i.e. generally between December and May), the thing to do is to seek out Captain Rister (or similar) at the port of Bellavista Nanay and in return for a small fee (perhaps S/.35 for a group of four) you will be treated to a leisurely three hour trip in his *irapay* canopied *botecito* along the Iquitos waterfront, guaranteed to be full of interest from beginning to end.

Travelling in the direction of *Puerto Productores*, first you will pass the numerous sawmills, *los aserraderos*, each accompanied by endless rafts of timber floating offshore, and you will be led to wonder for how long the forest can support this rate of timber extraction, day in day out? Foremost amongst the felled baulks are those of the giant *Lupuna*, towering trees of immense grandeur which have taken centuries to reach maturity and which are irreplaceable, now destined to become plywood for kitchen units in the so-called developed world. There has to be a better way.

Onward chugs Captain Rister, past the hollow vastness of the dumb lighters designed for transporting *petroleo*, past the floating docks used for the repair and maintenance of river craft of all tonnages, on to the fascination of the ferry-packed jetties of *Puertos Masusa* and *Henry*. Then to the Naval Base, where beyond historic BAP America (dealt with in detail separately – see *Plaza Clavero*), modern river corvettes are berthed, armed with business-like medium calibre mountings fore and aft, handy for frontier protection duty.

And all the while the birds come and go, and you will have no difficulty in identifying the ubiquitos *gallinazos*, the all-black, crow-like scavengers, with their red-headed cousin, the *rinahui*. The soaring sparrow hawk higher in the sky is the black and white, snake-eating *gavilán*, whilst at the other end of the scale you will spot the *touki touki* coots bobbing on the water. The distinctive heron are *garza*, the cormorant-style seagulls are *piebet*, whilst the yellow and black birds that flit past are banana-eating *paucar* enjoying a day out on the river but more usually associated with their nests that hang high above the

forest skyline on the topmost branches of the tallest trees.

The hanging nests of the Paucar birds – a common sight in the forest

Just before reaching the riverside offices of long-established **Explorama**[25] you will pass the fanciful flotilla of Brazilian cruise boats, with their promise of air-conditioned jungle adventure, fresh linen and haut cuisine. And then your eye will be distracted, first by the tower of the Church of Santa Fatima looming over Belén in the far distance, secondly by the derelict sky-blue emptiness of the architect's aberration (mentioned earlier) adjacent to the Plaza de Armas, and finally (as you pass along the boulevard, directly off the end of Putumayo Street), there will be the confectioner's spire of the

---

[25] Easily pinpointed when stately M/F **Amazon Queen** is alongside, painted in the Explorama livery of cream and orange. She was built/launched in 1997 as a cargo/passenger vessel, delivered on 27th August of that year, single screw, now converted to 6 cylinder diesel, acquired by Explorama 29th January 2001, and named *Rio Seco* at that time. The previous *Amazon Queen* was a wooden ship built/launched 22nd July 1967, owned by Paul Wright and engaged on taking tourists to Santa Rosa/Tabatinga/Leticia, but now no more.

cathedral, *La Iglesia Matriz*, framed between the *caucho*-epoch magnificence of the former Palace Hotel and the markedly less magnificent Hotel *Reál* (surely over-ripe for redevelopment, but where – in its pomp – Jennifer López supposedly stayed whilst engaged on the rigours of shooting 'Anaconda').

Onwards through the purple-flowering *huamas*, up the river Itaya into the floating village of Belén, the semi-see-through wooden houses thatched with the tradional *yarina* and *irapay* fronds. Past the ferries leaving for Tamshiyacu, and beyond, attended by a shoal of waterborne *vendedores*, weaving a course through erratic families canoeing out to bathe in the less polluted waters midstream or to wash their pots and pans. Photographs taken, save the upper reaches of the Itaya for exploration another day; now Captain Rister will reverse course and head towards *Padre Isla*, Iquitos Island, following the former course of the mighty Amazon before (having devoured the previous Iquitos boulevard) it changed its route and decided to cut the corner and flow directly towards Bellavista Nanay. As you pass the island you will see the float planes in their shelters on the shoreline. If you are lucky, one or other of them will oblige, taxi out and take off in a plume of spray. Or sometimes not, when the passenger count and cargo load is too great and the day too hot and windless. In which case the pilot will taxi back to base, one of the aircraft's two heavy starter batteries will be ditched and, with undiminished optimism, a further attempt may be made to get airborne.

Circumnavigation of the tranquil island completed, time to head for home. Point the bow at the great dome of the *iglesia católica Inmaculada de Punchana*, cross the turbulence between the black waters of the Itaya and the muddy brown of the Amazon, and keep a sharp eye out for the dolphins that frequent these parts. The sun will be hot now; be thankful that you set out at eight in the morning and that it is not yet directly overhead. Take a cooling *refresco* of *cebada* or *chicha morada* in the market once you are safely back onshore – and, thus re-invigorated, the rest of the day is yours to enjoy.

Morona Cocha

This village is situated just ten minutes or so from the centre of Iquitos (S/.2.00 by *motocarro)* to the west of the city on *lago Morona Cocha*, which in turn is connected for most of the year to the river Nanay. Consequently this picturesque and photogenic (westward facing – good for sunsets) waterfront district is readily accessible by water, and boats may be taken to other nearby villages. For example, *Don* Felipe will convey you to sleepy ***Santa Rita*** (where, sadly for some, oil has been discovered), and a similar 45 minute trip with *'capitán'* Jorge Aricari in his *bote motor de aluminio* (or with Gerald in his traditional wooden *lancha* with *irapuay* roof) to the hamlet of **San José de Lupuna** will take you through forest scenery in the company of darting swallows and brightly coloured butterflies. The tranquil waters en route are practically deserted apart from an occasional dugout loaded with firewood, and a few patient fishermen. Once in San José de Lupuna you can swim from the bridge over an off-shoot of the river, try your hand in a borrowed canoe, do some fishing and buy a sack of charcoal for your *tuchpa* BBQ at half the Iquitos market price. The round trip will be under S/.10.00 – perhaps as little as S/.2.00, according to your level of integration.

From the same embarkation point you can visit the river Momón which runs into the Nanay. This outing is rather more adventurous, the *'bote de madera con motor'* leaving at 0900 each day and coming to rest far up the Momón at around 1700, having stopped all along the way for passengers and produce. The return boat sets out the following morning to bring you home by the evening after 36 hours of sharing the lives of the indigenous people. To complete the evolution by nightfall on the first day, the trick is to switch to the Morona Cocha-bound boat half way…. (See Section VII for an account of an excursion up *El río Momón).*

There is a second river departure point at Morona Cocha just 50 metres from the first which serves the village of **Manacamiri** on the river Nanay, just one *Nuevo Sol* and 25 tranquil minutes distant. The boats run to and fro all day, passing en route the base for the *Grupo Aéreo 42* float planes (see next Section). Manacamiri is a happy place, popular at weekends and with a sandy beach exposed between July and November. The (occasional) Sunday food market on the grass at the side of the ever-active football pitch is full of interest: *juanes, empanadas* (yucca 'pasties' filled with egg, *aji dulce,* vegetables and beans), the yellow sweet-tasting *caimitos* fruits, the bright red *mamey, cocada postres* (cooked coconut and sugar balls), the citric lemon-like *cidra,* slices of coconut for 10 centimos, forest avocados, potent *masato de yuca* to drink, or *coconachado* liquor (*cocona* fruit and *aguardiente* femented cane juice). *Palometa* fish cooked in *bijau* leaves over charcoal compete with barbequed *boquichico* and there are mounds of the ever-present 'pine-cone' *aguaje* yellow palm fruit (remove the hard 'shell' with your fingers and reveal that you are from *la sierra* or a tourist; *Loretanos* always use their teeth).

Having made your purchases from the market, walk through the village to the renowned ***El Huerto de Mamá*** ('Mother's Orchard') and, if fortune is with you, meet *Mamá* herself ("No, I am not the owner here; He is looking down from above"). The passing years have taken their toll on this one-time Garden of Eden, but nonetheless you may still enjoy the one-and-a-half hectares of *tumbos, cocos, mandarinas, cidras, toronjas, aguajes* and *ungurahui* and admire the *piscigranja* fish farm before enjoying a fresh fruit juice of unrivalled purity ('*jugos dulces como amor sincero*') and even possibly conversing with *Mamá*. Mixed in with the philosophy and the theology, Sra. Aneliza Gonzales Tuesta will extol the virtues of the peel of the forest *mandarina* which can be made not only into marmalade and a flavouring for pastries but also serves as a repellent and a natural pesticide. And to complete the presentation, *Mamá* shows how the juice of the peel squeezed into the air can be ignited in a sheet of flame and a shower of sparks, the like of which few have seen before. Finally, whilst you are recovering your composure, you may learn how to skewer the scarlet flowers of the *cucarda* (hibiscus) on to a *palito* from the coconut palm as an ephemeral decoration for your house.

Puerto Belén

This is situated on the south east side of the city, fronting the river Itaya just above its juncture with the Amazon, and may be reached by walking down *calle* José Gálvez, crossing *calle* Pénjamo towards and through Venecia, the length of the walk and the amount of mud depending on the height of the river. Amongst other local destinations, this is the departure point for visiting the town of **Tamshiyacu** (literally 'Vine water'/River of the Vines – Quechua), 25 miles southwards up the Amazon. The public *lanchas* leave at 0930 and noon daily, and generally take three-and-something hours (depending on the number of en route stops), usually returning almost immediately (4 *Nuevos Soles* each way), although the schedule is variable. There is an *albergue* if you are inclined or have to stay overnight. Indeed, there is now a selection of basic *hospedajes/hostales* – minimal amenities, lots of atmosphere. Alternatively, if you want to spend just a few hours and have lunch in Tamshiyacu, you can take the *rápido* which leaves Puerto Belén at 1000 each morning (10 *Nuevos Soles*) and return on the afternoon *lancha*. Or the other way round. And if you arrive in Venecia with 10 minutes in hand, then you can have an *alfresco* haircut of great severity on the pavement of *calle* Gálvez courtesy of the barbers of Belén (price 2 *Nuevos Soles)*(say 75 US cents, 50p Sterling).

A Visit to Tamshiyacu

"We arrive in *puerto* Belén slightly behind schedule, aiming for the 1000 *rápido* to Tamshiyacu. In the excitement and the press of people we somehow end up on the delayed 0930 *lancha.* 'Florita' is slender, perhaps 20 metres long and today she is packed, the usual mountains of assorted freight, half a dozen sagging hammocks slung athwartships and maybe 50 passengers returning to their villages and to the town of Tamshiyacu, 40 kilometres to the south. Sister *lancha* 'Shishisco' is leaving simultaneously and together we are poled out from Venecia through the host of floating *vendedores*, including fired-up kitchen ranges precariously balanced in *canoas,* into the *Río* Itaya, taking on last minute supplies from the bread boat but having no luck in the quest for eggs.

I find a seat on a box on the roof of 'Florita' and settle down to enjoy the view as the waterfront houses of Belén and the bobbing *canoas* fall astern. We pass two timeless and characteristic balsa rafts used for transporting cargo, equipped with a makeshift shanty shelter in the centre and giant oars for propulsion. 'Against the current they need a *peque peque*,' explains my neighbour, Israel Ayambo, seated on the box next to mine and grower of pineapples on his *chacra* of 3 hectares in Tamshiyacu.

After 25 minutes we join *El Río Amazonas,* turn right and proceed up river, making good perhaps 12 miles an hour, heading east south east, then east. On the bank are black fish hawks (*Shihuango),* white heron and the scavenging *Gallinazos*. We pass banana plantations, occasional *aguaje* palms, *mamey* trees with their carpet of episcopalian purple, dark-leaved *mango* and the distinctive and imposing *árbol del pan* (an importation from the Pacific – horticultural globalisation). As we near the halfway point of our journey the sun is hot and this part of the river is narrow and scenic; as usual we hug the bank to avoid the current. In one of the thickest parts of the forest we come to a sign which reads '*Bienvenidos – Centro Industrial*'. Happily there is no sign of any industrial centre; all is deserted, apart from a prayer of four nuns gliding along the shoreline before settling themselves into a dugout canoe to engage on some dutiful excursion. Simply that and a joyful cluster of bright yellow butterflies holding their customary midday meeting on the muddy foreshore.

The wake of a passing launch causes us to rock in the ripples, causing alarm to one of the passengers. 'Don't worry,' the Captain re-assures us. 'This boat sank in Belén last month when too many traders came aboard but here there is no danger. Except it is best not to sleep in a hammock. Always stay alert.' In Tamshiyacu we have time for lunch and to admire the statue of Sergeant Fernando Lores in the main square before returning to Iquitos by *rápido*. Twice the price (S/.10.00) but half the time."

Other Local Venues

San Juan is the district to the south of Iquitos, towards the airport. At the Handicraft Centre (Av. Abelardo Quiñones Km.4) is a wide selection of authentic craft work from the Amazon jungle. There is an annual Fiesta on 24th June full of activity, displays, *danzas nativas y música folklórica* throughout the preceding week) in honour of the patron saint (St John the Baptist). **Punchana** (Quechua for 'small bird') is the district to the north west of Iquitos, originally home to the Bora people. The *Purisima* religious holiday in honour of the Immaculate Conception of the Virgin Mary is celebrated in Punchana annually on 8th December.

Rumococha is a small village 5 km south west of Iquitos on the right bank of the river Nanay. Access is by road or water. There is a lake which is ideal for quiet fishing trips. The village of **Santa Clara** is 15 km from Iquitos, also on the Nanay and again, you can go there by boat or by road. There are annual cultural exhibitions from 12th to 14th August and in the 'dry' season there is a natural sandy beach. **Santo Tomás** on the bank of **Mapacocha** Lake is in the same general direction, SSW 16 km from Iquitos near the airport. It was the original home of the indigenous 'Cocama' tribe; today the inhabitants produce clay crafts. It is an ideal spot for swimming, fishing and canoe trips. The feast of the Patron Saint Thomas is celebrated between 23rd and 25th September annually.

Zungarococha is a lagoon situated on the right bank of the River Nanay, 12 km from Iquitos and good for fishing and swimming. Take care: the mosquitos here are said to be malarial. The **Momón** River is a tributary of the Nanay offering beautiful landscapes and good swimming, accessible from **Morona Cocha** as previously explained. On the banks of the Momón is the **San Andrés** community of the indigenous **Bora** people. **Yarinacocha** is another quiet lagoon to the west of Iquitos, connected to the Nanay when the waters are high and like all the western locations mentioned, is (logically) an excellent site for wonderful sunsets. In the village of **Puerto Almendra** 30 km from Iquitos on the river Nanay (fork right off the road to Nauta) is the Experimental Farm/Botanical Garden of the National University of the

Peruvian Amazon, where it is possible to walk and see the cultivation of typical products of the region (take the *combi* from Próspero/José Gálvez).

Unsustainable timber extraction from the forest – day in, day out

A traditional Balsa Raft photographed in 2001 – but rarely sighted these days, perhaps extinct

Village life (and the population boom conundrum) – near Orellana

Section V
Travelling Further Afield

"Under the wide and starry sky ..."

General

The rain forest rivers of the Amazon basin (which covers more than a third of Perú's total area) are the arteries and highways of the region. The waters of the Amazon originate in part from the melting ice of the Mismi glacier far to the south of Perú in the Department of Arequipa, flowing via the Apurimac, Tambo and Ucayali Rivers to meet the Marañón River, which runs from Cajamarca, way to the west, and is fed by the summer thaw of the snows of the towering mountains of the Andes. From its point of origin the river Amazon flows 6,500 km to the Atlantic (4080 miles), and whilst previously not considered to be the longest in the world (the Nile was held to be 80 miles more; the Mississippi 340 miles less), it is certainly the river with far the greatest volume of water (but now see page 175 for the latest data!).

At the meeting of the Marañón and the Ucayali (just downstream from Nauta), the river width is about 4,000m, fluctuating en route between two and five thousand metres, and finally achieving 40km. At the mouth of the poetically termed 'Monarch of the Rivers' the delta width is 400km. From November onwards (the southern hemisphere summer) the river level rises steadily, peaking through March to May. Conversely, the water level drops progressively during the 'dry' season ('dry' as in river flow, rather than absence of rain), so that between July and October the river vista is markedly changed – and, incidentally, the concentration of the water results in abundant fishing (Navy records show a difference of over 14 metres between the highest and lowest marks recorded for Iquitos).

Grupo Aéreo No.42 (part of the *Fuerza Aérea del Perú)* run commercial flights to all parts of the region, operating a 14 seater Twin Otter and previously a float Pilatus for 4 passengers. Amongst the scheduled destinations are Santa Rosa, Angamos, Estrecho, Caballococha, Requena, Contamana and Pucallpa; other locations may be considered, on request. Sample single fares: Caballococha and Santa Rosa S/.200; Angamos and Estrecho S/.185. The office is at Sargento Lores 127 (telephone: 234632 or 234651 ext.181), open 0800-1300 and 1600-1900 Monday to Friday and 0900-1200 Saturday.

Pacaya-Samiria National Reserve

Eulogised (with good reason) by aficionados as 'one of the wonders of the world', and lying roughly between the rivers Ucayali and Huallaga-Marañón, about 300km from Iquitos and to the west of Nauta-Requena, this is 2,080,000 hectares (similar in size to El Salvador) of relatively remote and theoretically protected rain forest that still offers one of the few remaining truly authentic jungle experiences, with unique opportunities for primary research, being considered as one of the most important areas of unspoilt biodiversity remaining on the globe. It was earmarked for protection as long ago as 1940, and was officially recognised as a National Reserve on 4th February 1982 with ranger stations to monitor wildlife, enforce protection laws and promote research.

Colourful macaws[26], picturesque toucans, and in total 450 different bird species; over 20 kinds of orchids, more than 130 species of mammals: the range of the bio-diversity is seemingly endless, with reputedly 250 kinds of fish in 85 lakes, and 250 recorded species of reptiles and ampbibians. However, excessive hunting is an increasing threat to the existing wildlife, whilst illegal logging (including extraction of giant baulks of centuries-old timber towed underwater by canoe at night through boundary control posts where the staff are allegedly paid to look the other way) means that the existence of genuine, untouched primary forest is becoming progressively rarer and harder to find. Official rangers in the reserve estimate that a minimum of five years of the very strictest controls, anti-corruption measures, fencing and policing are required to give any hope of reversing the current downward trend of degradation resulting from the quest for short-term economic gain. Two of the starting points for adventure ecological tourism access to the region are Requena (Ucayali) and Lagunas (Huallaga/Marañon), whilst contact with official guides for individual tours, exploration and scientific expeditions is under the auspices of the *Instituto Nacional de Recursos Naturales (INRENA)* whose office is at Ricardo Palma No.113, fourth floor (telephone 232980), open 0730-1330 and 1530-1830 Mondays to Fridays. There is an entrance fee to the Reserve which assists in supporting the programme infrastructure, including promotion of awareness of the vital importance and vulnerability of the rain forest.

---

[26] Reported sightings down by 70% in recent years in the forest. A depressing statistic, even if lacking in precision. But worth remembering that the usual forest soil is reddish sand; wherever brief patches of yellow clay occur then huacamayos will be found.

Lodges and Cruises

Visiting a jungle lodge for a few days or taking a tour cruise along the Amazon can both provide memorable encounters with the rain forest. The lodge programmes are broadly similar in terms of walking the jungle trails with knowledgeable guides; fishing expeditions from dugout canoes and viewing the giant 'water lilies' (*Victoria Regia – 'una de las maravillas de la creación')*. There are opportunities to sleep under the forest canopy by the light of the dancing fireflies, the Southern Cross and a million other stars, or of listening to the rain pattering on the foliage punctuated by the alien noises of the night (*'el sinfonía de la selva'*). You may drift on the river in the morning mist to hear the dawn chorus, or in the hope of spotting a pink dolphin or a manatee, a three toed sloth and a variety of other wildlife. Menus are focussed on typical local dishes and foods. Activity details vary, depending amongst other things on the availability of facilities.

A few lodges have swimming pools, some have observation posts for bird watching (although it must be said that the most extensive *colpa* clay cliffs for observing the memorable and exotically colourful dawn congregation of macaws are to be found in the Tambopata reserve, for example on the River Heath bordering Bolivia, accessed through Puerto Maldonado without undue difficulty). '*Miradores*' – tranquil lookout towers – are also popular (and at least one has fallen into the river). Some lodges major on Shamanic ceremonies, led by *el curandero* or 'medicine man', involving *ayahuasca* (see under 'Medicinal Plants'). As a truism, the further you are from 'civilisation,' the greater the chance of seeing wild creatures, e.g. **Otorongo Lodge**, el Río Oran, 87kms downstream from Iquitos (office at Putumayo 163, 2nd floor, tel: 224192 or cell: 975-8658 – call Anthony and Ivy {Eve}, both with an encyclopaedic knowledge of *la naturaleza*; www.otorongoexpeditions.com).

In terms of capacity, breadth and range, scale and years of experience (the 50th anniversary is upon us) **Explorama** (<u>Explor</u>e <u>Ama</u>zonia) (Av. La Marina 340 - Tel. 065-25-2526/2530/3301) leads the field (www.explorama.com). They have a substantial luxury lodge at **Ceiba Tops**, near Indiana (40kms north east of Iquitos), whilst 40kms further down the river Amazon (just short of where the river Napo enters) is the more rustic **Explorama Lodge**, built as long ago as 1964 (adjacent to this lodge is the medical clinic established in 1990 by renowned Dr Linnea Smith, just three years ago re-housed in a fine new building, extensive and robust – see *Recommended Reading* at the end of Section II). On the Napo itself is **ExplorNapo Lodge** (Iquitos 157kms) with its unrivalled Canopy Walkway (at 500 metres one of the world's longest, reaching a height of 37 metres; the one at Royal Botanic Gardens Kew is 18m). Nearby was ExplorTambos Camp, a former rainforest research station for scientists and laymen alike which closed in 2013. ExplorNapo is a good place from whence you may hear the magical rumbling cadenzas of the howler monkeys.

Explorama's Amazon Queen berthed at the Ceiba Tops landing stage

The near-legendary (in these parts) Peter Jenson was the imaginative and far-sighted founder of Explorama all those years ago, when jungle tourism was truly a bold and pioneering venture. Nowadays Pam Bucur carries the Explorama baton bequeathed to her, in conjunction with Jaime Acevedo and the rest of the management team. One of the unique features of this enterprise is the extent of its integration and involvement with the river people, with materiel, medical and educational support being extended to literally hundreds of forest communities, including the provision of a 4,000-book learning and lending library (rare in these parts), together with music, computer, games, reading and, latterly, needlework programmes for children close to Explorama

Lodge. **Conapac**[27] is the name of the NGO founded in 1990 to work under the Explorama umbrella (they love clunky acronyms hereabouts – *Conservación de la Naturaleza Amazónica del Peru, A.C*). Features of the activities are Clean Water (via mini-water treatment plants), Adopt-a-School programme and school supplies, *Las Malvinas* garden project promoting environmental and ecosystem awareness, Fish Farms for families and communities, Education Workshops for teachers and community leaders, and Community Service Projects through international visitors to the region.

The **cruise options** (including the Pacaya-Samiria reserve) range from a leisurely excursion in a local *pamacari* river craft, sleeping by the river bank in a hammock under a roof of *irapay* palm leaves, to a more stately but equally enjoyable progression in a larger cruising boat, viewing the forest from the sun deck and resting in an air-conditioned cabin, again with professional guides and stopping at points of interest along the way. The Iquitos Tourist Office holds lists of the accredited lodge and cruise operators, but be sure to visit www.dawnontheamazon.com for details of **Dawn on the Amazon Tours and Cruises** (custom charter trips, and jungle cabin retreats), or ring the company President, **Bill Grimes** on tel.223730/cel.965939190 for bespoke advice and sage suggestions on how best to cover as many areas of interest as possible during your time in Iquitos. Also consult 'Ten Top Things to do' – www.dawnontheamazon.com/blog and advertisements and articles in the local papers.

[*In passing, note that the* ***Amazon Explorers' Club and Lounge*** *is located in the same building as Dawn on the Amazon at the corner of the Boulevard (Malecón Maldonado) and Nauta. Members have access to free wi-fi, trustworthy money exchange, a spectacular river view from the terrace, cold beer, Bill*[28] *& Marmelita's renowned restaurant, discounts and good advice and assistance booking jungle lodges, tours and cruises – see amazonexplorersclub.com*]

One of the latest cruise boats now on the scene (at 700 tons displacement

---

[27] "CONAPAC is a Peruvian non-profit organisation whose mission is to promote conservation of the rainforest through education of its stewards, the people who live along the Amazon and Napo rivers. The centrepiece Project is the Adopt-A-School programme, which is strengthened by workshops and complemented by service and sustainable projects in river communities."

[28] Also – as it happens – President of the little known Amazon Authors' Club

more properly referred to as a ship), is ***La Estrella Amazonica*** (Expediciones International), whilst three other relatively recent arrivals to join the seemingly ever-expanding armada of cruise vessels are the 130-foot-long M/V **Aqua** (*Calle* Huallaga 215) with 12 luxury suites and a crew of 15 offering three, four and seven-night itineraries (Bales Worldwide +44(0) 1306 732713 – www.aquaexpeditions.com), and M/Vs **Delfin I & II** (Av. Abelardo Quinoñes Km.5, 5115) operating from Nauta via the 1hr 40min road link with Iquitos, (www.delfinamazoncruises.com).

Amongst others available are **La Amatista, Turmalina, Esmeralda** and **Aquamarina** (www.junglex.com /Av.Quinones 1980), M/V **Arca** (www.TheArcaAmazonExpedition.com), and M/V **Amazon Explorer** operating handily out of Requena and connected to Iquitos by fast speedboat (www.travelvantage.com). See also www.latitudsur.org. for M/F **Selva Viva.** Website www.amazonriverexpeditions.com is a convenient catch-all for M/Fs **Spirit of Amazon, Flotel, Selva Viva, Arapaima, Delfin I & II, Aqua,** and **Aria**. A comprehensive compendium of all these assorted craft is now overdue! Two other vessels that may be encountered on the rivers are **Amazon Hope I & II** – not cruise boats, but engaged on the humanitarian provision of medical and dental care to remote communities; healthcare professionals interested in volunteering their services should visit www.vinetrust.org .

The historic steamboats rescued from the breakers' yard and restored by **AmazonEco** (see www.amazoneco.com) [29] merit a separate paragraph or two. The **Ayapua** was built by R.Holtz in Hamburg in 1906 and originally worked the rubber boom trade along the Purus, Japua, Jura, Putumayo and Yavari Rivers in Brazil and Peru. She underwent extensive restoration between 2004 and 2006 and now once again '*her steam whistle echoes through the forest in harmony with the howls of monkeys and screeches of macaws, dolphins swim under her bow and swallows flutter through her masts as gracefully she steams up the mightiest River on Earth*'. However, the operating costs of these old steamers are high; dry-dock preservation is a possibility that beckons, sooner rather than later.

[29] 'AmazonEco provides boats and logistical support for expeditions and projects to some of the remotest regions in the Peruvian Amazon. Services are provided to Non-governmental Organisations, Students, Volunteers, Universities, Schools, and Film Crews, among others. "We strive to help conserve Amazon rain forests by providing support for conservation and research expeditions ...".'

Historic rubber boom steamboat Ayapua 1906 together with Clavero 1876 – both presently operated by Amazoneco

The **Clavero** is the oldest boat still navigating the Amazon, having been built by Claparede Freres in Paris in 1876, then named *Cahuapanas*. Used by the Peruvian Navy in the campaign to expel the Ecuadorean invasion of the River Napo in 1903, two years later she was commissioned by the joint Peruvian-Brazilian frontier delineation expedition on the upper Purus River.

Her name was changed to *Clavero* in the 1930's when she was acquired by L.F.Morey (cf Section II *Plaza Clavero* and Section VII *Peruvian Navy*) and she was fully restored from 2007 to 2009 for expeditions to the Pacaya-Samiria Reserve and the Yavari River. The **Rio Amazonas** (at times in her history previously named *Braga Sobrinho* and *Arias*) was built on the Clyde in Scotland by Murdoch & Murray in 1899 as a rubber transport steamer for Miranda & Co of Belem, Brazil. In 1936 she was acquired by Adolfo Morey and operated on the 2,000 mile route between Iquitos and Belem on the Amazon delta. Restoration 'to her original splendour' is in hand under the auspices of AmazonEco. (See also website www.amazontours.net, Amazon Tours & Cruises/GreenTracks Amazon Cruises)(Requena 336, Iquitos, tel.065-231611).

Puerto Masusa and Puerto Henry

Puerto Masusa is way down Avenida La Marina towards Bellavista Nanay, turning right at the third set of traffic lights opposite the Hospital Essalud (2.50 *Nuevos Soles* by *motocarro* from the Plaza de Armas). In general terms, 'Masusa' is the long haul departure point for exploring the rivers and if you have strong bowels, then this is undoubtedly the economic way to go. For example, 4 days south up the Ucayali all the way to Pucallpa for 60 *Nuevos Soles;* 3 days south west up the Huallaga to remote Yurimaguas; 2 days and 2 nights east down the Amazon to Caballacocha on the Colombian border and then onwards to Brasil; 6 days north west towards Ecuador up *el río Napo* to Curaray; 2 days and 2 nights south west up river past Nauta on the *Amazonas y Marañon* and then turning northwest up *el río Tigre* to Intuto. The destinations are exotic and distant, the permutations many; the best thing to do is to visit Puerto Masusa with your hammock, read the sailing information displayed on the chalkboards and make your choice. Just before you get to Masusa (northbound along Av. Marina) is the 'newly' constructed turning to **Puerto Henry**, now used by the 'Henry' flotilla of ferries bound for Pucallpa and Yurimaguas (4-5 days in hammock or *camarote*); also look out for the *Eduardo* and *Voyager* boats. For Manaus there is *lancha Gran Diego*, leaving on alternate Mondays, 6 days, reportedly with en suite cabins (basic). For the overnight *lanchas* to **Pevas** go to **Puerto Pesquero** (between Masusa and Henry) – and turn two pages on for more about this destination.

Other Points of Departure

In addition to the *puertos* already mentioned, the *río Amazonas* waterfront has a number of other important embarkation points. Taking Raymondi from the Plaza de Armas will lead you initially into *calle* Requena, then Av. Coronel Portillo and finally Av. La Marina. First port of call (right hand side, where the river is) in the shade of a large *mangua* tree (under which Segundo will cut your hair for the standard street price of S/.2.00) and just before encountering Arequipa (coming in from the left) is the narrow entrance leading down to the **'private' pontoon** used by MVs 'Sofy' and 'San José' ('Madre Selva' has recently retired) running to **Requena** (14 or so hours, depending) at 1700 on Tuesdays and Fridays. And now there is another competing service leaving on Wednesdays and Saturdays: *Motornave/Fluvial* Vennor – 'newer and faster', ditto *MFs* Ninfas and Don José. Here you will also find MV 'San Antonio' sailing at 1700 on Thursdays and going double the distance up the Ucayali to **San Ramón**, 3 days travelling for S/.20.00, arriving back on Tuesday, perhaps on Wednesday according to how things go along the way.

Now walk on and immediately opposite *calle* Arequipa you come to the **Puerto de Productores** which quite apart from the boats and launches deserves a visit to view the cornucopia of forest produce in the *Mercado de Productores*: giant banana racemes; mounds of *pacay* pods; huge *toranja* lemons; *aguajes;* sacks of rice; oranges and mandarins all the way from the *la selva alta,* the 'high forest' of the *departamento* of San Martín. Down on the jetty, *lanchas* leave for **Francisco de Orellana** 6 hours downriver (S/.10.00) at noon on Mondays, Wednesdays and Fridays. Smaller faster craft leave all day long in the same direction but for only half the distance: 40 minutes to cross the isthmus to **Mazán** for S/.8.00, and 45 minutes to **Indiana** for S/.9.00; these *rapidos* are convenient but compared with the more leisurely standard 'ferry' services, they do not provide the same opportunities for meeting the 'real' river people. But no matter whether you are travelling or just people-watching, be sure you wander through to the back of the market. There, along the edge of the terrace housing countless food stalls, you will find a railing thoughtfully placed to provide support as you engage in idle contemplation of the panoramic river scene that extends before your eyes.

Confronted by all the other rival attractions on offer, visitors may be forced to forego the pleasure of undertaking a specific journey to visit **Indiana**, a *pueblito* of some 3,000 inhabitants. However, if passing on the river and opportunity presents, a tranquil hour or so may be passed strolling round the town (and then possibly visiting aptly-named **Monkey Island** across the water[30]). The river-front *plaza* contains an interesting monument to the life and work of *Monseñor* Dámaso Laberge, social architect of the town as it is today. Indiana was originally the *fundo* or estate of Don Pablo Morey (that previously mentioned family name much associated with the era of the *caucheros)* and took its title from Indianapolis, USA, where the owner studied in his youth. *Monseñor* Laberge bought the estate (on which 900 workers were employed) on behalf of the Church in 1948 with the aim of creating 'a model town that would be an inspiration throughout Amazonia' (reminiscent of the Jesuit 'spiritual collectivism' settlements of the 17th Century in what is now Uruguay, destroyed in 1820 by marauding Portuguese soldiers from Brazil). Twenty years later Laberge was buried in Indiana, the town to which he had dedicated his life, having died on Christmas Day 1968. Twenty years of quiet and solitary heroism. Maybe Indiana and its people do indeed have a special feel to them.

As mentioned above, across the isthmus from **Indiana,** 25 minutes and S/.6.00 by *motocarro* along the connecting ribbon of concrete *carretera*, is the delightful settlement of **Mazán** where there are a couple of *hospedajes* and a little market. From here you may board the 10.00 am *rapido* to **Santa Clotilde** up the Napo river, running daily except for Sundays. The journey takes 4hrs or so and costs S/.85.00 (single); it is not possible to return the same day. To reach **Roca Fuerte** on the border with Ecuador takes a further one and a half days, also by *rapido*, turning into *el río Curaray*; accommodation en route is rudimentary and security is problematic (for further details on this route, albeit in reverse - which is indeed a 'road less travelled' – see Section VIII [How to Arrive]).

Reverting to Iquitos, and continuing down Av. La Marina with *calle* Celendín (and *grifo* San Carlos) on your left you will find **Puerto el Huelquito** from whence you can take a local ferry boat over to **Padre Isla** and in 'summer' when the river is low you can reach the nearby sandy

[30] This sanctuary – yes, for monkeys – may also be visited as a separate excursion directly from Iquitos, about 40 minutes down river by *rapido*. The 200 hectare island provides a safe home for around a dozen species of primates, where the fruits that comprise their favourite diet have been specially planted. Access for visitors is free (take a few bananas with you); voluntary donations welcomed.

beaches for a similar charge of S/.1.00 *'y pasar un par de horas o todo un dia lleno de memórias.'* In Padre Isla itself, a one or two-hour excursion is well worthwhile: after a 10 minute river crossing you can look back at the city buildings in the distance and enter the world of the river villages and *los ribereños*: flimsy houses resting on stilts above the flood waters, shaded by purple-flowering *mamey* and dark-leafed *mango*; games of football that never end played on the mudflats, fishing and transportation in hollowed *canoas.*

Puerto el Huelquito also holds the key (or possibly did ...) to making a quick visit to **Pevas**, using the *Transportes Guacamayo* speed boat (office at 572 Av. de la Marina – Sr James Rojas & Sra Wendy – telf: 965764378/965616935/959772529) leaving at 1300 on Tuesdays and Fridays, departing from Pevas to return at 1100 on Wednesdays and Saturdays. Cost: S/.200 round trip; advertised duration 3 hours. Alternatively and more economically you may choose to take the regular *lanchas* bound for Leticia from *Puerto Pesquero,* Masusa, leaving in the evenings to disembark in Pevas the following morning.

Part of the same embarkation complex is ***El Embarcadero Turístico*** and as the name suggests, from here visitors can charter a fast launch for practically whenever and wherever they like – at a price. For example, a one-hour flip around the local scene for perhaps S/.70 for two; a day run to Francisco de Orellana for S/.400 for a party of 6; **Leticia** and back at high speed for S/.1,500. And if that is not enough, across the water from the jetty are a number of private float planes which can be chartered. US$150 for a half-hour overflight of Iquitos or trips further afield for $300 per hour (Hugo Pinero on 251291 is one such contact).

Just before you leave *El Embarcadero Turístico* do not fail to glance backwards and upwards to admire the magnificent **Felipe Lettersten** moulded sculpture of an *Iquito* native over the entrance arch. 'Sons of our Land' reads the tribute on the plaque.

Pevas

Reputedly a missionary settlement dating from 1735, the township of **Pevas** lies some 145kms down the Amazon from Iquitos, on the way to Santa Rosa-Leticia-Tabatinga (the 'triple-frontier' towns). The population has leapt from 3,000 to 7,500 in the past ten years – but one example of many of the unsustainable pressure on land and resources in the rain forest region ('*world population control*' – the elephant in the room). The grandiose ***Casa del Arte*** (residence and gallery of famed international painter **Francisco Grippa,** who incidentally and of interest to disciples, has his canvases made from the bark of the Oje tree) overlooks the town, and there are reportedly plans afoot to convert some of this extensive real estate into B&B facilities. Until that day the choices for overnight accommodation are somewhat limited. The former hilltop lodge *Casa de la Loma* wistfully and tantalisingly referred to in some guide books closed more than a couple of years ago, whilst *Hospedaje Rodríguez* serves to keep the rain out but not much else. For travel options to Pevas turn back two pages, to which may be added the daily jet-foil *dezlisador* to and from the frontier (USD $60.00 for a seat).

Nauta & Francisco de Orellana

Both Nauta and Francisco de Orellana (in opposite directions from Iquitos) merit a visit. Up until 2006 the *lancha* for Nauta left every evening from Puerto Masusa; an alternative was to use one of the *collectivos* leaving from Alfonso/Próspero/Gálvez (*El Paradero omnibus y combi)* throughout the day, taking about two and a half hours along the 'new' *carretera* (which at that time ran only as far as the *Río Itaya* bridge at Km 57), and finishing the journey uncomfortably on the bumpy and occasionally flooded dirt-track. There is a good selection of *hostales* in Nauta in which to stay, or the same night the return journey could have been made in the *lancha*, with all the excitement and colour of the riverside stops when produce for the city markets was loaded onboard. Sadly (and discounting the supposed 'development and economic' benefits), the overnight Nauta river service is now but one more nostalgic memory of the past, having been rendered redundant by tardy completion of the long-heralded 'new' tar macadam highway. In its place prosaic buses run from Próspero/Libertad every half-hour, journey time 90 minutes, fare S/.8.00. See below: *A Visit to Nauta.* In 2010 acclaimed international artist Francisco Grippa opened his second *Casa del Arte* at Nauta (the first of his extensive '*Galerías Grippa'* being at Pevas – see separate earlier entry), overlooking the river just 5 minutes walk from the embarkation centre. Formerly on the 'not to be missed when in Nauta' list, the building is now (2014) unfortunately closed and up for sale … .

Go to Francisco de Orellana to re-live the emotion of the *Conquistador* of that name who 'discovered' the river Amazon at the intended end of his arduous journey from Quito, Ecuador (which included receipt of a dart in his eye from a Yagua blowpipe en route). Rather more accurately, it was the adjacent village of Oran which provided the high ground where F. de Orellana initially disembarked and landed, but in any event he was the first intrepid traveller from the Old World to appreciate the immensity of the river network, voyaging as he did down the river Napo over 450 years ago (1542, as recorded in the one-time fast fading mural in the 'old' Municipal Building in the Plaza de Armas – cf Section II, Brief History of Iquitos, second paragraph), before sweeping onwards down the Amazon all the way to the Atlantic.[31] Less dramatically (but equally enjoyably), you can do some excellent fishing on the Napo. The township of Orellana itself is small[32] but picturesque and welcoming, the surrounds being planted with a great diversity of trees, fruits and shrubs. *Señora Sarita López* is an exceptionally knowledgeable guide in this respect; sadly the hitherto oldest inhabitant of the *pueblo, Señor Alberto López,* has just recently passed away in his late nineties – a poet of some note, he delighted in recalling making the gruelling two-day journey by canoe to Iquitos as a matter of routine, passing the night sheltering at Indiana. A fine hotel was built in Francisco de Orellana in 2001: The Grand Palace Hotel Municipal 'Las Amazonas' – read on and see below for further details.

A Visit to Francisco de Orellana *('En la boca del Napo')*

"We arrive nicely in time for the midday boat from *Puerto (Mercado) Productores* scheduled for Orellana. By 1230 we have slipped out astern through the water hyacinths (*huamas*) and we are on our way, making good a steady 10 knots downstream, thereby clocking in excess of 15mph over the ground.

"Our chosen vessel is some 120 feet in length, with perhaps a beam of 25 feet at the widest part. There must be around 100 passengers today, not too crowded but snug enough in the heat of the day. Down aft the motor throbs importantly, whilst somewhere above us we assume the Captain is directing our safe passage. Well, with a deadweight cargo of several tons of bricks

---

[31] In 1845 he mounted an ill-fated quest [from Spain] to locate *El Dorado* – the 'gilded man', transmogrified into the 'golden city'. But his expedition met with shipwreck, disease and Indian attacks. Francisco de Orellana 'died of fever and despair' and was buried by his wife on the banks of the Amazon wrapped in a Spanish flag. Poignant indeed, and it scarcely bears imagining.

[32] Perhaps approaching 200 households these days; a mere 30 years ago there were but a dozen families in the *pueblito* – compelling confirmation of population pressure on the rainforest.

stowed amidships on the main deck, we certainly hope so. In the event of a mishap, the negative buoyancy of that shifting, toppling load would effectively seal our fate – probably including those fortunate passengers who have managed to secure one of the ten lifejackets onboard. A dozen or so hammocks are slung randomly athwartships along the length of the boat, making movement fore and aft difficult. This constriction is compounded by the haphazard presence of the usual diverse types of goods and chattels that have found their way onboard, varying from a motley selection of free-range, balding chickens to eco-suspect drums of vital unspecified liquids, and even a substantial mound of dripping ice blocks, optimistically insulated in tarred hessian sacking. Vaguely located near the stern is supposedly *el baño,* but as it is not only out of sight but inaccessible and out of reach, it is best left out of mind.

"Onwards we go, and as with the normal run of river trips, nothing much happens for the next two hours or so. Along the river banks on either side every conceivable habitable spot is occupied; t'was not always thus, and there is an unpalatable and unspoken message here: there are just too many of us crowding onto this fragile and finely-tuned planet of ours. Setting this seemingly unsolvable dilemma to one side, we sling the family hammock directly above where the disconsolate blocks of ice are melting into their black bags, which is a shrewd move indeed and quite the nearest we will get to air-conditioning hereabouts.

"Our arrival at Indiana is the signal for the customary hustling incursion of *los ambulantes*, the nimble vendors of sustaining *aguaje*, *mandarinas*, *rosquitas*, *dulces*, *chupetes* and much more, especially the highly fortifying *turrones de mani* (peanut nougat) in which we invest heavily. Some families have brought their own selection of little pots and bowls of rice and beans, but there is really no need and no one goes hungry. Transient trading completed, the engine comes back to life and at this juncture I see that I am quite mistaken about the general conning arrangements for our craft, and the assumed existence of a well-sited, all-seeing wheelhouse. In fact, the way it's done is that at the back end (with v.limited visibility) Mr Mate is manning the motors – two 40HP outboards in tandem – whilst up in the bow stands our Captain, discreetly placed just to one side of the main deck entry port. For the travellers down below all that can be seen is a pair of legs, but these exude undoubted authority, and on close examination and scrutiny it can be observed that command and control is exercised by the merest lift or waggle of a finger or two, the hand silhouetted against the sky in the square of light that filters through the hatch. Nothing more than an authoritative and eloquent gesture to assure and chart our safe passage, as the occasion demands.

"Another couple of hours pass serenely, the way they do in these parts. We nose into various *ribereño* river bank settlements and people jump for the shore with their possessions, offspring leaping in turn behind them. Some pirouette shyly to wave us goodbye, *ciao*, bon voyage, and to send us on our way before the jungle swallows them whole like a giant caiman, and they disappear from view as though they had never existed. Finally the sun grows tired of all this to-ing and fro-ing, and releases its hold on the day. But not quite; the best of the light has gone yet there is still half an hour before complete darkness presses in, and the solitary canoes hurrying across the unruffled waters of the river from distant *chacras*, from fishing trips and after visiting friends and relations will still just make it home before nightfall. The stilt-borne, palm-thatched houses are few and far between now; just a thin, spiralling haze of tell-tale smoke from the *tuchpa* revealing their whereabouts, or on occasions, a thicker plume billowing from a pyramid of *carbon* – the charcoal burner's sand-covered cone – indicating the presence of human activity on shore.

"We too just make it to Orellana before being overtaken by darkness. We swing to port into the mouth of the Napo to come alongside directly below the *malecón* of the historic township, the promenade itself fronting the spacious *plaza* planted with scarlet hibiscus, purple *mamey*, and venerable glossy-green mango trees. These in turn are dominated by the colossal monument (donated and sporadically maintained by the Spanish Crown) to the founding father and 'discoverer' of the river Amazon, *Conquistador* Francisco de Orellana. Our arrival is serenaded by the resident colony of green parrots squawking and whirling above us before settling for the night in the spectacular *Amasiza* trees that border the river. There must be two hundred of them circling and swooping overhead – as good as a *colpa* clay lick; the birds are protected now, and 'parrot soup' is happily becoming an aberration of the past.

"We make our way to the Grand Palace Hotel Municipal '*Las Amazonas*', built with 20- odd rooms over two floors in 2001 in an architectural style that can only be termed 'Minimalist Cauchero Revival'. There we find that previous clients have purloined all the towels and much else that was portable, and that the *chatarra* water pump has long since ceased to function. However, with a little coaxing, ingenuity and instant retail investment at the village store mosquito nets are rigged and we come into possession of an electric fan – this latter springing to life on the stroke of seven when the local generator is fired up and power provided. The downside to this is that the illuminations in the main square and along the boulevard mean that we lose sight of the wondrous canopy of the myriad stars in the sky overhead. An additional setback is that our hitherto successful policy of 'living off the land' falters at this point and we are thankful for the bag of *mandarinas* that we bought earlier in the boat, and for the memory of those exceptional *turrones de mani* acquired in Indiana.

"By 0515 the following morning there is sufficient natural light with which to start the day. Breakfast is not part of the inventory of the Grand Palace (Administrator: Sr. Segundo Perez), but by some unfailing *milagro de la selva* the fruits of the earth appear in abundance and all is well. By 0700 we are back on the river, *peque-pequing* up the Napo, courtesy of Tío Mayar and his *deslizador*, with an additional canoe in tow astern. Unfortunately our quest in search of the giant Amazon water lily (*Victoria Regia*) in flower is thwarted by new reed and *huamas* growth blocking access at the entrance to the chosen *cocha*, so we engage in some serious fishing instead, using the classy rod kindly made available by Mad Mick before we left Iquitos.[33] The water is like glass, perfect for water skiing, except that it would be sacrilege in such surroundings. As we drift, we pass not one but two, and then more of the normally infrequently sighted *punga* trees, easily distinguishable by the bright red fruits the size of cannon balls hanging from the upper branches. When ripe they are much loved by parrots, but the forest people dry the fruits, which then open to produce a fine yield of cotton, 'softer than swansdown', ideal for filling pillows and cushions. As for the fishing, we catch *sardines*, *pacos*, *chambiras* and *pirañas*; no records broken but satisfactory.

The Napo fish are renowned as being the tastiest of all: fish soup (*caldo de pescado*) from here is vastly superior to that of Iquitos. Yet now it is the familiar global-story – fish stocks have plummeted in recent years and the waters no longer teem with the former plentitude. To improve our chances we take to the little canoe that has been trailing behind, and glide silently into the flooded forest, through the trees, around the roots and creepers, under the magical canopy. But to no avail, the sun is high now and the placid *tuki-tuki* birds and the heron watch sleepily and without undue interest as we make our

[33] Mike also does a unique bespoke line in hand-made fishing lures, which he personally authentically shapes and paints.

siesta-way back to Orellana.

"Later in the afternoon we stroll the length and breadth of the settlement – a *pueblito* particularly well-presented and maintained, not only brimful with trees and plants of interest, but also with vestiges of the now fast-disappearing, long-established practices of rural life. Such as the production of *fariña* (manioc or cassava flour) by soaking *almidón de yuca* (ground yucca 'starch') in a canoe filled with water prior to drying, and use of the *pilo-maso* cup and 'pounder' in the preparation of rice. They rightly say that in Francisco de Orellana little changes; perhaps the trees get a little taller and the children grow a little older, 'but the smile remains the same'. Which brings us back to the riverside trees, the branches above us full of evening parrots passing and bartering news of the day. Who knows where those comical birds have journeyed between dawn and dusk, and on what impulse? The daily *lancha* from Iquitos is late today but it matters not; there is no hurry, the generator throbs in the distance, the townsfolk promenade, the children play and the insects cavort in the looms of the lights. We pass the time by making acquaintance with a big-jumping Smokey Jungle Frog, and then have the good fortune to find a lime-green Giant Monkey Frog – venomous, in spite of his smiley face and easy-going temperament.

"During the night our friend the rain sends greetings, and then stays to accompany us during our homeward journey upriver, so that the sky is blessedly overcast, the air soft and gentle. We sail in advance of the advertised hour of 0630, no fuss, the cargo all quietly stowed (including several large plastic bowls of green and red *camu-camu* fruits), not many fellow passengers at this juncture. Of the parrots in the *Amasiza* trees there is no sign, although much scuffling and scrabbling indicates that they are actively making their plans for the day; the stately trees themselves are known as the 'oak of the river', and are cherished for their natural beauty and also for their medicinal value. In season they are covered in red flowers in cockscomb form – *gallitos* – which fall romantically to the surface of the river and drift away on the current, provoking all manner of poetic images.

"Not long into our journey we make our first stop – the first of many; the charcoal-maker waves his shirt frantically from the river bank and in we nose. Twenty blackened sacks of *carbon* laced with vines across the top (to be sold for S/.5.00 each in Belén) thud on to the roof above our heads, the branch that had become entangled in the propeller is removed, and once again we push onwards, upstream against the current. So the process repeats itself, more and more cargo, ever more people. There are minor variations to the theme: twice we are skilfully intercepted by intrepidly managed canoes midstream, and precious items are tossed or passed onboard for sale in the Iquitos markets – animal skins, chickens, *masato*, and much more (the fermented *yuca* brew is handled with especial care). Truly a fine-tuned waterborne network of co-operation and communication, no paperwork or administrative overheads, all in the *ribereño* family.

"Midst all the bundles of *guabas* (long bean pods with succulent 'cotton' packing), racemes of green bananas (each identified with the owner's initials carved into the stem), the baskets and bowls of red and yellow *cocona* fruits, the papaya and so forth, breakfast arrives: *piraña* and *carachama* wrapped in *bijau* leaves and cooked over charcoal. Delicious. There is also roasted splayed *sajino* on offer – a dog-sized hairy little peccary pig – but we don't go for that. Throughout all, the rain continues pleasantly, helping to engender the shared community spirit of the colourful voyage. Moreover, by now the close-packed sense of cosiness onboard is magnified by the presence of scores of chickens and roosters tethered along the gunwhale of the vessel (the side-coaming), overlooking and closely observing the scene with bright-eyed curiosity, backsides strategically sited outboard.

"The only impediment to our smooth and somnolent homeward passage is the ailing state of the motors. First one, and then the other, stutters to a halt, reluctantly re-starts, falters and fades. Against the current we have scarcely sufficient power to advance, so that when we eventually put in at Indiana to clear the contaminated fuel lines we lose no time in jumping ship. We gladly pay the additional S/.10.00 to whiz back to Iquitos in a flurry of spray, completing our outing in a noisy but convenient *rapido*."

[Addendum – Another Visit to Orellana, January 2014:

"Perversely and contrarily, I decide that the most expeditious route to Orellana lies through Mazan. Consequently we embark early in the S/.15.00 *rapido* from Puerto Productores, but then lose the best part of an hour waiting for the boat to over-fill to ultra-economic capacity. A 40-minute ride followed by a speedy *motocarro* across the isthmus separating the Amazon from the Napo and we are on the Mazan waterfront, ready to negotiate the next step of the adventure[34].

"There is indeed no regular service to Orellana, and the array of small craft on

[34] Sr.José Ramírez (Cel.997280066), self-appointed boat agent, is your man

the foreshore looks decidedly unpromising. In the end the choice lies between Sr.Colley's 2-hr rusty roofless *rapido* (a *chalupa* if ever there was) at S/.1,000 *ida y vuelta*, and *Capitan* Jaime in his 6-hr (estimated) *peque peque* powered period *pamacari* at an equally exorbitant S/.500. As usual, the peace of the *pamacari* prevails over the speedboat (never mind the finances) and Capt. Jaime gets the contract.

"With no time to lose if we are to arrive before nightfall, jerricans of gasoline are loaded, together with a bag of bread, a couple of bottles of water and some stale packets of soda biscuits from the nearest vendor. That completes the expedition catering arrangements; simplicity is all. Six members of Jaime's family appear like genies out of a bottle, plus the obligatory chickens secured in sacks with just their startled heads protruding. And finally three reverberating oil drums are loaded – those clumsy homeless oil drums that are never in the right place and are forever in transit.

"Eleven o'clock strikes (metaphorically – Mazan is as yet without a clock tower), the headrope is slipped and we are on our optimistic way down the river. Perhaps 5 knots from the straining *peque peque* (on which so much depends), and a further five knots from the flow of the lower Napo. Say 12mph, speed made good ... Our departure goes un-remarked by the disinterested residents of Mazan; the weather is clear for the moment, pleasantly fresh, and our craft is called *Mi Amorcito*.

"Hardly more than an hour later we run on to our first sandbank. Captain Jaime leaps overboard, weight is shifted from for'd to aft and we float free. Free to proceed, but for how long? Anyway, another hour and we drop in to the village of Tamanco; the oil drums disembark, followed (unexpectedly) by the bread and then all the extended family. On we go, willy nilly. Until our gallant boatman reveals that he is worried about his return trip and declares that he would like to find a companion for the voyage. The river being about 2km wide at this point we look at him blankly and then at the equally blank banks of the distant forest encircling us. Fortunately Jaime pulls himself together, sensing the reality of the situation and we settle down once again, willing the distant rain clouds to go away.

"The *pueblito* of Puinahua comes and goes. Then the rain comes and stays and the temperature drops ten degrees as we huddle under the *irapuy* roof. Finally the rain does stop and Captain Jaime cuts the motor and starts to bale in earnest, so we relieve him of his secondary duties and take over with the bucket so that progress may be resumed. It takes quite some time to empty the bilges, and closer inspection confirms our suspicion that *Mi Amorcito* is leaking like the proverbial sieve. Oh well, nothing is perfect, and that explains the earlier hope for additional crew.

"Four o'clock. Five hours into the journey. The river is beautiful here, wide and tranquil; the sun has re-appeared but the wooden seats in *Mi Amorcito* are getting harder. Time to empty the bilges again – there seems to be even more water than previously. Mid-task we are slowly overhauled by *Bote Fluvial Milagritos* from goodness knows where bound for Masusa, due there in the morning. On we go, village San Alejandro moves from ahead to astern, there is still rain around, but not overhead.

"Gone five. Cold breeze. The day is fading now. Six hours on passage, perhaps 70 miles under the keel, twisting and turning along the serpentine Napo. On the far horizon appears a pencil thin radio antenna; we strain hopeful eyes to pinpoint the Orellana obelisk, at first without success until finally there it is, right on the nose. In the sternsheets one can sense Captain Jaime's relief and *Mi Amorcito* surges happily down the home straight, but not before we have baled the capacious bilge for a third time. Like Francisco de Orellana before us, we have done it – well, some of it. Verdict: can be done, was done. But best think twice before pioneering new routes that lie beyond the local inventory. Indiana to Orellana is quicker and more direct, but via Mazan is a picturesque little meander along the way less travelled. And just one final detail that may avoid disappointment: bear in mind that the 0630 *lancha* for the return trip to Iquitos always sails *en punto* at 0615, sharp.]

A Visit to Nauta

"We board the waiting bus at Próspero/Libertad soon after eight in the morning, and in our wake the vehicle fills rapidly with the familiar array of families and attendant bulging bags, plants, implements and impediments. As always, there is no shortage of the usual bewildering assortment of travellers' fare on offer; this time we sample the local pâté *cerdito* wrapped in the inevitable *bijau* leaf and accompanied by *pan de cerveza*, followed by *dulces de almidon*, the sweetened *yuca* derivative. '*Ocho y media – vamos!*' chorus the passengers, on the stroke; the driver takes his time to finish his cigarette and only then do we edge out of cluttered Belén to rattle down the length of Av. Abelardo Quinones, past the turn to the airport and on to the Nauta Highway – the long-awaited open road. First up is the municipal land-fill site, the very same *gallinazos* lazily circling the ill-sited rubbish tip as those that habitually hazard daytime flights to and from the nearby runway through fear of catastrophic bird-strikes.

"Moving on, a frisson of excitement runs through the passengers as we overtake a posse of head-down racing cyclists, but aside from that, the view through the bus windows is of a uniform succession of bedraggled villages and homesteads, once shadily remote and nestling amongst the trees of the forest, now exposed to the glare of the world. This is the inevitable result of the unequal struggle between conservation and development – and a sad and unwelcome reminder that once the projected tarmac road extension from Nauta to Pucallpa becomes reality, that will be the beginning of the end for happily isolated Iquitos as we know it today. As for the repetitive line of recreation centres and *albergues* that we are passing – the scourge of ribbon-development, that well-known syndrome – all are empty, even though it is the weekend. Overkill, and lack of market research in the race to make a swift, short-term profit.

"By and large, the rolling landscape that we traverse no longer rates as forest, not secondary, not even tertiary. Not even woodland, it is more akin to urban parkland – pock-marked with bald areas of total erosion. Will we never learn? At intervals the bus halts to set down and pick up travellers and labourers employed on the various *fundos y fincas,* the farmsteads and smallholdings which have emerged since the highway was built, but in environmental terms the cost of this admitted feat of civil engineering is beyond reckoning. The further we travel, the sight of the hideous scarring left by the widespread felling and burning of the forest appears to increase in scale and frequency. The enforcement of planning controls – if indeed they exist – will come too late to save this region, hell bent as it is on replacing the priceless treasures of *la selva* with a few unimaginative and uninspiring fields stocked with herds of methane-emitting cows.

"Then – here we are in Nauta, population estimated at 20,000 and growing – one hour and 30 minutes on the road as advertised, S/.8.00 per head paid to the *cobrador* and we dismount. Accommodation can usually be found in the Nauta Inn or in *La Granja Azul* (slightly away from the centre), or in Hotel *Iranuka* (meaning 'pretty house' in the Cocama language) on the Plaza and near the river (*el río Marañon*), except that today the town is celebrating its 177th Anniversary (including a Grand Beauty Contest) and everywhere is fully booked. We pause at the highly recommended Snack Restaurant *Rosita* (*Calle* Ayacucho, opposite the Market), where our enquiries as to how we might return to Iquitos by ferry are met with incredulity. Why would anyone want to travel by river when you can go by road? – thus re-confirming the repercussions of *la carretera*, which is not only dealing a death-blow to the adjacent forest but is also inexorably eroding the traditional Amazon way of life, with the river as the central artery of communication and transport.

"Happily we have the great good fortune to chance across Sr. Winter Fausto Gonzales and his well-found, newly constructed 30-foot *peque peque*, *irapay*-roofed and with space for two hammocks slung amidships, fore and aft. By 1230 we are off, chugging down the Marañon, Señora Winter and 6-year old son Joyner accompanying. With the favourable current we might get back to Iquitos before 2000, just two hours after dark; then Family Winter will battle homeward upstream for perhaps a further 13 hours; the asking price of S/.250 is handed over readily and without demur. We certainly prefer the romance of the river to that of returning by road, and although there are still ferries from Yurimaguas which pass Nauta in the *madrugada* (0400 is mentioned), no knows when the next boat is due until it arrives. It seems an uncertain business, particularly as the weekend holiday and the Beauty Contest have ensured that beds are at a premium.

"Forty five minutes out of Nauta and we reach the confluence of the Marañon and the mighty Ucayali. Thereafter, following this union, we proceed on the combined waters which form the River Amazon, and just a quarter of an hour later we pull into *Communidad Grau* on the left bank, where – behold! – we encounter a finely constructed *Mirador Touristico*, of such imposing grandeur as to excel all others. Thirty metres in stature, 10 floors to ascend, made in metal to endure 100 years or more, started on 21st November 2005, completed and opened Autumn 2006. All done under the seal of approval of President Alejandro Toledo himself. In fact, there should have been a few floors more – up to 40 metres in height – but this plan was foiled when the lighter bearing the final quarter of the required girders, metal spars and framing unexpectedly foundered en route from Brazil. Notwithstanding, three cheers for development on the positive side of the balance – the 360 degree view over the three rivers and as far as Nauta and beyond is truly magnificent. Perhaps *la carretera* and the Beauty Contest did us a good turn after all. (The mobile/cellular number for Sr. Winter[35] is 9762748; Nauta landline 411.298).

"Ever onwards: Winter reads the current to take maximum advantage of the flow. This puts us amidst the purple puffs of drifting *huamas*, the baulks of timber and the general debris of the river – a sure sign that the river is in

[35] Worth a try, although at the time of writing he is 'between boats'. Stop press: Moved to Pucallpa; his replacement is Sr. Juan Tapullima Leonardito, cel.944933589

flood. The surface of the water is deceptively smooth, only occasional swirls, back eddies and ripples revealing the presence of treacherous under-tows and whirlpools: bathing hereabouts is definitely contra-indicated. We have the vast expanse of water almost entirely to ourselves, just the odd glimpse of distant craft. Our passage takes us past a balsa raft – an increasingly rare sight these days – the giant oars inert on this occasion: no point in paddling when the river is being so obliging. The weather is fine, the breeze engendered by our forward passage is balmy, the two *hamacas* are a boon. What's more, the surrounding trees have been untouched for centuries – truly glorious primary forest, the stately trunks glistening as the sun moves westward.

"Night falls as we pass Tamshiyacu, as forecast, some two hours short of our destination; it is like a midsummer's evening on the Norfolk Broads. Now our way is starlit, the waxing moon one third in size. All the constellations are in their appointed places: Ursa Major on the bow; the Southern Cross low over the stern. That fits – we are heading north. At 1915 we catch sight of the loom of the lights of Iquitos, fine on the port bow. Half an hour later the lights themselves become distinct. Now there is a fresh head wind and the moon glistens on the wavelets. The low silhouette of Padre Isla appears and we come round to port in a wide arc; whereupon our Captain nudges us cautiously into the quiet end of Puerto Masusa and we make fast. Eight o'clock precisely. Señor Winter is proud of that, and rightly so."

A Visit to Requena

"Arriving at Puerto de Productores (Avenida La Marina) two hours before sailing time, we join the waiting throng of passengers at the top of the steps leading down to the pontoon. Almost simultaneously, *lancha Sofy* comes alongside: more battered than beautiful, odorous but willing; around 180 tons, single shaft, V8 diesel giving perhaps 14 knots on a fine day. A couple of sturdy planks are set ashore and we go onboard, jostling with the other travellers and assorted vendors to secure a comfortable spot for the 12 or 14 hour passage up river. Not knowing the ropes, we opt to go aft in the belief that there we will get a good view and a fresh breeze, only to find that we are immediately above the heat and noise of the engine and that we are surrounded by several hundred disconsolate chickens.

"The *lancha* is filling fast so we hurry forward again and come to rest on the left of the main deck, and sling our hammocks adjacent to a large open port. Orlando, our immediate neighbour, tells us that he is in the fish business and is regularly visiting his Aunt in Requena and that we have made a good choice. Particularly with being on the port side, thus securing shade for the duration of the daylight hours of the voyage, and especially protection from the fierce early-morning sun for the 3-hour run in to Requena (and vice-versa for the return trip, although less important as it will be late afternoon; confirmation of the old posh-adage: Port-out, Starboard-home). The bustle is unbelievable, and good choice or not, we are in the thick of it. More and more stores come on board, some disappear into the holds, some are stacked on the deck below our hammocks and more and more passengers arrive to occupy every conceivable space. We stay put and guard our territory but have to raise our hammocks to make room for the growing mound of boxes immediately below us.

"Five o'clock in the afternoon and we sail on time, past *Isla* Iquitos and heading upstream more or less SSW in the direction of Requena some 300 kilometres distant. Orlando undertakes to keep an eye on our rucksacks and we duck under the jumble of sagging hammocks to climb to the upper deck and note that the area abaft the cabins is the spot where the cognoscenti make their pitch. Fresher air, better view, removed from the cargo. Next time. There is an hour before nightfall and we find a seat on a wooden bench just in front of the bridge. The river must be two miles wide here and away to our left a 20,000 ton ocean-going cargo ship, 2,000 miles from the open sea, is discharging into lighters, derricks working, possibly bringing sugar from Brazil and definitely replenishing all those Asian goods that are on sale in the Iquitos markets.

"It is April and in consequence the river is high and the adverse current all of 6 knots. The Captain hugs the shore, and forest dwellers fishing in canoes dart for cover to escape our wash, their wooden houses sitting on stilts to avoid the flood waters. Night comes quickly and along the river bank the occasional kerosene lamp flickers from a *ribereños* dwelling and a large nocturnal bird is caught for an instant in our lights. There is no moon and rain threatens. No radar either but somehow we find our way without slackening speed, possibly because our pilot has a diet high in carrots or *camu-camu*.

"On the upper deck the occupants of the cabins take to their *camarotes*, paying 25 *Nuevos Soles* for the privilege[36], whilst on the main deck, where

[36] Once again follow the time-honoured British-India Empire adage of 'Port Out, Starboard Home' when booking (hence: *Posh*), thereby ensuring your berth is on the shady side of the steamer.

there must be sixty or seventy hammocks squeezed down either side, the charge is S/.10.00. 'Very few passengers,' grunts the Purser. 'Beginning of the week,' he explains, in case anyone doubts his word. Everyone settles for the long night. A chill wind comes through the access port and in the inadequate cocoon of our hammocks we remember the unheeded advice to bring a blanket. Our course takes us first to one side of the river then to the other, so that at times the dark line of the far bank is scarcely visible low on the horizon whilst at other times the forest is almost within touching distance and we can look directly into the little huts that glide past our view in the gloom. The rhythm of the throbbing diesel is soothing and sleep comes easily. First we tie our rucksacks together, and then I tie the end of the rope round my foot in the hope that anyone attempting to make off with our belongings will encounter unexpected hurdles. Then we have second thoughts and sleep less comfortably but with greater peace of mind with our bags in our hammocks.

"The night is pitch black but we forge on at full revs, although with the current against us our speed over the ground is at least five or six knots less than our speed through the water. Periodic changes in the note of the engine followed but a vibrating rumble as the Captain goes astern herald our arrival at riverside settlements. Cargo is disembarked and passengers slip over the side and disappear quickly into the darkness of the vegetation. Then everyone twists and re-settles in their hammocks, watching our lights gleam white on the trunks of the forest trees slipping past until sleep returns. This is the signal for the Purser to do the rounds with a posse of assistants, waking everybody up again to extract the ten *Soles* toll.

"The first shards of dawn appear soon after five and before six we move back to the wooden bench in front of the bridge. In response to a huddle of waving figures on the shore our *lancha* nudges into the river bank. 'San Genaro' says the crooked sign and as the current swings us downstream, passengers come and passengers go, boxes and bags are thrown ashore, sacks of papaya and yucca and huge stems of bananas are loaded together with a batch of *irapay* frond roofing panels for some up-river client. There is no ceremony and within minutes the propeller is thrashing astern to take us off the mud so that we can be on our way. One of the porters slips and falls on the dew-wet deck, and the early morning solemnity is disturbed by a burst of appreciative laughter from his colleagues.

"We buy a baked fish wrapped in a *bijau* leaf with a boiled banana for company in exchange for one *Sol* and eat our breakfast as we pass *Esmeralda,* a large three-deck tourist cruiser, the guests still resting, their breakfast awaiting on the fresh linen of the sun deck aft. We enjoy our fish with our fingers without envy and then open *pacay* pods to eat the sweet white fibre surrounding the giant beans as we watch the procession of birds overhead. *Gaviotas,* the ubiquitous seagulls, the yellow breasted *Víctor Días*, gangs of screeching parrots, *gavilán,* the scavenging black sparrow-hawks. White egrets watch our progress cautiously from the reeds fringing the river banks and Orlando points out the hanging nests of *paucars* (the yellow-chested Amazon blackbird, with a distinctive call akin to a tap dripping intermittently into a resonating bucket of water) on the branches of the *Punga* tree, as *golondrinas* (swallows) skim the surface of the river. Without stopping we pass the settlement of Panyallpa, sitting in the shade of the feathery fronds of tall breadfruit trees, *árbol del Pan.* Further on, a waving child signals from the shore and in we go to a single wood and thatch stilt house. One passenger jumps ashore and as father is welcomed home without words, a bag of *harina de yuca* (cassava root flour, also known as *almidón*) comes on board, either for use as a talcum powder substitute or to make *rosquillas,* the biscuit-like white rings on sale in the market stalls. During the brief halt we are able to smell the vegetation of the forest, still humid and damp from the recent rain and we are visited briefly by two or more pink dolphin, those elusive creatures of the river with mystical powers of fertility that reach out to village maidens passing along the shore.

"Village Genaro Herrera (situated on the SE border of the Pacaya-Samiria National Reserve) is reached at about seven in the morning. This is a substantial settlement (Population: '*Bastante*' – ask anyone), renowned for its daily production of fresh cheese, reputedly unique in the Amazon region. Berthing is the signal for a frenetic stampeding invasion of massed ranks of *vendedores* bearing more fish, coconuts, fruit in general (including the fantastically juicy, sweet, health-giving, yellow *taperiba*), and every other conceivable necessity of life. When we slip and proceed 20 minutes later, half of the sellers are still onboard; in this way the leisurely passengers are able to sample a little bit of everything over the course of the succeeding couple of hours. Added to which, *Sofy's* gallant galley crew conjure up a mug of porridge ('Quackers') and a slice of bread for the steerage class passengers, whilst cabin class receive a glass of coffee and a slice of toast – prepared in that much-loved Peruvian gadget, the *wafflera* (in which, by chance, the sole of the modern-day running shoe was evolved). With two or three hundred (who knows exactly?) souls onboard, this is a feeding evolution approaching biblical proportions.

"Soon after nine in the morning we finally sight Requena, low on the horizon far ahead. The adverse current has indeed been fierce and our journey upstream of 200 miles has taken 16 hours. In town we stay at the *Hospedaje río Seco* [now surpassed by *Hospedaje Sadicita*, tel.41-2677/41-2499], visiting the river to swim and travelling to a nearby *camu-camu* orchard of 54 hectares with a fruit yield of 10 tons to the hectare, no fertilisers, no spraying. And in no time at all we are embarking for the return trip to Iquitos, this time in *lancha 'Madre Selva,'* sailing at three in the afternoon. As an aside, as we step onboard, the discarded debris in the waters below the gangplank reminds us that the Loreto authorities need to engage on a determined educational campaign against 'plastic pollution' – the unthinking and random disposal of lethal, non-biodegradable bags and bottles in the river and elsewhere.

"Underway on time, we enjoy the scenery from the upper deck until dusk, and then watch the sunset. There is a full moon through patchy cloud and Ursa Major appears low in the night sky. Along the way we stop and load more branches of green bananas, sacks of yucca and papaya, lines of ducks suspended from poles, fluttering chickens, fish and more fish. As we touch into the river bank everything is thrown on board on to the foredeck in disorder and then off we go again and everything is sorted out. Sometimes in the haste of our departure villagers become stranded on board and have to be rescued by anxious friends in canoes. At other times the water is insufficient for us to get alongside, and the transfer of passengers and goods has to take place precariously in mid-stream.

"Now the decks are crowded and there is no space between the hammocks, drooping low in the Loreto fashion. Mothers sleep with their children, head to toe, and one large hammock shrouds at least four sleeping forms. Everyone needs to be fresh for the morning market, selling all the produce in return for kerosene and other essentials of modern life in the forest: matches, corrugated metal sheets, new machetes, fishing hooks, new shoes and sugar and clothes. At one point we pass naval control and our Captain returns with an officer who checks the ship's papers, guarded by an armed marine. Food vendors take the opportunity to swarm aboard and nobody goes hungry: smoked fish, rice *juanes,* fried chicken, *juanes de yuca,* smoked chicken, *plátanos fritos, aguaje,* and *cigarillos* sold individually for 10 centimos.

"On this journey the current is with us and we make good time, arriving at four in the morning, or perhaps it is only three o'clock. Difficult to be sure in the dark. The market-goers are keen to be on their way but we stay in our hammocks for an extra hour or so, and in *la manera selvática,* nobody minds."

[*Requena has an endearing time-warp feel to it; the settlement was officially founded in 1907 and the century-old Franciscan Mission building (now a school) dominates the skyline, but in general the houses are of simple and traditionally rustic construction. There is talk of opening up an overland route through to the Brazilian frontier, a distance of some 130 kms; no doubt this would be an attractive commercial proposition, but so far as conservation of the rain forest is concerned long may it remain but a dream. To re-iterate, Requena is a good jumping-off point for the Pacaya-Samiria reserve – e.g. Shapshico Tours, www.viaje.selva.peru.com – and as indicated in the foregoing account, there are many things to do during your stay, including visits to the market, the aguaje plantation and the camu-camu chacras, a trip out to the old (1930's probably) sugar cane mill which still operates just outside the town (take plenty of mosquito repellent) and Los Delfines recreation park (which is on the way to the mill). Located at the cargo pontoon 'Sinchi Roca' (also used by the Henry boats traversing to and from Pucallpa) is El Muelle restaurant (Sra Gladys Castro Chávez – tel.41-149) with its grand vista over the river Ucayali and the best menu in Requena. Radio Energia FM 93.1 run by Sr. César López is the local radio station and welcomes the opportunity to interview passing travellers. Nowadays a rápido leaves Requena at 0830 daily except Sundays and arrives in Nauta 4hrs later; from there the journey to Iquitos is completed on the 'new' highway, arriving at 1330 – an unimagined leap, even five years ago, and the reverse journey is of course equally bookable, all inclusive for S/.80. courtesy of Transportes Rápido* "Jaen", *Luciola and Srs. César Galan & César Torres, cel.961980026 & 965875112. Similar service also available from Gaby Express, www.gabytours.com.pe*]

The colourful fish market at Requena

Section VI
Fish, Fowl, Flora and Fauna

"Here grow as many things as there are stars in the sky."

General

The Amazon basin contains 25,000 recognised species of plants; the rivers contain some 2,000 kinds of fish; there are said to be 4,000 different birds and (apparently) the same number of different butterflies, the greatest diversity of the latter in any region of the world. In the area of Iquitos alone there are reputedly 141 types of reptiles. Only a very few of all these varieties are mentioned here. For further natural history reading, visit *La Biblioteca Amazónica* (Malecón Tarapacá) and consult *'Así es la Selva'* by Avencio Villarejo. For butterflies, *La Pequeña Enciclopedia de Mariposas* by Dr V.J Stanek is recommended (1990 Aventinum Praga – Spektrum Brno).

Fish and Fishing

Fish are synonymous with the Amazon basin. For the indigenous people of the rain forest they are a central ingredient of their staple diet and the principal protein source. A handful of the commonly encountered names are given below. But first a few fishy facts.

The river Amazon and its many tributaries (estimated at 1,400) are at their highest level during the summer thaw in the Andes and the 'rains' of February, March and April. The rise of the waters in some years is said to be as much as fourteen metres and can last until the end of May, during which time it becomes more difficult to catch fish. From July until December when the rivers are low (and the catch is concentrated) there is an abundance of fish in the markets and the price tumbles.

In *el río Amazonas* itself, the fishing is not as good as in the more tranquil tributaries, and in the even quieter *cochas,* the lagoons and 'tributaries of the tributaries'. This is as a result of the combined effect of the destruction of river bank trees and vegetation (thus depriving the fructiferous fish of their prime food source of berries and seeds), the accumulation of *barbasco* in the waters (the poisonous vine the villagers use to catch fish – it kills via asphyxiation, hence the dead fish may be consumed with no ill-effects; ditto for the caustic resin/sap of the *catahua* tree, another 'naturally derived' poison which is illegally used in the same manner), and the contamination and disturbance caused by ever-increasing present-day river traffic (not to mention the illegal practice of *bombeando*, the use of explosives to kill and stun fish). In turn, the river Napo has the reputation of being home to the tastiest fish (for example, the fine *Peje Amarillo*, the 70cms 'yellow fish' that is especial to the Napo). This is partly on account of its relative remoteness but mainly due to the prevalence of *tahuampas,* concentrations of trees, general vegetation and grasses extending into and over the river, and thus supplying a rich food source of fruit and berries for the fish. (The 'blackness' of certain rivers is evidence of countless years of vegetation falling into the waters, with *el río Pucate* perhaps being the blackest of all).

Sadly, the double earthquake in Ecuador on 5th March 1987 (6.9 and 6.1 on the Richter scale) resulted in vast quantities of industrial pollutants contaminating the once abundant waters of the Napo. In Peru *los ribereños* downstream of the quakes, all the way from Roca Fuerte on the border to Francisco de Orellana at the Amazon confluence watched in despair as oily man-made detritus drifted relentlessly downstream for days on end, killing millions of fish and causing immense ecological damage that still exists today. The days of returning from a fishing trip with perhaps seven or eight huge *gamitana* in the bottom of the canoe are now but a memory, and is something which will not recur in our lifetime, and indeed probably never again. Truly a disaster, natural yes, but the effects of which were grossly distorted and exacerbated by human disregard of the environment.

The enthusiastic fisherman visiting the region will probably come equipped with all the accoutrements of his pastime. But if not, keen anglers may well find exactly what they are seeking in the way of rods and reels, unique handmade lures and flies and so on at '**Mad Mick's Bunk House and Trading Post**,' twenty paces down Putumayo (Number 163). For amateurs, a simple hook, line (green for the black waters of the tributaries, clear line for the Amazon itself) and cane can be bought for two or three *Nuevos Soles* from 'Commercial Florindez' or neighbouring shops in Belén Market (*Pasaje* 3 # 172 Belén, continuation of Abtao/16 de Julio*).* For bait, bread paste is one solution but more effective and traditional is grated *pijuayo* (palm fruit) bought from the market, mixed with water to a compact paste and then cooked lightly in a *bijau* leaf over a barbeque. Or if that seems too complicated, use earthworms or scraps of fish. And of course, follow local practice and be aware that fishing under a full moon will generally result in a disappointing catch. When you are out and about, it is generally not too difficult to borrow a *canoa* and a paddle for a spot of fishing in exchange for a few *Soles*; however, if you really want to buy your own canoe, go down to the Belen waterfront with 40 or 50 US dollars in your pocket and half an hour to spare and ask around.

The fish most likely to be encountered in the markets (or possibly on your hook) are as follows. *Paiche* – only in pieces, as the biggest specimens can grow to 2 metres; nowadays all *paiche* on sale should come from local fish farms, it having been legally protected for at least a decade. *Dorado* – a metre or so long, few bones, tasty and much favoured for *cebiches. Corvina* (River Bass) – perhaps half a metre, also with few bones, fine white flesh. *Sábalo (el oveja de la Amazon* – 25 to 50cms, red-tailed and black tailed, fewer bones than *Boquichico* and therefore preferred. Folklore has it that those who eat *Sábalo* (including the head) will stay for ever in the land of *la selva.*

Tucunaré – up to half a metre in size, not especially tasty but renowned under the name of Peacock Bass as an outstanding and favourite 'sports' fish – a game fighter, much sought after by North American anglers; few bones and easily identified by the large 'eye' marked on the tail (for information about the **Peacock Bass Club**, co-located with the Amazon Birders' Club at 101 Nauta under the auspices of Captain Bill Grimes and a 'must' for enthusiasts, go to www.peacockbassclub.com). *Gamitana* – can be nearly a metre long and 30kg in weight, always in demand in the market place, fresh or dried; fructiferous, eating seeds and fruits. *Paco* – very similar to *Gamitana,* although smaller. *Palometas* – 20cms, abundant and sometimes seen as an ornamental fish. *Paña* or *Piraña* – not for eating, but could well appear on your hook (25 separate species have been identified); they have a voracious appetite for bloody meat but tales of them stripping a human or animal to bare bones within seconds are fantasy (it takes several minutes, at least). *Sardina* – abundant, and the most probable catch of the hook-and-worm amateur; very popular with the river bank dwellers.

Carachama – curious and distinctively whiskery in appearance (downright ugly, actually), black, much sought after for its high mineral content; named after the unfortunate *Chama* tribe. During the 'low-water' season, round wicker baskets of this fish appear in the markets in writhing abundance (it lives on for a day or so after being caught and removed from the water). The fish live in burrows on the river mudflats; the boys of the villages wade into the water and feel for the *Carachama* with their toes, hoping not to encounter a vicious *fasaco* by mistake, a fish with the ability to inflict a severe wound.

The local custom is to serve the complete fish prostrate on the plate, which sounds fine until you actually come face to face with it. Definitely not for the faint-hearted; on the other hand, fortalise yourself with a protein-rich '*caldo de carachama'* (fish-broth) whenever opportunity offers. *Acarahuazú* – up to 400grams of tasty white meat; grown in fish farms and when used ornamentally known as *Oscar;* not dissimilar to *Carachama* in appearance, except dark greeny-yellow in colour and rather larger. Measuring up to one metre in length with distinctive scales patterned in reddish-brown is the *Arahuana*, delicious eating but rarely found in restaurants or indeed in the market-place.

Canero – tiny (but up to 5cm) and slender but devastating, with a predilection for entering the bodily orifices of humans or animals when motionless in the water; has little spines which facilitate its ingress and oppose its departure. This specie has a 15cm cousin, more robust, which devours fresh and putrefying meat. Moral: swim as fast as you can. Another aggressive (unpleasant) biting fish found in Peruvian rivers is the Blue Whale Catfish (Cetopsis), up to 20cm. At the other end of the size scale is *Saltón*, the huge leaping fish of up to 3.5 metres peculiar to the river Marañon (bigger than the *Paiche*), with tales of children having been found in its stomach (and one French explorer taken from his raft in 1989). *Anguila Eléctrica* – the electric eel can grow up to 2 metres in length, discharging several thousand volts, more than sufficient to paralyse a man and cause heart failure. A wet rope or a fishing line can serve as a conductor; they favour still, shaded waters. To finish on a more positive note, try *Doncella,* another flat-headed fish (as is *Carachama)* and one of the very best for eating. Easily distinguished in the market-place by its long 'whiskers' and white body with surreal zebra-like stripes; much favoured by the housewives of the region for *cebiche.*

Birds of the Region

Space precludes listing all the 4,000 species of birds in the entirety of the Amazon basin, many with exotic names to match their exotic plumage, such as the Plum-throated spangled Cotinga. There are 1816 confirmed species in Peru alone, including 50 species of Parrots and Macaws. However, the first lesson may be taken in the Municipal Natural History Museum. On display are hawks and eagles of the region, grey-winged and pale-winged *trompeteros* and colourful Toucan, owls of the forest, *condor de la selva, guacamayos* (macaws) and the sad-songed *Ayaymama;* in total 55 kinds of bird. Second lesson is at the Quistococha National Tourist Park (cf Section IV). Advanced studies for serious birders can be undertaken in *La Biblioteca Amazónica* reading *Así es la Selva* and related tomes.

Less technically, in and around Iquitos and other towns and villages, the large (ugly) black scavengers with heads like a grey vulture are known as *gallinazos.* The tiny humming bird (120 species) taking the nectar from bougainvillea and hibiscus flowers with wings fluttering at 4500 rpm is a *colibrí,* known locally as a *picaflor.* The yellow-breasted bird with brownish plumage is a *Víctor Día* – 'everybody knows Victor Día' say the locals ('*Victor-victor-día*' they call: 'Praise-praise-the-day; hip-hip-hooray'). The little blue bird that you see is the onomatopoeically named *Suisui*, and the doves are *palomas mensajeros.* Another 'onomatopoeic' bird is the *Panguana* – the Gray Tinamou – a cross between a wild chicken and a pigeon calling *phoo, phoo, phoo-ah, huu, huu, huu-a,* and thus fatally revealing the presence of this unfortunately delicious-tasting partridge-like fowl to the hunter; in consequence it is less often encountered in Loreto these days, although still found in relative abundance in the Mariscal Caceres region of San Martin province. Along the river banks the solitary big, black red-headed birds are fish hawks *(Shihuango);* there is also a yellow-headed variant. Neither should be confused with the dark brown/blacked plumaged Turkey Vulture found throughout the Americas with its featherless, purplish-red head, hooked beak and six foot wing span.

The colourful, medium-sized bird with beautiful wings (beloved of artists) is the *Hoatzin* (locally *Shansho*), directly related to the dinosaurs. Parrots in general can be identified by their swooping flight as they pass overhead; they have set routines, the villagers tell the time by the passing of the parrots. The small green parrots are known as *Pihuichos* or *pericos*; their singing is a harbinger of rain to those brought up in the forest and versed in reading the distinctive notes. To sight the national bird of Perú, the elusive scarlet Cock of the Rock, the waterfalls around Tarapoto provide one of the best venues. The guides at the jungle lodges and in the Pacaya-Samiria National Reserve are experts in bird identification and their calls. (For information about the **Amazon Birders' Club** with its well-appointed HQ at 101 Nauta, located just around the corner from the **Dawn on the Amazon Café** on Malecón Maldonado 185, go to www.amazonbirdersclub.com).

Wildlife

Amongst the most commonly encountered mammals of the forest are: Amazonian tapirs, jaguars, ocelots, forest deer, *majas*, many types of monkey, *agutis*, manatee. The largest crocodile (*lagarto negro*, up to five metres in size) is now endangered. Of the other reptiles, the Green Anaconda is also noteworthy for its size (thick bodied, and up to 5m/16ft in length – mythical tales in excess of this have never been scientifically confirmed). Another capable river swimmer is the Boa Constrictor (*mantona*), albeit slightly smaller at 4m fully grown. The bite of the adult and aggressive *shushupe* (the feared Bushmaster, 2.5m to 3m long, which raises its body to strike and will attack repeatedly) is almost invariably fatal, whereas the venom of the *Fer de Lance* (1.25m, hides in banana plantations) is treatable if action is taken rapidly, although permanent memory impairment can result. There are examples of most of these creatures in the Municipal Museum. As previously mentioned, in Iquitos alone, 141 species of snakes have been recorded. As for elsewhere in the region? Still counting.

Trees

For academic study, *'Así es la Selva'* is again the best starting point for the trees of the forest. Additionally, the Municipal Museum has an excellent presentation of some of the different woods of the region adjacent to the display of animals, with natural history professors on duty. Quistococha is the place for practical study prior to visiting the rain forest. At the end of this process you will be familiar with everything from *caoba* (favoured by cabinet makers) to *cedro* (one of the most useful and economically valuable woods of the region), *palo cruz* and *palo sangre* (woods of beautiful grain and texture used for marquetry, carvings and walking canes) to *lupuna* (the 60-metres high giant of the forest, three metres in diameter, cut and extracted for the production of *tripley*, or three-ply), *jebe, caucho* and *chicle* (latex and chewing gum) to *topa (palo de balsa)* and *tangorama* (large tree with a saucer-sized creamy white flower, much favoured by ants). For the making of canoes and paddles, the favoured woods are *caspi* and *cedro.*

In more detail, and for the record and reference purposes, some of the principal *Maderas de la Selva* are as follows:

Aguanillo: 30m in height; medium density; easy to work. Used for cabinet making and decorative carvings.

Almendra: 25m high; upright and cylindrical. 'Good for construction.' Bark: medicinal.

Azucar Huayo: 35m; hard wood – difficult to work. Used for parquet flooring, as well as for furniture and carved pieces.

Boa Caspi: 15m; grows in flooded areas. Medium density – general carpentry.

Brea Caspi: 'medium height'. Good for housing and 'all aspects of roofing, poles and columns'. Because of the straightness of the limbs of this tree, *caspi* is the wood of choice for making blowpipes (*picuna*). The leaves have 'aphrodisiacal powers'. The latex/sap resin is used to treat herpes, dermatitis and eczema.

Canela Moena: 33m; for carpentry and canoes.

Caoba 'Aguano': 50m (over 150 feet), a true 'giant of the forest'. Esteemed and prized as one of the highest quality woods in the Peruvian Amazon. Used widely for furniture, for decorative laminates and for handles for tools.

Capinuri: 30m; high density. Plywood and planks. The latex (sap resin) is 'good for hernias and the treatment of dislocations'. (The suggestive appearance of the end of each and every twig of this tree provides a never-ending source of ribald entertainment for the small boys of the forest – and for *malcreados* in general).

Carahuasca Negra: 25m; low density, easy to work. Poor resistance against insects and fungus, but is used with a preservative for planking and furniture.

Catahua Blanca: 25m; medium density. Good resistance to humidity. Much used for boats, and for rafts for floating homes. The latex in the bark is caustic, and is used as an illegal asphyxiant for fishing and 'against anacondas and insects'; contact with the skin (or eyes) is caustic.

Cedro Rojo: 40m; medium density; resistant to termite attack. Considered to be one of the finest woods of the Amazon. All-purpose, including ornamental laminates. The bark is utilised in the treatment of urinary ailments, and the leaves for the alleviation of arthritis.

Cetico: local name for that medium sized tree with frond-like leaves (a favourite food of the sloth) and white wood that springs up all along the river banks. Makes for poor firewood but good paper pulp.

Chonta: the straightest of all the forest trees, and is seen as a symbol of military obedience, the name deriving from *Chunta Whuachu*, legendary Inca warrior. This is of course the palm that provides the *chonta* salad on your plate, the harvesting of which 'heart' destroys the tree; now cultivated 'sustainably'.

Chontaquiro: 20m; high density. Used for railway sleepers, heavy construction, posts and furniture. The powdered leaves are mixed with the flowers of the *yuca* to deal with 'infirmities of the blood'.

Copaiba: 40m; high density. Used for planking, parquet flooring, construction and decorative laminates. The sap is a strong disinfectant and is 'an effective curative for healing wounds and animal bites, acne, haemorrhoids, psoriasis, skin and nail fungus, and is also used for infirmities of the womb'.

Cumala Colorada: also known as *madera liviana*, much in demand for export to USA, Mexico and Europe. The bark is used in a variety of ways medicinally – for stomach pains, malaria and fungal infections.

Cumaseba: flexible wood from which the tools for hand net-making are made.

Cunchi Moena: 25m; medium density. Easy to work, resistant to fungi and insects. Good structural wood for houses; also for cabinet making and general furniture.

Huacapú ('Fierro Caspi): 25m; high density. The best wood for posts, sleepers and piles (for stilt houses and jetties); lasts for 30 years or so when in contact with the earth. Hitherto, the Quechua and the Guaraníe tribes used a poison derived from the bark for fishing.

Huacapurana: high density – columns, posts and firewood. Bark extracts plus *aguardiente*: treatment of arthritis, rheumatism, malaria

Huacrapona: A dark, yellow-lined, heavy wood. Used for rural flooring and by the parquet industry. In the forest it is the first-choice wood for making spears, bows and arrows, and *pucuna* blowpipes. Also serves as an ingredient in the popular aphrodisiac *'Rompe Calzón'.*

Huingo: The saplings provided the cane of choice for disciplining unruly children in more enlightened days gone past.

Huito 'Jagua': 15m; construction, carpentry and artefacts. Has an edible fruit which in various forms is reputedly 'good for bronchitis, cancer of the uterus, inflamed female genitals, gonorrhoea, extraction of teeth – and as body paint'.

Lagarto Caspi: the bark has a reptilian appearance, hence the name; it is boiled to produce a medicinal infusion. A high density wood used for the keels of boats and canoes, and for decorative trellised balconies. Burns slowly and with great heat and is much valued on this account. Used for railway sleepers.

Lupuna: 40m; low density. Botanical name: *Ceiba.* Widely exported for making plywood. Grows along the river banks, thus sadly facilitating its extraction and annihilation. These magnificent trees, centuries old, are being eradicated as a result of uncontrolled and illegal logging. Formerly they were useful for river navigation, serving as leading marks and points of reference. Because of their size, *Lupuna* have long been associated with *los espíritus de la selva* (forest ghosts and spirits) who seek refuge in the depths of the branches, and in conversation you may be advised that 'these trees provide a home for our ancestors'. Bathing in the macerated, stewed bark can be effective in reducing fever; the flowers of the *Lupuna* give way to a form of cotton which is used on the flights of hunting arrows. The flowers are also used in the preparation of medicine with diuretic and emetic properties.

Machimango Negro: 30m; high density. Used for construction and supports. The bark is utilised to make improvised rope.

María Buena: 25m; medium to low density. Susceptible to insects and fungi. Firewood.

Mari Mari: good for poles and strong posts. From the leaves and the seeds is produced an ointment with which to treat skin eruptions.

Marupa: good resistance against fungi and insects. Used for interiors, furniture, plywood, and also as pulp for paper. The macerated bark is mixed with rum as a prophylaxis, and a tonic against malaria and dysentery.

Marupa Amarillo: 25m, low density and easy to work. Good insect and fungal resistance. Used for carved work, planking and furniture.

Oje: a tall, graceful tree. The resin is used medicinally '*por el estomago*', especially in the treatment of intestinal worms. It is recognised as an *anti-parasitario de gran potencia*, and mixed with warm water the sap (milk) is a pungent purgative indeed: best not to leave home, cancel all appointments for the day.

Palisangre: this is the high-density red-coloured wood familiarly used for tourist artefacts. In 1985 it was memorably used to make a giant cross in honour of the visit of Pope John Paul II. Commercially it is used to make decorative laminates and also for tool handles. When combined with *aguardiente* the resultant brew 'fortifies the body after giving birth'.

Papelillo Caspi ('Cachimbo') – high density wood, growing in non-flooding areas. Used for construction, planking and parquet flooring.

Parinari Colorado: 30m, high density. Poor insect and fungal resistance. Used for firewood and charcoal, and also for roofing supports and beams.

Pashaco Blanco: 25m; medium density, easy to work, good resistance. Good for wood murals and furniture. The flat seeds are strung for curtains, lampshades and decorations generally. When skated across the rivers, the number of skips will indicate the number of children to be expected in a household.

Pashaco Colorado: used for construction, plywood, canoes and general carpentry. Potions made from the bark are used to treat diarrhoea and ulcers.

Polvoro Caspi: 25m; low density. Low insect and fungal resistance, but with preservatives can be used for roofing (beams and rafters); also used for firewood and charcoal.

Puma Caspi: 6m only – firewood and charcoal. The sap is used for diarrhoeal treatment.

Pona (palm): exceptionally hard and durable, making it ideal for flooring and spears.

Quillosisa ('Sacha Alfaro') – 35m, high density. Good for panels, ceiling panelling and boxes. The powdered bark is used indigenously for the promotion of abortions.

Quillosisa Colorado: medium density – housing (ceilings and skylights); chipboard.

Quinilla Blanco: good wood for parquets, and notably, nautical 'blocks and tackles'.

Quinilla Colorado: high density hardwood for posts, parquet flooring and construction.

Remo Caspi: high density and with good insect/fungal resistance. Housing purposes, firewood and paddles ('*remos*'). Bark latex used as a prophylaxis for malaria.

Renaco: The Sacred Tree of the Amazon. 'If you use, you will lose all your family'.

Sapotillo Colorado: 20m; low density. Used for housing: roofing, beams and rafters. Also for firewood and charcoal.

Shiringa Roja: 25m, low density. General carpentry and construction. Ceiling panelling. Formerly the latex (*jebe*) was tapped and collected commercially (cf: rubber boom).

Shiringa Masha: 25m, low density. As for *S.Roja* above, and for boat building.

Tangarana Amarilla: 30m; high density. Good general resistance. Favoured for construction and furniture, particularly veneers and lacquer work.

Topa 'Palo Balsa': 12m, low density. Aero-models, fish floats, rafts (*flotadores,* and hence 'raftwood tree'). The cotton from the seeds is used for stuffed toys, cushions and pillows.

Tornillo 'Huaira Caspi': 40m; grows in poor soil. Used for carpentry in general, and construction (less expensive than '*cedro*').

Violeta Nazareno: 25m; high density wood growing in flooded parts of the forest. Useful for house construction, furniture and ornaments.

Wuira Caspi: 6m to 20m; low density; good resistance to insects and fungi; easy to work, used for furniture, and firewood. The bark is stewed as a tonic for children, and for diarrhoea.

Yacushapana: 30m; very tough wood, used for tool handles and parquet flooring.

Flowers and Medicinal Plants Etcetera

The "*Inventario Taxonómico de la Flora de la Amazonía Peruana*" available from CETA at 355 Putumayo is for serious students of this subject. The orchids of the rain forest, a subject of attraction to many, can be studied prior to visiting the jungle in *Las Orquideas Silvestres* (Arend Job de Wilde) available in the *La Biblioteca Amazónica* (the spacious wood-furnished reading room overlooks the river). One of the best books on medicinal plants of the Amazon region, first alphabetically arranged plant by plant detailing uses, and then cross-referenced against a comprehensive list of illnesses and ailments is '*Plantas Medicinales de uso Popular en la Amazonía Peruana'* by Kember Mejía & Elsa Rengifo (ISBN 9972-614-00-5), also available in the *Biblioteca Amazónica.* A similar treatise on medicinal plants as used by the Shipibo-Conibo tribes of the Amazon is *'Las Plantas Medicinales y su beneficio en la salud'* by Guillermo Arévalo Valera.

Notwithstanding the above, ***Ayahuasca*** receives a separate mention here. The Quechua word translates literally as 'rope of death'; conversely, it is also referred to as the 'spiritual vine'. Regardless of perspective, this creeper is a narcotic of unusual power, inducing delirious and supposedly telepathic fantasies, which are a feature of the *Shamanic* ceremonies (for the cognoscenti, it contains dimethyltryptamine, which has been likened to 'a sort of psychic depth-charge'). Through prolonged cooking of the fibre it is possible to extract a coffee-coloured infusion which promotes hallucinatory dreams, at times sensual and of extreme beauty but interspersed with monsters and other horrific images. The control of this aphrodisiac and the attendant erotic images depends on the 'skill' of the *ayahuasquero* and also the preparation and quality of the narcotic. The onion-like bulb of the *piri-piri* reed is used to help counteract any feelings of nausea, whilst the onset of diarrhoea and vomiting is a not uncommon feature of the hallucinogen; a strict meat-based diet is recommended for eight days following the use of *ayahuasca.*

A particularly fine example of the innocuous-looking Ayahuasca vine growing but a short distance from the centre of Iquitos

As with all drugs, the dangers inherent in 'incorrectly' administered *ayahuasca* should not be under-estimated; cases of death are not unknown. Which brings us back to the translation of the Quechua name. On the other hand there is no gainsaying that *ayahuasca* has a substantial and growing following from outside the region; an increasing number of lodges cater for these visiting adherents seeking tranquillity and anxious to explore their inner selves (at a price). Much has been written on this controversial subject, readily available via the Interweb, where differing personal experiences abound. *Ayahuasca* was of course hitherto the exclusive province of indigenous *curanderos*; somewhat predictably, the latter-day influx of external practitioners has not been universally well received locally. (NB. In Columbia the vine is known as ***Yagé***).

The list of plants of interest in an ethno-medical context is lengthy; here are just a few samples (entries marked with an asterisk were kindly contributed by Cliver Rioja Acosta, Naturalist Guide, Explorama Lodges):

Abuta: a vine from which is made a 'cure' for tense muscles and for the relief of sprains.

Achiote: a large shrub/small tree (*urucú*) with pink flowers and inedible bright red spiny fruits 'resembling in shape that of a chestnut', indigenous to the Amazon rain forest 'from which may be extracted a potion with anaesthetic and aphrodisiacal properties'. More definitively, when stirred in water, the red seeds of the fruit provide the red dye that was previously widely used by many tribes as a body paint, particularly for the lips (hence the common name: Lipstick Tree). Nowadays this natural pigment is used equally widely, but as a colouring for foods ('jungle paprika'). From the sap of this shrub and other parts of the plant are derived treatments for 'sunstroke, tonsillitis, burns, leprosy, rectal discomfort and headaches'. Also makes an effective repellent.

Camu Camu: already mentioned under "Frutas y Refrescos" – very high ascorbic acid content and growing only in well-watered areas. Should be harvested long before dawn (*en la madrugada*) to obtain double the content of natural richness.

Caña Brava: A riverside plant, the 'fusion of the shoots' results in a 'viagra variant'. The wispy flowers and seeds are used for decoration, the stems as spears, fishing rods and fencing (as in palisade) sticks.

Chancapiedra: A little plant that grows underfoot throughout the rain forests of the world. A preparation made from the leaves is used for a wide range of medicinal treatments, including urinary and bladder ailments, Hepatitis B, the liver, hypertension, prostate, gonorrhoea, dysentery, fever, dyspepsia, malaria – the list is seemingly endless.

Chia: Salvia Hispanica – very much an intruder in this list, but it needs a home, so here it is. A member of the mint family grown by the Aztecs (rather than the Incas) in pre-Columbian times as a food crop equal in importance to maize and included because it is now grown commercially not only in Mexico but also Bolivia, Ecuador and the Argentine, enjoying popularity as one of the latest 'wonder foods'. About a metre tall with purple and white flowers, the harvested seeds are said to reduce inflammation, improve heart health and stabilise blood sugar levels, with nutritional content akin to that of salmon (Omega 3), spinach and human growth hormone combined, resulting in muscle building, lowered cholesterol, and reduced risk of heart disease.

Chiric Sanango: this is an ornamental plant with abundant white flowers; the macerated roots of this shrub are the source for 'an additive to the *ayahuasca* potion administered by *Shamans y Brujos* (Witches)'.

Chulla-Chaqui shrub (so-called)*:* Extracts from the cooked bark 'serve as an excellent tonic for adults when taken to coincide with the new moon'.

Clavo Huasca: a creeper; the vine is shredded/macerated and drunk with *aguardiente* as a stimulant and to ward off rheumatism.

Cocona:* a type of wild tomato (*Solanum Sessiliflorum Dun - Solanaceae*) grown throughout the Amazon Basin, the juice (high in Vitamin C) squeezed from the fruit being used for the treatment of Diabetes, to alleviate vomiting and, externally, as a scalp treatment and for insect bites; the liquid extracted from crushing the leaves is used for the treatment of burns, to reduce pain and to avoid blistering and scarring.

Cotton Plant: A fusion of the leaves 'provokes the onset of childbirth'.

Fer-de-Lance:* Jergón Sacha (*Dracontiun Loretense – Araceae*) – a drink made from the large, bulbous root cut into pieces and boiled in water is used for the immediate treatment of a snakebite; the tuber may also be heated and applied directly to the wound itself.

Forest Mistletoe: in this instance, a fusion of the leaves acts as a contraceptive.

Green Toad: indeed not a plant – but gets a mention because 'the saliva when rubbed in the eyes improves the hunter's night vision'.

Guarana en Polvo: this powder comes from the red fruit of the small-sized *guarana* tree, which when mixed with water is claimed (by the vendors) to be beneficial for all of the following: energy, circulation, rheumatism, active sex life, mental tiredness, stomach pains, diarrhoea, headaches, alcohol dependency, feminine problems, moderation of the appetite, haemorrhoids, and pimples. Oh yes – it is also a diuretic and general tonic.

Guisador: the root is used for the treatment of hepatitis.

Hierba Luisa: also known as Scented Verbena, Fever Grass, Lemon Grass. The infusion is used 'to relax and tone the nerves, to lower the blood pressure, digestive, and stomach acidity'. Supposedly a constituent of Inca Kola; also plays a part in New Year's Eve 'good luck' superstitions.

Hilupuro/Iporuro: the bark and leaves of this swamp-growing tree are macerated in alcohol to provide protection against rheumatism, arthritis, colds and 'general limb pains brought about by the toil of fishing'.

Jengibre:* Ginger (*Zingiber Officinale Roscoe – Zingiberaceae*) – this plant is used as a spice and flavouring agent, using the dried or fresh rhizome. The crushed rhizomes in *agua ardiente* (from sugarcane) are taken for rheumatism and arthritis, and to increase virility. The rhizomes are also used for diarrhoea and stomach aches, headaches and bronchitis. Extracts have shown anti-inflammatory activity comparable to aspirin. Indigenous women use *jengibre* for colic, sore throats and menstrual cramps.

Lobo Sanango: the leaves are heated and softened for the alleviation of rheumatic pains.

Manteca de Boa Negra: a serpentine intruder in the medicinal plant list, included here for convenience – evil-smelling bottled boa fat derivative used to alleviate aches and pains in the joints. Disappointingly applied via a chicken or parrot feather, rather than by an obliging *charapita.* Then bandage the affected area to allow the charm to work … quite amazingly (and given time and patience) the concoction will pass right through the troublesome limb to emerge on the far side in little droplets. Truly astonishing, but beware of placebos.

'Monkey Tail': provides a medicine for renal problems (*coto chupa*).

Motelo Sanango: the macerated leaves of this herbaceous shrub are used in conjunction with *aguardiente de caña* to treat 'muscular colds, bones with rheumatism, and to re-energise and improve the vitality of the man and the woman'.

Noni: Fist-sized irregular green fruit with wart-like markings, apparently originally from Polynesia, Malaysia and the Philippines. Eaten raw after peeling (but not the seeds) as a general health tonic for all ailments. Much sought after, and it was previously expensively imported from Central

America until large quantities were discovered growing in Peru.

Ojé:* medicinal fig (*Ficus Insipida – Moraceae*) – the sap of this species diluted with sugarcane or orange juice (as well as that of many other figs) has widespread use throughout Amazonia as a purgative against worms and intestinal parasites.

Pajaro Bobo: looks like a little Christmas Tree; the 'cones' are pulverised as a treatment for acne.

Pan de Arbol: the fruits are eaten cooked or baked before they are completely ripe. The resin from the tree is used to treat fresh cuts and wounds, as a palliative for hernia, and also to 'extract worms and maggots from the skin'. The ripe seeds are eaten cooked (and sometimes added to *masato*), and are recommended for indigestion and flatulence. This large tree, readily recognisable from the frond-like leaves and hanging fruits, is not native to the rain forest – 5,000 plants were imported from Polynesia in 1875

Quinoa: another intruder in the list, but it crops up in the South American context so it gets a mention. This crop of edible seeds (the name is a Spanish derivation from the Quechua '*kinwa*') has been grown in the Andes of Peru, Ecuador, Bolivia and Colombia for thousands of years. Termed a pseudo-cereal, now sought after globally as a good source of calcium, phosphorous and iron. (Also *Quinua – trigo inca*/Inca wheat); pronounced 'kinwa' regardless.

Retama Amarilla:* Wild Senna (*Senna Reticulata – Caesalpiniaceae*) – This plant has a variety of medicinal uses; the flowers are used to treat liver problems as well as upset stomachs and malaria Both the leaves and the flowers contain antibiotics that are effective against certain bacteria and useful in treating kidney inflammations. Wild senna is also used to treat venereal and skin problems, and as medication against ringworm and other fungal infections, being made into dermatological soap.

Ruda: Dark green bunches of this strongly scented, feathery plant are to be found on sale in Belen and elsewhere throughout the region, although in fact it comes from Huanaco in *la selva alta.* Reputedly it provokes menstruation, kills lice and nits, is useful in treating heart palpitations and nervous diseases, and provides good luck for good measure. Small wonder that it sells well.

Sacha Ajo: Wild garlic, growing as a creeper. Makes an excellent repellent against mosquitos and bugs in general (and – unfortunately – all your friends).

Sangre del Grado:* Dragon's Blood (*Croton Lechleri – Euphorbiaceae*) –

the resin of this thick-trunked tree with copious foliage, some five or six metres in height, is taken orally in hot water to hasten internal healing following an abortion and for stomach ulcers. The sap is also used to staunch the flow of blood and heal wounds and skin cuts. It is used as a vaginal douche subsequent to childbirth. Dragon's blood is a great coagulant and antiseptic.

Tagua: 'vegetable ivory' – not medicinal, but well merits recognition; when hardened in the sun, the seeds were formerly used to make beautiful buttons, which were sent through Lima to London. Sadly, the trade collapsed through maladministration. Now the selfsame seeds are used for carvings on sale to tourists.

Toe Plant: the six-leafed foliage can be used as the basis for a hallucinogen.

Uña de Gato: Cat's Claw (*Uncaria Spp. – Rubiaceae*) is another vine (woody liana) of especial interest, typically found in old secondary growth forest, the properties of which in respect to the prevention and treatment of cancer and the amelioration of arthritis, rheumatism and internal wounds have excited worldwide interest and are the subject of international seminars and scientific studies (ongoing, and as yet without definitive conclusions). In addition to 'powerful anti-carcinergetic (*carcinogenic*) properties' it is also recommended for 'anti-inflammatory use, female uro-genital treatment, gastritis, stomach ulcers, prostate and kidney problems, cirrhosis and gonorrhoea', the inner bark/stem being traditionally taken as a weak, slightly bitter-tasting tea re-inforcing the immune system against illness.

Decorative gardening and floral arrangements are not amongst the strongest cultures in Iquitos. However, magnificent blooms of locally grown red and pink *Bastón del Emperador*, stems of Pineapple Ginger as though freshly sculpted from pale yellow wax, and scarlet and yellow 'Bird of Paradise' *Heliconias* (best on Fridays) can be bought from Cecilia in ***Floreria Exótica/Hogar Moderno*** (Av.Grau No.1043, tel: 233744, cel.965935194). Also, ***Amaranthos*** (Sra. Ericka Reyna) at *Calle* Fitzcarrald 174 (tel: 065-232562) receives fresh flowers by air from Lima three times a week, including roses from Ecuador. Another option is to visit the flower sellers outside the city cemetery, *el Cementerio General,* at the junction of Alfonso Ugarte 8 and Fanning 12. Most of the flowers (with notable exceptions, such as the sweetly scented white *margarita* and the dramatic and aptly named scarlet *gallo cresta*) come up from Lima by air on Tuesday and Friday evenings. Hence, for the freshest bouquet, make your purchases on Wednesday or Saturday morning. To buy a potted flower as a gift for your balcony, or plants for your garden/*chacra*, the best selection is to be found in the Central market (*Sras.* Rosita y Sulema): *croto, bouquet de novia, jazmín del cielo, bougainvillea, cucarda* and so on.

"Manos Amazonicas" – Village appliqué workshop, Río Yanamono

The Aguaje palm and highly popular ubiquitous 'pine cone' fruit

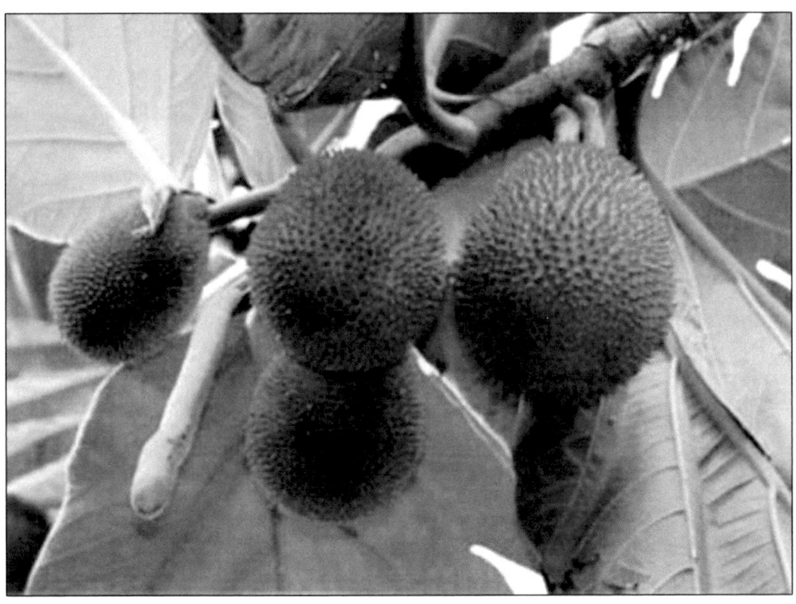

Pan de Arbol: the distinctive breadfruit tree, originally from the Pacific Islands but now widespread throughout the region (also known as Pan de Dios)

Section VII
Loose Ends

"The last wilderness, land of the hurricane lamp and the manguare drum."

Tribes and Languages of the Forest

This is a huge subject. It is estimated that the Peruvian rain forest was once populated by more that 1,000 distinct tribes – even making allowance for the fact that sometimes the same group of forest dwellers received a separate name from different missionaries or explorers, and that on occasions the confusion was compounded by alternative transliterations of the same name. Nor is this a static subject; over the years many tribes have changed their primary locations for a variety of reasons, principally associated with survival. For example, stemming from the Putumayo genocide[37] of the days of the 'rubber boom' in which upwards of 40,000 indigenous people are estimated to have died (and in which crime against humanity the name of *cauchero* Julio César Arana features large), members of the ethnic groups Huitoto, Yagua and Bora are today encountered in regions far removed from their original ancestral lands. Moreover, some tribes have remained relatively isolated whilst at the other end of the spectrum other groups have been more or less absorbed by and integrated with national society, with consequent loss of identity. In this manner, even by the time of Spanish colonisation, the process of extinction and absorption had reduced the number of tribal groupings to less than eight hundred.

The highly complex ethnic tapestry of Amazonia defies satisfactory simplification, the subject demanding much detailed study. However,

[37] Extract from Report by C.Reginald Enock published 1912: "It was averred that the peaceful Indians were put to work at rubber-gathering without payment, without food, in nakedness, that their women were stolen, ravished, and murdered, that the Indians were flogged until their bones were laid bare when they failed to bring in a sufficient quota of rubber or attempted to escape, were left to die with their wounds festering with maggots, and their bodies were used as food for the agents' dogs, that flogging of men, women and children was the least of the tortures employed, that the Indians were mutilated in the stocks, cut to pieces with machetes, crucified head downwards, their limbs lopped off, target shooting for diversion was practised upon them, and that they were soused in petroleum and burned alive."

accepting the shortcomings of generalisations in this area, the following are broadly the basic linguistic families of the Peruvian Amazon:

Jíbaro; Cahuapana; Huitoto; Arahuaca; Harakmbet; Pano; Tacana; Tucano; Tupi-Guaraní; Zaparo; Peba Yagua; Quechua.

Similarly, the following are the principal tribal groupings (but bearing in mind that this is a condensation and contraction from several hundred tribes):

Achual, Aguaruna, Amahuaca, Amarakaire, Amuesha, Arabela, Ashaninkas, Bora, Campa, Candoshi, Capanagua, Cashibo, Cashinahua, Chayahuita, Cocama, Culina, Huachipaire, Huambisa, Huarayo, Huitoto-Muinane, Huitoto Murui, Iquito, Jebero, Jíbaro, Lamista, Machiguenga, Marinahua, Mayoruna, Ocaina, Orejón, Piro, Quechua de Napo, Sharanahua, Shipibo-Conibo, Ticuna, Urarina, Witoto, Yagua, Yaminahua

Four tribal names (and indeed, tribal people) frequently met by visitors to Loreto are: *Bora, Yagua, Shipibo* and (yes!) *Iquito.* For anyone wishing to delve deeper into this fascinating subject, the following steps are recommended. Firstly, study the Tourist Office ethnic map. Secondly, read the appropriate sections in *Así es la Selva* and *Panorama Histórico de la Amazonía Peruana* (both in the Recommended Reading list). Thirdly, re-visit the Municipal and *Amazonica* Museums, and finally re-visit the two Iquitos Libraries.

(Note: When Pope John Paul II dropped in on Iquitos in February 1985 he expressed the wish that his greetings should be received by every member of the indigenous native community of the forest, and to this end – and no doubt guided in his wisdom from above – he specifically identified the following groups: **Campa-Asháninca Aguaruna Humbisa, Cocama-Cocamilla-Omagua, Quichua-Lamista, Shipibo-Conibo, Machiguenga-Napo, Chayahuita, Ticuna, Amuesha, Candoshi y Piro.** *There is to this day no known record in the Vatican of any complaints having been received from anyone who felt they had been inadvertently omitted from this list; it may therefore be concluded that possibly the Pontiff's groupings are all-inclusive).*

Legendary Inhabitants of the Forest

In addition to the nocturnal *tunchi* ghosts and *los espíritus* of the departed that abound in these parts (and who are particularly fond of making their homes in the furthermost branches of the mango and the *lupuna*), there are a host of other creatures and monsters that dwell in the darkest depths of the forest, some benign but the majority fearsome. These are but rarely encountered by visitors, but are well known to the people who live in the remoter regions. It is possible that you will hear tales of some of the following:

Amaru: In the Quechua and Aymara tongues this is the name given to the 'sacred serpent' that represents infinity and which is entwined with the blessed waters that irrigate the farmlands, symbolising the vitality that maintains the existence of the people. Thus the deity *Amaru* dwells invisibly in the water that runs through the rivers, the brooks and streams and irrigation channels, making it possible for the seeds to become plants. Also, it is said that everything which comprises life itself is written on the scales of the *Amaru*.

Ayaymama: The plaintive call of the onomatopoeically-named *Ayaymama* bird, strikingly sad and melancholic, is most likely to be heard on nights when the moon is full. Back in the mists of time a destitute mother left her two children in the forest whilst she went in search of fruit and shelter. After five days without food the little boy and the little girl, lost and abandoned, managed to climb a tree, calling for their mother. But to no avail. Whereupon the children grew feathers and became birds, who to this very day may be heard endlessly calling '*ay-ay-mama, ay-ay-mama, ay-ay-mama*'.

Ayapullito: This little bird of the forest is rather more than it might at first appear (named from the Quechua: *aya* = dead; *pullito* = bird), for it acts as a spy for witches, anxious as they are to observe all things. Thus, and in their turn, wizards are able to foretell sorrow and misfortune.

El Barco Fantasma: A spectral happening, rather than a lurking monster or sinister creature, obviously, but included here for the sake of completeness. This is the Amazon equivalent of the *Marie Celeste* ghost ship, a vessel without a crew to be seen but briefly, gliding through the mists of dawn or half obscured by a rainstorm before disappearing from view.

Bufeo Colorado: Although strictly speaking hardly falling within the confines of this section, the strange powers of the Pink Dolphin (also *Bufeo Rosado*) are included here for want of a better home. These are best conveyed in the words of ancient *Abuelita* Beatita, wrinkled beyond belief, speaking to the young girls of her village on the upper reaches of the river Pintoyacu[38]:

"*Now that you are growing up so fast, you should be aware of the compelling*

---

[38] Text © John Lane from his book *Homeward Blows the Wind*

spell that is cast by the Pink Dolphins that swim here in the river. You will have seen them countless times passing and playing innocently during the day. But by night, subsequent to the setting of the sun it is another matter. Some say it is only a legend, but you may judge for yourselves. Many are the young maidens who have walked alone on the river bank in the darkness, only to fall to the seductive and enticing embrace of the Pink Dolphin. Those unfortunates so entrapped and beguiled have returned to their homes long after the expected hour, bearing with them but bemused and hazy recollections of what has befallen and occasioned such delays. However, as the ensuing months have passed, the stars in their eyes have been dulled and diminished as the regrettable reality of their condition and destiny arising from the warm company of the passionate Pink Dolphins have become increasingly evident to all. Some say it is only when the moon is full that such violations occur, but from my personal observations over the years I would advise that the state of the moon is an irrelevance. New moon or full moon, waxing or waning, the outcome is the same. It is a matter of biology rather than astronomical astrology."

What Granny Beatita fails to mention is that when the Pink Dolphin is engaged on his nefarious business he generally wears a hat to cover his long nose.

Chullachaqui: 'Diminutive and repulsively hairy little men with one foot bigger than the other who live secretively in the darkest part of the jungle, alone with the jaguar and the serpents. It is said that they delight in appearing before lost travellers, mischievously giving 'false directions to worsen their plight.' The name of this demon of the jungle derives from Quechua: *chulla* = uneven; *chaqui* = feet. 'According to popular belief, the *chullachaqui* goblin has the ability to transform itself into the form of any person, making a fool of the inhabitants of the jungle by introducing himself as a family member or friend and taking them out of their way. The only way to establish his true identity is through his feet, which he tries to keep hidden; when his trickery is revealed, he flees through the trees.'

Huancahui: A bird similar to the sparrow hawk, whose cries possess occult powers and with the ability to devour the most ferocious of snakes. The sorcerers of the Amazon must learn and master the calls of the *Huancahui* in order to dominate the serpents. He who fails to do so will be beset by snakes, resulting in death.

Janulf y la Warmiboa: Amongst those who supposedly emerged from the fertile depths of Quistococha Lake was Janulf, the forgotten mythological god distinguished by his high cheek bones and powerful muscles. Together with

Warmiboa, the beautiful native half-woman, half boa, Janulf delighted in performing the ritual dance of the anaconda (also known as 'mother of the water'). According to the information provided at the entrance to the Park, Warmiboa 'dances sensually, rubbing the snake between her legs'.

Lagarto Negro: The Black Lizard, the largest crocodile of the Amazon by far, reaching up to eight metres in length. Is possessed of supernatural powers, is extremely aggressive, and is much feared by the people of the jungle, not least for its voracious appetite.

Mayantu: A goblin with the face of a toad. It lodges in the tree tops, blending with the bark. Despite this unpromising description, the *mayantu* is the 'god of the good in the jungle and this goblin helps the needy man'.

Motela Mama: The Giant Turtle, mother of all *chelonians* (i.e. the order of reptiles with 'horny shells', viz. turtles and tortoises) of the Amazon forest. Stationary for unbelievably long periods, to the extent that plants take root and grow over its recumbent form, thus deceiving victims who approach without fear. When this immense creatures moves, the resultant upheaval of land and water is akin to an earthquake; its life span is infinite, and it has existed since before the beginning of time

Runa-mula: A monster, half-human and half with the head of an ass that appears to haunt those who have cheated in love. If bidden, it will also come to those who choose to commune and converse with lost ones beyond the grave, to reach out across the Great Divide.

Sachamama: Disguised as a fallen tree in the shadiest parts of the forest, and camouflaged by the vegetation that grows on his body, this gigantic, snake-like beast presents itself as a comfortable and welcoming place of repose for the weary traveller. As soon as the unsuspecting hunter is seated, the branch-like arms of the *Sachamama* whirl around the victim, pinning him in place and preventing all further movement. To struggle is futile; the end is nigh.

Shapshicos: Beware of these 'little people of the forest' who may appear at your side at any moment and who may, unfortunately, rob you.

Tanrrilla: A relatively small bird of the Amazon but with surprisingly long legs, it lives on the banks of the rivers. When at rest its plumage is unremarkable, but when its wings are spread it displays an exquisite combination of shades of grey, black and white. The point is, should you chance to behold your beloved through the legs of this enchanting bird, your loved one will in turn become wholly enamoured with you.

Tunchi: Meriting inclusion and a second mention, the *tunchis* are 'disturbed souls wandering in pain and grief in the depths of the darkest nights; above all, when the silence most lugubrious reigns, they re-trace the steps and paths that they trod in their past lives, announcing their presence close at hand with a sharp whistle so alarming that your skin creeps and your blood runs cold – and then they are gone again, lost in the forest depths'.

Yacumama: The mother of all Giant Boas. Once they have been constricted, and consumed, victims are sometimes regurgitated, to be encountered at a later date in a sorry state on forest trails.

Yacuruna: A greatly feared scaly denizen of the deep whose habit is to entrap virginal maidens bathing at the riverside, seizing and submerging them to dwell at its side in the sediment of the watery depths for all eternity.

Yanapuma: The name means 'Black Puma' in Quechua. This vicious member of the cat family has an excess of black pigmentation, a rarely encountered aberration and a strangely compelling oddity that has lead to the belief that the *yanapuma* has diabolical powers and hypnotises its victims before devouring them.

Yara: The temptress of the deep who steals young men to devour at her leisure in the innermost chambers of her palace on the river-bed.

Yashinga: A diabolical creation, a dwarf with one enlarged foot (yet not to be confused with the *chullachaqui*). These hideous demons have the capacity to enter the being, sequestering persons for sexual purposes. Ghoulishly, they also have the ability to commune with dead spouses.

La Marina de Guerra del Perú en la región Amazónica

The Peruvian Navy has been active in Amazonia from the early days of the formation of the Republic in 1821, although one of the first recorded 'naval' travels in the region was made by Lieutenant Henry Maw of the British Royal Navy. He nonchalantly journeyed from the Pacific Ocean to the Atlantic in 1827 'crossing the Andes in the Northern provinces of Perú (Lambayeque and Cajarmarca) and descending the rivers Marañón and Amazon'. In 1834, two more 'enthusiastic English mariners', Lieutenants William Smythe and Frederick Lowe from HMS SAMARANG, anchored at that time in the port of Callao (Lima), set out with Lieutenant Ramón Azcarate of the Peruvian Navy and Sergeant Mayor Pedro Beltrán to reconnoitre the area of the river Pachitea, travelling via Cerro de Pasco,

Huánuco and Pozuso with the hope of arriving at the river Ucayali (at the confluence due south of Pucallpa), and thence downstream to the distant Amazon. As it happened, they failed to reach their ambitious goal, but the account of their epic adventures awakened still further interest in *la Amazonia Peruana.*

Thus it was that in 1843 Captain Francisco Carrasco was tasked to lead an expedition from Lima through Cusco to explore the headwaters of the rivers Urubamba and the Tambo, and then voyage on to the mighty Amazon via the Ucayali. Somewhat amazingly, this he duly did, his expedition comprising four canoes and two balsa rafts. The resultant map was included by the Italian Antonio Raimondi (who gave his name to the 'wild west' giant cacti to be found in parts of the Andes) in his book entitled 'The History of the Geography of Perú'. For half a century this was acclaimed as the best depiction of Amazonia until Coronel Pedro Portillo (one time distinguished *Prefecto de Loreto* 1901-1904) published his *Mapa del Perú* in 1906.

In 1853, prompted by the catalytic activities of Carrasco and Raimondi, the then President of Perú, General José Rufino Echenique, commissioned the construction of two steam boats in the USA, the ***Huallaga*** and the ***Tirado***. The working lives of these vessels were unfortunately very short, the former being lost at Omaguas in 1857 and the latter sinking at Nauta the same year, these mishaps being 'the price of inexperience and their hull forms not corresponding to river navigation'. [*In keeping with the often contradictory records of this period, some accounts state that these pioneering steam boats 'arrived at Nauta on 14th March 1852'*].

In his second Presidential term of office, the farsighted Mariscal Ramón Castilla (*cf Plaza Castilla*) created the *Departamento Marítimo Militar de Loreto* in 1861, decreeing that the assets to give effect to this vision should comprise not only ships but logistical back-up[39]. The necessary orders were lodged with the engineering firm of Samuda Brothers in England, noted builders of some of the very first iron steamships from 1843 through to the

---

[39] Coincidentally, and as recorded by English Heritage researcher and author Serena Cant, this was at the height of the extraordinary trade in *guano* seabird-droppings (circa 1840-1880) between Peru and Great Britain, when as many as 70% of the ships in the port of Callao would be British, and the Royal Navy's South Pacific Squadron 'was the local coast guard and debt collector'. Accordingly, both diplomatic prudence and a desire for regional naval supremacy led President Castilla to look to Britain for the provision of Peru's new warships.

1880's, whose shipyard at that time was on the River Thames at Millwall on the Isle of Dogs. Hence the historic arrival in Iquitos in 1864 of the frigate '***Arica***', the barquentine '***Próspero***' (more correctly: 'brig'), the schooner '***Teresa***', and the smaller gunboats '***Napo***' and '***Putumayo***', plus the necessary materials from Britain with which to construct a floating dock and a naval factory in support of the vessels. Also in 1864 came the '***Morona***' (Captain Ferreyros) and '***Pastaza***' (Captain Raygada) of 500 and 300 tons [*or possibly both of 500 tons: records differ on this point*], having crossed the Atlantic from England and sailed up the Amazon under their own steam. It was these two ships with their naval crews that immediately opened up the routes for commercial traffic from Iquitos to Tabatinga some 300 kilometres to the east (i.e at the frontier with Brazil) and to Yurimaguas lying over 400 hundred kilometres to the south west, up the rivers Marañón and Huallaga.

[*Even by the standards of an era in which men were giants compared to their latter day counterparts, the successful construction, marshalling and final assembly of the components of the* Marina Fluvial del Perú *was an evolution of heroic proportions. As previously mentioned, the 'Morona' and 'Pastaza' were of sufficient size to cross the Atlantic to the mouth of the Amazon under their own steam. However, the smaller 'Napo' and 'Putumayo' were dismantled by the Samuda shipyard and the pieces stowed onboard the Peruvian frigate 'Arica' under the command of Captain Frederico Alzamora, which had sailed all the way to England round Cape Horn at the southern foot of the South American continent from Callao on the west coast of Perú expressly for the purpose. The large quantity of materials destined for the fabrication of the floating dock and the factory with its steam engine, foundry, ironworks, sawmill and carpentry workshops required the charter of various freighters, one of these being the sailing brig 'Próspero'* (illustrated p.4) *of 192 tons, built in Jersey and on her maiden voyage from the Channel Islands* (see also boxed text below). *The 'Simbad' and the 'Elisa', both chartered by Captain Alzamora, were two other British freighters that featured in the complex logistical operation; however, on arrival at the Amazon delta their cargoes of factory parts were transferred to the schooner 'Teresa' which Perú acquired from the Brazilians.*

BRIGANTINE PRÓSPERO

In the mid-nineteenth century the boatyards in the Channel Island of Jersey had the advantage over other English yards in that oak and fir for ship building was imported from France and the Baltic free of English timber duties. Simultaneously and

subsequent to that, salt from the Jersey mines was exported to Newfoundland for use in the preservation of the vast quantities of cod then being fished from the North Atlantic; after discharging this cargo, the Jersey owned and operated vessels returned from the Americas having first proceeded south to pick up ballast from the New World in the form of hardwoods such as mahogany, green heart and teak, again for use by the local shipbuilders (and also in house construction) - the so-called 'cod triangle'.

One such shipyard was F.C. Clarke's at West Park in St Aubin's Bay, where 62 vessels were built between 1844 and 1867. In 'Jersey Sailing Ships', compiled by John Jean (published 1982 by Phillimore & Co. Ltd, ISBN 0 85033 464 0), the brig *Próspero*, 192 tons, is shown on page 104 as having being built in 1862 for George Malzard, who owned her from that time until 1870 when she was sold in Adelaide, Australia for £3,000 to a Mr Joseph Storm. In corroboration of this, the *Próspero* features in the records of the Mount Nelson signal station and coastal lookout, Hobart, Tasmania: for example on 22nd July 1880 'bound for Port Pirie' some 200kms north of Adelaide, and again on 11th February 1891 as '198 tons (sic), arriving from Newcastle, New South Wales' – 162kms north of Sydney, all faithfully announced in the columns of the Mercury, the local newspaper of the day (closed 1954).

In the 1920's and 1930's *Próspero* was apparently still active in the Sydney area, but returning to the initial period of her surprisingly long life, when Captain Malzard sold her in 1870 he happened to retain her figurehead (see following picture herein) as a keepsake. This decorated the corner of his residence, Prospect House, in the district of St Peter, Jersey for many years, from whence fortuitously in due course it found its way to the Maritime Museum in St Helier to be preserved for posterity, and where it occupies pride of place in the exhibits. The accompanying inscription reads: 'The *Próspero* spent most of her time trading in China and Australia, but in 1864 Captain Malzard took her from London to Belém and she was towed by paddle steamer over 2,500 miles up the Amazon ["farther than any British ship had ever been before"] to deliver a cargo to the Peruvian town of Iquitos'. Author's Note: This is the first time that all these facts relating to the brig *Próspero*, iconic vessel in the formative years of the city of Iquitos, have been assembled, co-located and related, including that of the continuing existence of her figurehead in Jersey. It is of course, merely a matter of time before this material is plagiarised and re-used in other publications and widely on the web without copyright permission or acknowledgement, like most of the original material in this book – including even multiple theft of the title.]

The figurehead of Próspero, currently on display in the Maritime Museum, St Helier, Jersey (Channel Isles) – where the ship was built in 1862

The 2,000 mile journey up-river to Iquitos presented different challenges. Against the current, in dangerous shoal waters with shifting sandbanks and with little wind, the sailing craft were unable to make headway. In consequence, the 'Próspero' was towed to Iquitos by the 'Pastaza,' arriving of 25th February 1864, and it was a further three months before the 'Arica' arrived, towed in by the 'Morona' on 25th May. The 'Pastaza' then returned to the delta to collect the 'Napo,' completing the tow on 6th November 1864 accompanied by the 'Putumayo' which made the journey under her own steam. The 'Morona' also retraced her steps to tow the 'Teresa' up to Iquitos, the last ship and the final part of the grand venture to arrive. As a postscript, it has to be recorded that, once again, not all accounts agree on the precise timing and sequence of these events, but the foregoing is the generally accepted version].

The stage was therefore set, and from the moment of the timely and auspicious arrival in 1864 of that naval flotilla under the subsequent overall command of *Capitán de Navío* Federico Alzamora, the activities of the Peruvian Navy based at Iquitos became central to the history and development of the region. Daring voyages of discovery were undertaken to the remotest and hitherto unknown corners of the territory, and one of the earliest tasks was the demarcation of the border with Brazil, a mission undertaken by the experienced and previously mentioned *Capitán de Navío* Carrasco. The river Huallaga and the smaller Aypena (which runs from Jeberos, parallel to the Marañón) were explored by Lieutenant Gregorio Pérez, whilst Lieutenant Luis Sandi went by canoe up the Ucayali and Pachitea to pave the way for the exploratory voyage of the 'Putumayo' under the command of Captain Mariano Vargas. Whilst in the river Pachitea, the 'Putumayo' collided with an underwater palisade and had to be beached to effect repairs to the hull. This in turn led to an attack by the aboriginal members of the Cashibo tribe in defence of their territory; Petty Officers Juan Távara and Alberto West were killed in the ambush and subsequently devoured by the Cashibos. A punitive expedition consisting of the 'Morona', 'Napo' and 'Putumayo' was launched in 1866 but was not altogether successful. The 'Putumayo' ran aground in the river Ucayali and stuck fast for a full year, not regaining Iquitos until February 1868.

Quite apart from the ferocious attacks of the natives, the other dangers and hardships attendant on these journeys in the 'counterfeit paradise' were equally daunting: wild animals, immense reptiles, and deadly tropical diseases, all without the medicines and technology that are taken for granted nowadays. Plus of course, the constant 'perils of the deep' ('these waters appear quiet, yet all the time they claim lives'). Many are the illustrious names recorded in the Amazonian annals of the Peruvian Navy of this époque, not least being that of *Capitán de Navío* Germán Stiglich whose extensive hydrographical surveys embraced the Pachitea, Ucayali, Mishahua, Serjali, Caspajali, Manu and Alto Madre de Dios.

The work of the Navy continued unabated throughout the second half of the nineteenth century, opening up the waterways, controlling and monitoring the river traffic, promoting integration of the region, carrying aid and support to the civil community, providing hydrographical services including navigational charts, marking and policing the frontiers. Outstanding in this latter context was the combat performance of the armed launch ***'Cahuapanas'***[40] in the river Napo during the actions at Angoteros and Torres Causano in 1903 in pursuance of the conflict with Ecuador. The valiant deeds and contribution of the Peruvian sailors led to the Government reinforcing the river flotilla and by 1909 it comprised the following units: 'Estrella, Pizarro, Orellana, Requena, Cahuapanas, Iquitos and América', the latter vessel being dealt with in more detail below, in particular the outstanding action at *La Pedrera* in 1911 against Colombian forces.

As an aside, the delivery of these relatively small vessels to the Amazon (and elsewhere, as part of President Ramon Castilla's grand strategy for Peruvian regional naval supremacy following the defeat of Peru by Bolivia at the Battle of Ingavi in 1841) from their mainly European building yards (principally British) continued to pose challenges, bearing in mind that many of the craft were specifically designed for use on inland waters rather than the open sea, and that they were particularly unsuited to transiting the inhospitable and unpredictable Atlantic Ocean. In some cases (as aforementioned) they were transported intact as deck cargo on freighters, and even (in some reports) 'lashed to the side of a mother ship', although the seamanship practicalities of this are questionable. Carriage of all the component parts of some vessels in kit form as freight for re-assembly on arrival was another device employed, notably and memorably in the case of the British built steamships ***Yavari*** and ***Yapura*** in 1862 (destined in this instance for service on Lake Titicaca, where in the event, llama dung was used in the ships' boilers instead of scarcely available coal). It took eight years before these diminutive ships were re-assembled in Puno on the lakeshore to make their maiden voyages in 1871, not least because of the necessity to manhandle all the pieces (in 2,766 numbered boxes) from Lima over the towering obstacle presented by the Andes, aided by llamas employed as pack animals. Today the *Yapura* is still in service with the Peruvian Navy, albeit renamed as BAP ***Puno***; the *Yavari* was saved from the breaker's yard by formation of a conservation project (directed by renowned Ms Meriel Larkin of Putney, London) some two decades ago, and is now poised (with diesel engines instead of reciprocating steam, but still as the world's oldest – and

---

[40] Built by Claparede Freres in Paris in 1876, her name was changed to ***Clavero*** in the 1930's. From 2007 to 2009 she underwent extensive restoration under the auspices of **AmazonEco** and is said to be 'the oldest boat still navigating the Amazon river'.

highest – working single-screw iron ship) to enter commercial passenger service on the lake.[41]

However, not all such undertakings had successful outcomes and happy sequels. One unfortunate example was that of the 'gun brig' ***Loreto*** in 1903. Built by the firm of John Jones at Birkenhead, this 150 foot river gunboat destined for the Amazon had a designed speed of 16 knots and was armed with a 2-pounder deck gun for'd and assorted machine guns, which would have made her a potent adversary at the time on the inland waterways being defended and patrolled by Peru in the north of the country. Unfortunately she sank on her maiden voyage on 25th May 1903, getting no further than '40 miles NW off the Isles of Scilly'. The delivery crew (believed to have been from Liverpool) took to the boats and were fortuitously picked up by a passing French trawler and later landed at Plymouth. Her wreck has never been located, but it is surmised that *Loreto* was swamped by heavy seas, being of but shallow draught, although it is conceivable that she sprang a leak – or possibly suffered a combination of these setbacks. Certainly such minor vessels were vulnerable on the open seas and 'insurance on the *Loreto* was deemed a massive risk, although finally cover of £12,000 was obtained', equating to more than a million pounds at today's prices. Certainly the news of the sinking caused considerable and understandable dismay in Lima – and no doubt, in Naval HQ Iquitos, still located on Avenida La Marina.[42]

The year 1926 saw the inauguration of the first float plane services on the river by the Navy and in 1935 further modernisation of the flotilla took place with the arrival of the gunboats '***Amazonas***' and (a new) '***Loreto***' from the USA, in good time for them to participate in yet another conflict with Ecuador, that of 1941, and then to take part in the lengthy process of the subsequent border demarcation. In 1951 the gun boats '***Marañón***' and '***Ucayali***' were acquired from Britain and these units took their place in the order of battle for the 1981 hostilities against Ecuador referred to as

[41] My most grateful thanks to historian Paul Goulder for consolidation, prompting and provision of many of these fascinating historical gems. For further information and pictures, start with his article 'Ramon Castilla's Dream' in the Peruvian Times of 21.3.2009. As a first step on her touristic career, bed and breakfast is now available to visitors onboard the *Yavari* berthed alongside in Puno.

[42] Further gratitude and indebtedness for all of this to English Heritage scholar Serena Cant, author of 'England's Shipwreck Heritage: from logboats to U-Boats'

Cordillera del Cóndor (the Paquisha War), and that of *Cenepa* (a brief and localised conflict) in 1995. Since that time the Peruvian Navy has continued with its role of public service, promoting safety on the rivers and the prevention of contamination of the waterways, and above all, maintaining national security and the integrity of the frontiers of Perú.

Peruvian Gunboat 'América'. This illustrious vessel occupies an almost legendary place in the annals of the history of the Peruvian Navy in Amazonia. Displacement of 240 tons, length 135ft, beam 20ft, twin screw, steam driven, reinforced plough-bow for ramming, with galvanised ¼ inch thick steel plating, a complement of 28-30 officers and ratings, top speed variously cited as between 11 to 15 knots, shallow draught of 3½ feet for river work, and most importantly, initially armed fore and aft with two 37mm Armstrong Whitworth guns (plus 48 rifles and 48 sabres – subsequently augmented by rapid fire 47mm Vickers Maxims and much later in the mid-1930s by Finnish 20mm Madsen anti-aircraft machine guns). She was built and launched by the Tranmere Bay Development Company (shortly to become Cammell Laird) of Birkenhead (near Liverpool), England in 1904 and arrived in Loreto on 11th May 1905 having crossed the Atlantic and journeyed up the Amazon under her own power. To the delight of nautical historians, the long list of the varied makers of her auxiliary machinery and ancilliary components reads like a Who's Who of British engineering firms of the Edwardian era.[43]

Following service in opening navigational routes in the rivers Napo, Marañón and Curaray, fame came six years later in action against Colombian forces on the river Caqueta in a vast region known as *La Pedrera* [*north of the river Putumayo, subsequently to be ceded to Colombia in 1922 in its entirety together with Leticia by way of the infamous Treaty Salomón-Lozano, allegedly in obeisance to North American pressure – see below*]. Initial attempts to dislodge the occupying Colombian force from Peruvian territory were unsuccessful, until on 12th July 1911 BAP América under the command of Lieutenant (First Grade) Manuel Clavero defied both the fierce currents and whirlpools of the river, and heavy enemy fire to disembark Peruvian troops

[43] For example: triple-expansion engines by Plenty & Son of Newbury; steam windlass by Emerson Walker & Thompson of Gateshead and London; single-cylinder steam engine by H.T.Boothroyd, Hyslop & Co. Bootle; chain-operated steering by Armstrong Whitworth of Tyneside; single-ended boilers by the Stirling Boiler Company, etc.

from Chiclayo in the rear of enemy positions. This audacious action, considered to be impossible in the face of the obstacles, so demoralised the invaders that they fled, many being captured together with their equipment, and the National flag was once again raised over the Peruvian outpost.

The victorious force, with 'América' in the van, returned to a jubilant reception in Iquitos on 31st July 1911 but unfortunately, Lieutenant Clavero was amongst those onboard suffering from a multitude of tropical diseases ranging from beri beri to yellow fever, and after struggling for life for ten days he was buried on 13th August 1911. The epitaph on his monument in *Plaza* Clavero reads: 'In recognition and gratitude to the naval hero commanding BAP America, victor of the battle of *La Pedrera* and example to future generations who offered his life for his country.'

Museum ship América berthed at the Iquitos naval base, open to the public on Navy Day, 8th October and by written request; seen here in her authentic original white livery.

As for gunboat 'América,' as a result of her exploits she earned the title of *El Huáscar de la Amazonía* (cf *Plaza* Grau, Section II) and incredibly continued in service on the rivers of Loreto for at least another four decades, well into the 1950's, before going to Callao (the port of Lima) into reserve during the Sixties and Seventies. She then returned to Iquitos via the Panama Canal to become a training ship for new entry naval recruits. In June 1987 the decision was taken to save the ageing vessel from a watery grave in the depths of the Amazon, and the necessary restorative work was set in hand to convert the historic gunboat into a floating museum. In particular, after over eighty years the hull plating was wafer thin, not from the corrosive effects of salt water normally encountered in sea-going warships but from the continuous abrasive action of the sediment in the rivers of Amazonia. On completion of her refit (some of the bullet holes being preserved for posterity), 'América' was at first anchored permanently off the city. This was then limited solely for the duration of Tourist Week when she was towed into position, but nowadays she is normally berthed at the administrative HQ of the Navy on *Avenida* La Marina. Written applications from groups interested in visiting this maritime 'museum' are welcomed and should be made to the Admiral Commanding the Fifth Naval Region and the Naval Forces of Amazonia at least a few days in advance.

[*Just for one moment we must succumb to the temptation to 'revisit' the fascinating background to* El Tratado Salomón-Lozano *of 1922 – Alberto Salomón being the Peruvian Minister of External Relations of the day and Favio Lozano being his Colombian counterpart. However, responsibility for the Treaty, which ceded this immense tract of Peruvian territory totalling 113,912 square kilometres (i.e. over one and a half times the size of Ireland) to the 'enemy' of the day, lies squarely with the then President of the country, Augusto Bernardino Leguia, whose track record in this respect was a national scandal. In his first term of office he donated 169,977 sq. kms to Brasil and then 91,726 sq. kms to Boliva; not content, he followed up with the 1922 Treaty which was kept secret until 1927 (and the process of ratification not completed until 1930). This in turn provoked the re-taking of Leticia from the Colombians in 1932 by a 50-strong group of patriotic Loreto civilians acting unilaterally, followed by a predictable period of rising tension and finally war in 1933 between Perú and Colombia (and, incidentally, not for the first or the last time, discontented rumblings hinting at the possibility of the secession of Loreto from Perú to form an independent state).*

President Leguia's claim that he acted under pressure from the USA, whilst being insufficient justification for what many termed as 'treason', is apparently not without foundation and curiously, was linked to the construction of the Panamá Canal. The story goes as follows. In 1880 Ferdinand de Lesseps started work on the construction of the waterway across the Central American isthmus, a project of inordinate strategic and economic importance to the United States, the chosen route lying through what was the then Colombian province of Panamá. Malaria decimated the workforce and de Lesseps was beset by financial and contractual problems; the US Government, maintaining a close eye on events, made proposals to the Colombian Government to resolve matters, but the stringent demands were rejected in Bogota. Whereupon the USA set about motivating and promoting a separatist movement in Panamá, achieving this objective in 1903. Thereafter they had a free hand to oversee completion of the canal in the newly independent state to their own specifications and on advantageous operating terms and the canal opened successfully in 1914.

Needless to say, the Colombians were unimpressed by these contrived twists of fortune and equally, the US Government, having won the day, was now anxious to heal the wound. Hence the pressure on President Leguia to sign away territory that had long been sought by Colombia. In return, the US persuaded the Chileans to return Tacna to the Peruvians, although not the territory containing the rich nitrate deposits, symbol of Perú's humiliating defeat in the War of the Pacific. A foretaste of the shape of things to come, say some, but who can judge how it was and how it all happened getting on for 100 years ago? At the time, President Leguia was probably quite relieved to be rid of an ungovernable and lawless tract of remote forest, up to seven weeks distant from Lima in those days, and scene of part of the horrendous 'cauchero' genocide. Nowadays with the benefit of hindsight it is not too difficult to see who got the worst of the deal.]

Oil Exploration in the Peruvian Rain Forest

After the initial confirmation of the existence of oil deposits in the region, following the chance discovery by *cauchero* José Angulo Rodríguez near Contamana in 1917, success in the search for commercial quantities of oil did not come rapidly or readily. Analysis of the first samples was completed in 1920 and between 1922 and 1930 eight years of exploration by the immediately formed Standard Oil Company of Perú was largely un-noteworthy. Similarly, it took 12 years of exploration and the drilling of more than 16 wells before the first 'gusher' was achieved in the *Oriente* concession in 1957 on the river Maquia, to the west of the Ucayali. Nevertheless, by 1967 the combined extraction by the former companies of *Ganso Azul* (whose first wells date back to 1939-40) and *El Oriente* had amounted to over a million barrels.

Conversely, in 1971 the newly formed national company of Petroperú enjoyed almost instant success with their Trompeteros drilling on the left bank of the Corrientes river and this was quickly followed by the successful exploratory bore at nearby Pavayacu, also in the river Corrientes region. Oil extraction in 1973 was 40 million barrels; in 1974 this figure rose to 512, stemming from further exploration in the Capirona, Yanayacu and Valencia sectors, amongst others.

The year 1976 brought the opening of the oil pipeline *Norperuano* connecting the Marañón oilfields with the port of Bayovar on the Pacific Ocean, a major feat of civil engineering over 800 kilometres (discounting feeder pipelines) through virgin forest, over the Porculla Pass across the Andes at nearly 8,000 feet and into the Sechura desert. "Almost heroic was the daily toil of the workers" reads one account, "who with great stoicism and Titanic force succeeded in opening a path through the forest vegetation to rescue the petrol, mud up to the waist, machetes in hand, to put in train the progress of Peru." All of which took Peru into the league of oil-exporting countries. That was until 1984 when home consumption again exceeded production, a situation which persists today in spite of the Corrientes-Pavayacu Project opening up several new wells since 1992.

Although situated some 800 kilometres due south of Iquitos, a long way from Loreto, no account of oil in the Peruvian rain forest is complete without mention of the giant *Camisea* field in the Shell concession, 500 kms east of Lima, with an estimated 13 billion cubic feet of gas and well over 600 million barrels of liquid products. This has given rise to optimistic expectations for the coming years (at least in the narrow context of marketable resources), even though the project has been bedevilled and delayed by a succession of contract disputes – and grave fears for the ecological impact and the well-being and future of the affected people of the area. The controversy continues – and grows; visit the Internet to get the flavour.

The real and over-riding challenge presented by the rich oil reserves which undoubtedly exist in Amazonia is not simply a matter of exploration, discovery and extraction. It is the immensely more demanding question of how to achieve these economic aims with minimal damage and destructive impact on the ecological integrity of the magical and fragile environment that is *La Selva Amazónica,* the irreparable loss of which will be vastly and immeasurably more costly than any short term financial gains.

The Provincial Capitals of the Department of Loreto

Yurimaguas. Capital of the province of Alto Amazonas, situated on the bank of the Huallaga river (which flows into the Marañón). The name originates from the '*Yuri*' and '*Omagua*' tribes. Renowned for the beauty of the landscape, it is euphemistically known as the 'Pearl of Huallaga'. Access to the town's port of *La Boca* is by boat upstream, e.g. *Botes Eduardos* from *Puerto Henry*, Iquitos (4-day trip, en-suite *camarotes matrimoniales* reportedly available). Alternatively by air, Iquitos to Tarapoto, thence 50km northwards on the 'new' tarmac road; or direct by float plane (Yurimaguas Inn; Hotel El Luis Antonio; Hotel El Naromji). The sometimes mooted *Ferrocarril Iquitos/Yurimaguas* is anathema to forest conservationists, although it must be conceded that it would certainly make for a fascinating journey.

San Lorenzo. Capital of the 'new' (2005) province of Datem del Marañon (formerly all part of Alto Amazonas – above).

Nauta. Capital of the province of Loreto, 84 km from Iquitos on the left bank of the Marañón river, seven miles from its picturesque confluence with the Ucayali river. Strategically placed and in consequence an important centre of commerce and communication from early times, although not designated 'capital' until 3rd May 1955, indicating the relatively recent development of the regional administrative infrastructure. The scenic tarmac road link with Iquitos, mooted over many, many years (and delayed by financial problems) was until the end of 2006 still some way short of its destination, although vehicles (including '*collectivos*') could generally complete the journey in two to three hours, although not without difficulty after heavy rain. However, finalisation of the *carretera* was finally achieved in 2007, resulting in dramatic changes in accessibility. Buses leave from the junction of Prospero/Libertad every half-hour throughout the day and complete the journey in one hour and 30 minutes (fare S/.8.00). An 'express' service leaves from *Av.Aguirre* 1495, rear of *Mercado Sacha Chorros* (1hr, S/.10.00).

Prior to this engineering feat (to the grave detriment of the adjacent forest) it was customary to reach Nauta by water, via an easy overnight river journey by *lancha* from Masusa, with a daily return trip early every morning. With the coming of the highway, this service is no more. See also Section V (Travelling Further Afield) – *A Visit to Nauta*. Moreover, think on this: 'The

Amazon rainforest faces destruction if plans by South American governments to improve transport and communications go ahead, environmentalists warn. Scientists at Conservation International say (Oct '07) the plans would involved widespread deforestation and the jungle could be lost within 40 years.'

Requena. Capital of the province of Requena, with origins dating back to 1750, 316kms from Iquitos, lying at the mouth of the Tapiche river at its confluence with the Ucayali river (See Section V – *A Visit to Requena*). The overall atmosphere in the town is tranquil, this peaceful spot currently being very much off the usual tourist trail; this means a welcome paucity of tour operators and the attendant tourist infrastructure, but nevertheless, the organisation of economical (and rewarding) fishing trips and excursions into the neighbouring Pacaya-Samiria National Park is perfectly feasible (for M/V Amazon Explorer – see Section V). The Requena market is a colourful experience (some of the *venderdores* reputedly still travelling for five or six days from afar with their produce). As for accommodation, the *Hospedaje Sadicita* has overtaken *Hostel Palo Alto* as the best place in which to stay. The local *Los Delfines Recreation Park* is worth a visit; at the other end of the challenge and excitement scale, the Brazilian border can be reached in a *deslizador* in two and a half days of rapid travel up *El Río Tapiche.*

The town, like the province, is named after the Spaniard *Coronel* Francisco Requena, famed for his 'dissemination of culture and education to all the zone'. In particular, *Don* Francisco de Requena as Governor of Colonial Maynas between 1779 and 1794 prevailed upon King Carlos IV of Spain to return the administration of what is now Peruvian Amazonia to the jurisdiction of the Viceroy in Lima. This was done by Royal Decree in 1802 thus preventing the inadvertent transfer (by default) of the region to Portuguese control and subsequent permanent distortion of the political map of the continent of South America.

Contamana. Capital of the province of Ucayali and one of the principal ports of the river Ucayali, 12hrs by boat downstream from Pucallpa (and not to be confused with the *Contamana colpa* which is on the Heath River). The name means 'Palms Hill' in the Shipibo dialect. From Contamana visits can be made to the local ferrous thermal springs and to the native community of the 'Chamas.' (cf Fish & Fishing, Section VI – *carachama*).

Ramón Castilla. Capital of the province of Ramón Castilla, lying way down the Amazon in Caballococha lagoon. A Peruvian bastion against frontier incursions from Colombia.

Iquitos. At this stage, no further introduction is necessary. However, it should perhaps be explained that the province of Maynas (of which Iquitos is the capital) takes it name from the Mayna tribe of the *Selva Baja* (Lower Forest), who in turn took their name from Mayno, their Chief. The Mayna people resisted the advances of the Spanish *Conquistadores* with great fortitude and tenacity, gaining the respect of the invaders who invariably referred to the region using the name of the indigenous inhabitants.

Folklore – Dances of Loreto

Far removed and quite aside from contemporary dancing styles of the discotheques, tropi-cumbia (tecno-cumbia) and salsa and so on, visitors may encounter the following traditional dances of Amazonia, particularly during festivities and fiestas.

Changanacuy. The name originates from the Quechua words for leg (*chango)* and caress (*nacuy).* Consequently and predictably, the dancers interlace their legs and through a gymnastic process of small jumps achieve the caressing effect.

Sitaracuy. This name comes from that of a biting ant. More jumping, and the couple coquettishly exchange pinches, simulating the painful bite of the ant. Allied to this dance is of course *La Dansa de los Sancudos y Hormigas.*

Chimaychi. A dance derived from and similar to the *Huayno* dance of the Peruvian *sierra* (highlands). Popular for the celebration of village and river town anniversaries.

Pandilla. A typical 'comic' dance of the jungle, appropriate to the '*carnival*' holiday (February/March – moveable feast) and danced in jolly pairs around the '*humisha*', the festive central palm tree implanted and decorated for the occasion and hung with presents.

Cajada. Used for *fiestas* in honour of the Saints; the rhythm is slow with sad melodies.

Aficionados of this aspect of the historic culture of the Amazon region may choose to contact Professor Walter (or Nestor or Javier) in the Music Department of UNAP (*Universidad Nacional de la Amazonia Peruana*) to see a display by the colourful and accomplished dancers of *Tierra Magica*, or to obtain more information on the arcane art of Amazon drumming and its complex rhythms.

"Iquitos in Rubber Times"

(Re-printed by kind courtesy of the Fitzcarraldo Restaurant Bar – Napo 100/Boulevard – one time headquarters of the Orton Bolivian Rubber Company)

"By 1850, Iquitos was no other than a 'sparse and miserable hamlet.' In 1854, a traveller that visited this place wrote in his diary: 'I counted 33 houses and one straw-thatched church … except for half a dozen white and mestizo families, the population was of no more that 250 Iquito Indians.'

"Fifty years later, in the first years of the 1900's, when rubber tapping was in full swing, Iquitos grew into a prosperous and cosmopolitan city, with 20,000 inhabitants, of which 4,000 were immigrants from Europe, Asia, and Peru's neighbouring countries. In the 1880's, from the initial years of the rubber boom, Iquitos became the administrative, financial and commercial centre of business and the seat of the most important firms directly connected with foreign banks and holdings.

"The most diverse European products inundated the region. They were introduced through the wharf built in 1864, which became the shipping port of rubber exports and the port of arrival of these imports. English ships crossed the Atlantic and sailed up the Amazon to Iquitos, creating an active traffic between England and the jungle. Witnesses of the time tell that 'boxes of sterling pounds could be seen lying on the boardwalk' and that 'this was the currency regularly used.'

"The rubber boom left a lasting mark on the Peruvian jungle. It gave way to a traumatic migration of the native population and the immigration of people from elsewhere in the country and all over the world. This had an ineffaceable impact on the urban profile of Iquitos and the racial, cultural and social map of the whole region.

"***The History of Fitzcarrald.*** Isaias Fermin Fitzcarrald was the oldest of the seven children of an American navy man who had established himself in the mining district of San Luis de Huari in the central Andes of Perú (in Ancash). He was born in 1862 and studied first in Huaraz, near his birth place, and later in Lima. He lived a tempestuous youth during the years of the war with Chile and the Chilean occupation of Lima. Of him it is said that after finishing school he was seriously injured in a gambling quarrel in which he almost died, that he had been looked for as a Chilean spy and that he changed his named to Carlos Fernando.

“Actually, in his young years he went into the jungle trying to run away from Lima, the war or maybe his own demons, which judging from his agitated, adventurous and short life had apparently never stopped troubling him. He started working in the jungle by joining forces in the Higher Ucayali with a veteran Brazilian rubber tapper. In 1883 he sold his first ‘good remittance of rubber’ in Masisea, near the place where the Pachitea drains its waters into the Ucayali. The map exhibited on one of the walls of the present day Fitzcarraldo Restaurant Bar marks the most significant dates of Fitzcarrald’s adventures, outrages and feats since that year up to the year of his tragic death when barely 35 (sic).

“It is really amazing what this man achieved during his short time in the jungle. At 26 he was known as the richest rubber man in the Ucayali and at 31 he was recognised as the discoverer of the isthmus that today carries his name. According to the historian Jorge Basadre, this was in Perú ‘the most important geographic discovery of the nineteenth century.’ During his life in the jungle until his death at 35, he revealed himself as a tenacious man, a brave colonizer and an exceptional leader and organiser. He mobilised more that 300 people of different races and temperaments from the central jungle and the northern coast of Perú, to put them to work with the Campas (Ashaninkas) of the Higher Ucayali-Urubamba and the Piros of the Mishagua-Madre de Dios, forming an army of thousands of men that thanks to Fitzcarrald’s attributes and no doubt with the help of some Winchesters, he had managed to ensure their blind obedience, as otherwise it is difficult to understand how the natives could have followed him in rubber tapping expeditions of so many years. With these contingents he established a series of stations along the banks of the rivers at distances of 20 to 30 miles. This scheme allowed him to count with intermediate points of support for the long and strenuous navigation throughout such a vast region.

“Coronel La Combe, head of an expedition to the eastern region of the country wrote in 1901, referring to such achievements: ‘only a giant of the stature of Fitzcarrald could have accomplished such a task in so short a time.’ For others, however, Fitzcarrald was nothing but another predator of the Amazon jungle, a vulgar adventurer, a simple pawn of English colonialism [!], who with his unscrupulous greediness destroyed the native cultures and displaced the indigenous tribes from their territories. This controversy has been open since his tragic death when only 35 years old.

“***The ‘Fitzcarraldo’ Restaurant Bar’ – a place with a history.*** When opening the isthmus route, Fitzcarrald came into contact with the big Bolivian rubber tappers who operated in the Beni, Madre de Dios and Orton rivers. Amazed by this deed and the economic significance of the new route, they were eager to associate themselves with Fitzcarrald. As a result of the discovery, Antonio Vaca Diez 'an extremely wealthy rubber businessman of Riberalta, Bolivia, decided to travel to Europe to bring goods through the Atlantic and Amazon to the port of Iquitos and then carry his cargo to Bolivia through the route opened by Fitzcarrald. In April 1897 he arrived in Iquitos to establish a partnership with Fitzcarrald. On April 30 that year 'The Orton Bolivian Rubber Company for London and Iquitos Trade' incorporated to that effect, established its commercial place of business in the corner occupied today by the 'Fitzcarraldo Restaurant Bar'. On 9 July 1897, little more than two months later, Vaca Diez and Fitzcarrald were drowned in the Urubamba when the vessel which was carrying them to the isthmus was wrecked. Fitzcarrald was 35 years old."

[*Thus Fitzcarrald is presented as a legendary, charismatic and even almost mythical figure. Indeed, some of his undoubted success is attributed to the fact that he managed to deceive the Indians of the forest into believing that he was the re-incarnation of Juan Santos Atahualpa, the revolutionary who led the 1742 rising against Spanish domination (and was hung, drawn and quartered for his pains). Be that as it may, in the process of achieving his ends, analysts estimate that deputies acting on behalf of Fitzcarrald killed anything up to 10,000 people of the forest; the arrow was no match for the rifle*].

"Visiting El río Momón"

"The 0900 *bote con motor* sails from Morona Cocha dead on 0945 with 20-odd passengers onboard, returning to their villages along *El río Momón*. It is cool under the *irapay* roof, the sun obscured by the morning clouds. The July river is low, the waterfront wooden houses perched aloft on their precarious stilts, the floating houses marooned on their balsa rafts high and dry along the foreshore. Our *capitan, Señora Griselda,* navigates cautiously down the lagoon, with *Enrique* the mate standing on the bow indicating the route, not altogether successfully. We touch bottom, bump again and then run firmly aground. *Sra. Griselda* cuts the engine. The mate feels we should turn to starboard, the general consensus amongst the travellers is that our best course lies to port. In the event, the current swings us off the sand bar and we run on to join the breeze rippling the surface of the river Nanay. "When the river level falls like this, where does the water go?" muses one traveller.

We pass our old friend, the happy village of Manacamiri, and now that we are in deeper water the mate abandons the bow in favour of a vast platter of rice and rolls. He glances round happily at the envious onlookers before starting his late breakfast. "More food than work," declares one passenger and everyone laughs. The mate, his mouth full, doesn't trouble to reply as we pass Padre Cocha on our left and the beginnings of Bellavista Nanay appear downriver to the right. But before reaching there we turn sharp left into the high banks and black waters of the mysterious river Momón.

We discuss the construction of our *bote motor,* 10 metres long, 25hp, 30 pax max (but more on occasions). Four thousand *Nuevos Soles* to build the boat in Morona Cocha, six thousand *Soles* to mechanise the craft; life on the river perhaps 10 years. "What type of wood is this?" we ask. There is a lull in the conversation. "Good wood," we are told. Everybody nods. Good wood.

We glide past a huge tree, hung with the nests of the black and yellow *paucar* birds, followed by the sites of the local Bora and Yagua communities, much commercialised. On we go, twisting and turning our way up the river at a peaceful 8 knots. Now the trees are taller and overhang the water; the village of San Andrés comes and goes, whilst at the *Caserio del Porvenir* sacks of charcoal are stacked waiting for the return boat to Iquitos and subsequent sale in the market of Belén. More settlements, more *quebradas,* minor streams and brooks running into the main river.

"The end of *El río Momón* is high in the mountains, but *El Río Nanay* has no end," explains Enrique. "*El río Momón* is passable only by canoe from some time in July until November," he continues. Indeed, the sand banks are already emerging at intervals along the shoreline. From time to time fish jump ahead of the boat and under the trees an occasional canoe is tethered. Here on board, all is tranquil. A radio plays quietly and there is a low hum of conversation. There is the flash of a vivid aquamarine kingfisher and an equally vivid blue butterfly hovers past, followed by green, black and red cousins. Iquitos has been left far behind, the forest is closing in on us. More birds, sand martins from the river banks, yet more butterflies, yellow and celeste; now the river is barely 20 metres wide as we glide quietly through the water, the splash of the wave under our bow in harmony with the symphony of the forest. Enrique converses with a passing canoeist, paddling hard. "This man left at dawn," he explains. "He will reach Iquitos by nightfall. He is carrying *animales silvestres,* we call them *sajinos,* for roasting. They are like small pigs."

After 20 miles or so and three hours we nose into the river bank and drop our first passengers. The shore is still sandy, good for swimming but there is no time. The departing passengers disappear into the undergrowth and we press on, a united band of river travellers. The owner of the radio adjusts the volume a fraction higher to fill the space left by the leavers and everyone settles again. A flock of large fan-tailed birds agitate in the trees, black and glistening. *Vacamuchacho* the locals call them, birds of superstition and ill-fortune. The river continues to shrink, now it is scarcely 15 metres wide and we proceed with caution. Around one o'clock we meet two Iquitos bound *botes,* heavily laden and making best speed. With a desultory wave as they pass we are committed, no chance of returning home today and we are beyond the last *albergue*. The high cloud of the morning has given way to bright sun and cumulus but on the river in the shade of our frond roof it is still cool. A few dragonflies keep us company but otherwise we are insect free today.

Another family disembarks, a confusion of bags and babies. "How far to your house?" we ask as a *Tuqui Tuqui* bird looks on, a *pescador,* a fishing bird like a short-legged Heron. "Oh, just an hour or so," reply the family, shouldering the bags and babies. *Pueblito Grau Pampa Hermosa Pop.80* says the sign, and the mate pushes us clear of the bank and on we go up river, ever narrower. "Maybe two weeks more and we will finish," says Enrique. "Then it is difficult for the river people without the river. They cannot move their products." Indeed, the trees are almost touching now across the water, shutting out the sky except for a thin ribbon of blue. All is quiet in the launch, the radio is off and everyone is contemplating the silence of the forest in the heat of the day, broken only by the purr of our outboard motor. The air is still except for the slight breeze of our passage rustling though the fronds of the roof, *la sinfonía de la Irapay*. The trees tower over us, more canoes drawn up on the sands, children swimming; the air is fresh, softly scented. The engine cuts and we glide to the shore, hearing the parrots in the distance. Rolls of bread are delivered in a plastic bag and off we go again.

Enrique is back on the bow now, *Sra. Griselda* controlling our advance with care. Our progress becomes ever more uncertain. Then we come to a fallen tree blocking three quarters of what remains of the shrunken river. *Sra. Griselda* steers for the gap but is defeated by the current and we become wedged in the branches. It takes ten minutes of discussion and pushing and rocking to free us. Time enough to admire a large clump of Heliconias on the river bank and to ponder how things will be for our return journey on the morrow. The general philosophy seems to be to leave tomorrow's problems for tomorrow. For our next stop, no chances are taken. *Enrique* hurls two plastic bags ashore before we touch bottom and we are already going astern as two small children emerge from the forest to collect their prize. "A pity about the eggs," says one of the passengers, and just for a moment *Enrique* is disconcerted.

Another halt, seven hours into our journey and only six passengers left, the sun slanting in sideways under the roof. We pass stationary rafts comprised of giant baulks of timber: economic pressures competing with preservation. Their passage downstream will have to await the November rise in the water level, as now we are passing between high river banks as though entering a canyon. A chameleon scuttles across the mud; maybe an alligator next, for we are deep into the forest and we have seen scarcely half a dozen people on shore in the last two hours or so. We follow the serpentine curves of the river ever onwards, until on rounding one tortuous bend we encounter a large launch broadside on across the river, impaled on a sunken tree, wrecked and abandoned. *Enrique* precipitately announces that we are at our journey's end but fortunately he is wrong and there is just sufficient room for us to squeeze past to arrive at our true journey's end half an hour later, *Pueblito* Sargento Lores, Pop.350. "How many miles have we travelled?" Pause. "Kilometres?" Nobody is sure. "Quite a few." Yes, quite a few. Maybe 50, possibly.

Darkness comes quickly. There is no accommodation for us in the village so we sling our hammocks under the canopy of the boat to pass the night. Looking out across the blackness of the river and the forest it seems that the village of Sargento Lores must have more stars overhead than any other place on earth. The night is restful, as it should be, if unexpectedly cold. We rise at dawn, awakened by some mindless gunman blasting *Pihuichos* – sparrow-sized green parrots – out of the *Amasiza del Río* trees bordering the village. The birds are breakfasting on the colourful *gallito* coxcomb flowers that adorn the branches, and in turn find that they themselves are being favoured for soup by *los indígenos.* The hunter proudly displays a bird in his hand as we pass, the breast blown away to reveal the heart pumping frantically. "*Sopa,*" explains the assassin. Parrot soup.

By 0700 the outboard is propelling us homeward. The water level has dropped dramatically and the villagers are anxious to use what could be their last opportunity to transport goods to Iquitos. We load *Irapay* roofing, bananas and yet more bananas, yucca, cocona and much more, plus three dozen passengers. The *bote* is not only lower in the water, the roof panels stacked on our canopy have reduced our stability. At last we can load no more and down river we go. That's until we arrive at the fallen tree of yesterday.

The trunk is now high and dry across our track. The outboard is put hard astern but this time its puny efforts are no match for the current. We are swung round and swept down on to the obstacle. For one brief moment, just before the impact, there is complete stillness on board. Fearful silence. Then we crunch on to the fallen tree and lurch violently, first towards, then heeling back the other way towards the water. Above the sound of the cracking branches and the breaking of our canopy comes the screaming and shouting of the passengers. Some of these river folk carry scars and memories of previous capsizes, and of loss of life. Then there is a repeat of that eerie silence. The cockerel tethered on the far side of the boat flaps its wings nervously as the boat steadies, and a beautiful blue 'Morpho' butterfly passes, unheeding and untroubled. The confusion subsides and amid much conflicting advice we eventually extricate ourselves from the unwelcome barrier and back off upstream. Three heroes come to the fore and swim to the fallen tree with machetes. Nonetheless, things don't look too hopeful, and our thoughts turn to the traveller of yesterday canoeing to Iquitos in his dugout.

However, an hour later the three labouring stalwarts have achieved the impossible, and the boat is being manhandled through a narrow gap. Miracle of miracles, we are clear. Just one further brush with an underwater obstacle that nearly succeeds in capsizing our confused craft and then we are in the lower reaches of *El río Momón* and all is well. Everyone relaxes and we listen drowsily to the music of the water on the hull and re-enjoy the vistas of the river and the huge trees of the forest. Moronacocha is reached uneventfully just before sunset. We thank *Señora Griselda* and we pay our fare to *Enrique*: 10 *Nuevos Soles,* there and back, *ida y vuelta*.

The Annual Great River Amazon International Raft Race

This competition, brainchild of founder and organiser **Mike Collis**, was inaugurated on 29th July 1999 with 42 teams of four representing three countries: Peru, Colombia and Great Britain. The winning raft with a crew of Bora Indians completed the 20km course from Santa Clara to Bella Vista Nanay in 3hrs 20mins.

The year 2000 Second Amazon Raft Race comprised 64 teams from Perú,

USA, Australia, Norway, Italy, Israel, Russia, Uruguay, Argentina, Great Britain, France, Germany and Canada. The winning team were the reigning 1999 champions, the four Boras completing the course in a record 3hrs and 6mins. The winning Ladies team, *Las Virgenes* representing the village of Santa Clara with a declared average age of 54, finished in an astonishing time of 3hrs 20minutes, thus straining the bounds of credibility even further. The first foreign crew home were from Uruguay in 4hrs 12mins.

Since those early beginnings, the event has gone from strength to strength, and the Annual Great River Amazon Raft Race Adventure (GRARR) now runs over three days in stages from Nauta (Pescadoras Island, Nueva Esperanza) on the Marañón river, down into the Amazon, via Porvenir and Tamshiyacu to finish at the *Caza y Pesca* Club, Bellavista Nanay, Iquitos, a distance of approximately 112 miles (180 kms), making it 'the longest raft race in the world on the largest river in the world', as acknowledged in the Guinness Book of World Records in September 2013. For further details on this unique competition, and the results and pictures of previous years, visit www.iquitostimes.com.

The Amazon Golf Club

Another **Mike Collis** inspiration, conceived on 24th January 2004 in the fertile bar of The Yellow Rose of Texas. The 10 hectare, 2,340 yard, nine hole course is just off the Iquitos-Nauta Highway, 10 minutes beyond the airport (proceed 5.5kms to Quistococha Village, then turn off the tarmac road right towards Zungarococha for 500 metres). The course (funded by some 60 founder members from 14 different countries worldwide) is now well established, having opened officially on 1st May 2008, four years since inception. The tree plantings are maturing, a fine Club House has been built, and a tennis court and swimming pool are in the offing (or rather, on the drawing board ...). It is reputedly 'the only golf course in the Peruvian Amazon and one of the most remote golfing destinations on offer; it is a difficult 9-hole par 5 course landscaped on 24 acres with hazards that include caiman sunning in the sand traps, piranha lurking in the waterholes and red-tailed boas constricting in the rough' – see www.amazongolfcourse.com for further details of this unique facility.

Stop Press

The story of how Adolf Hitler escaped from the ruins of his bunker in Berlin in 1945, eluding the advancing Allies to cross the Atlantic by U-Boat (long range type XXI) to the mouth of the Amazon and live for more than 20 years in the rain forest (being buried near Iquitos in 1969), will be published separately in "Herr Hitler Lies ©John Lane" as soon as ongoing research is completed. The submarine used in the escape was subsequently run ashore not far from Manaus and was broken up and the parts sold and dispersed in the ensuing years, whilst the second-in-command of the boat (Mannfred Nietsky) took up residence in the city, also having married locally, subsequently dying in Brasilia in 2007 at the age of 83 years.

Typical Boa habitat – Pacaya-Samiria National Reserve

Not perfect, but a rare photo of the Peruvian Corsair fighter squadron engaged in the 1933 war against Colombia, commanded by Colonel Francisco Secada Vignetta

Petroperú Refinery, opened in 1982 with a capacity of 10,500 barrels per day

Section VIII
Putting it Together

"No horizon is so far that you cannot get above it or beyond it ..."

How to Arrive

If you are reading this, the chances are that you have already found your way to Iquitos ('the largest city in the world that cannot be reached by road'), probably by flying north from Lima, possibly having arrived in the Peruvian capital by KLM, Air France or Iberia direct from Amsterdam, Paris or Madrid, or by Avianca via Bogotá. One thing is certain: you didn't arrive in Iquitos by bus or car. Alternative routes lie through North America (e.g by Air Canada via Toronto, or US airlines via Houston, Newark, Atlanta or Miami). Travelling via Mexico City is another colourful option, or you might even have considered taking in La Paz or Santiago en route. From Australia the LAN/Quantas A380 runs from Sydney to Santiago, usually via New Zealand.

Less likely, perhaps you came up the river in leisurely style from Brazil, having journeyed the whole way on the Amazon, starting at Belém on the Brazilian eastern Atlantic seaboard. A swifter option is to fly from Europe to São Paulo (stay at *Pousada Dona Zilah*, Alameda Franca 1621, tel: 0055-3062-1444), and to take an internal flight to Manaus (try *Hotel Manaus*, opposite the historic *Teatro Amazonas*, splendorous relic of the rubber boom). Thence an economic six or seven-day river ferry (for instance, a comfortable double cabin in MV *Monteiro* for under £300 all-found, or a hammock for considerably less, bookable on the Manaus waterfront) through to Tabatinga (sample the *Hotel Takana*, Room 219, www.portaltabatinga.com.br), adjacent to the Brazilian/Colombian/Peruvian 'triple frontier' and to the towns of Leticia and Santa Rosa.

To reach Iquitos from here (but first allow time for a visit to *El Museo Alfonso Galindo* to see the collection of artefacts of the Mayoruna and Ticuna tribes) you may opt to take another river ferry from Santa Rosa (3 days and 2 nights), choosing from *Gran l'Oretana* or *Gran Diego* sailing on Fridays, or *Manoel* departing on Saturday evenings. Quicker (but noisier and devoid of charm) is the 12-hour endurance-test transit by 70kph *dezlizador* Volvo Penta-powered jet-foil in return for USD$60.00, leaving Santa Rosa (where the Peruvian Immigration Office is situated) at 0500 (try Cynthia at *Hospedaje*

Las Hamacas – mosquito net, fan, shower, battery-lights after 2130, all for $10.00, or *Hostal Diana*), and arriving Iquitos mid-afternoon, deafened and vibrating (*Expreso Golfinho* on Wed/Fri/Sun – Iquitos office at Raymondi 378, tel.225118 – or *Trans Turismo Amazonas Express[Transtur]* on Tues/Thurs/Sat)[44]. The option of flying exists sporadically, depending on prevailing airline economics. How ever you decide to depart, remember to get your passport stamped at the office of the Brazilian *Policia Federal* in Tabatinga before leaving (the formality takes about two and a half minutes).

Yet another scenic and adventurous route to Iquitos is down the river Ucayali from Pucallpa (reached in 1hr 15mins by air or 16 to 24 discombobulating hours by bus from Lima)(Hotel *Sol del Oriente* is the place to stay, hsoloriente@qnet.com.pe and www.soldelorientehoteles.com; restaurant *El Encanto de la Selva*, Av. Inmaculada 191, is the place for your fish supper), a 3-day trip on one of the *Henry* boats (supposedly sailing on Saturdays; bookings are made directly on board, don't trouble to search for shore offices or internet reservations). The permutations are many and varied, and even include a diversion for a few days of Pacific Ocean beach time and sunshine at Mancora (e.g. Mancora Beach Bungalows – see Web, and reserve through: reservas@mancora-beach.com), reached by air to Piura (Hotel *Los Portales* – tel: 073-321161) followed by 3-hours on the bus (or even a taxi for S/.180). Once the tanning is up to scratch, re-trace your steps by bus through Piura (S/.12.00) directly onwards to Chiclayo (S/.15.00)(6-hours total journey time)(try Hotel *Casa de la Luna* – www.hotelcasadelaluna.com.pe; there are many others, obviously). Once there, allow time to see the picturesque *tortora* reed-rafts at Pimentel – *los caballitos del mar* (also the location of the former home – now a museum – of air force hero Abelardo Quiñones) and be sure to visit the outstanding Museum of the 'Royal Tombs of Sipán' at Lambayeque (just 12km distant), a World Heritage site.

All that done, take a deep breath and cross the Andes by bus (S/.60.00) through Chachapoyas and Moyobamba and on to Tarapoto (Hotel *Río Shilcayo*, tel: 042-524236, hotel@rioshilcayo.com, or *Puerto Palmeras*, reservas@puertopalmeras.com.pe). The advertised journey duration is 14-hours, but in the event it may extend to 20-hours, depending. After recovering

---

[44] A quarter of the way along this route, and halfway between Caballococha and Pevas, lies the generally unremarkable village of San Pablo, but noted for its leper colony and where *ancianos* amongst the inhabitants can apparently still recall Ché Guevara passing by...

in *la selva alta*, you may decide to fly to Iquitos by Star Perú, or to take the 3-hour bus ride on the 'new' road to Yurimaguas (Inn *Puerto Pericos*), voyaging from there first on the river Huallaga and then the Marañon to the confluence with the Ucayali upstream of Nauta, and thence to Iquitos.

Should none of that appeal, you could always fly into Quito (Ecuador), and after a few days luxury at one of the well-advertised *haciendas* find your way to Nuevo Rocafuerte[45] by bus and boat, and after obtaining your Ecuadorean exit stamp from the immigration officials in the police station, move onwards by the river to Cabo Pantoja on the other side of the frontier with Perú. Then, re-tracing the path of Francisco de Orellana (who beat you to it by nearly 500 years), you may take a series of *rapidos* or other more sedate river craft (e.g. the periodic *lancha* which takes four or five days) downstream along the Napo through Santa Clotilde (S/.75.00 to this point) to meet the Amazon just beyond the town of Orellana itself. Alternatively, you may hop off at Mazan and take a 20-minute *motocarro* across the isthmus to Indiana before boarding a final one-hour *rapido* to Iquitos, thereby saving at least the best part of one day's travelling – but missing the delights of historic Orellana (cf Section V).

If (after all that) you are still set on coming up from Lima, amidst the countless hotels from which to chose, the economic **Hotel Antigua** Miraflores at 350 Av.Grau is recommended, or for convenience use the excellent **Ramada Costa del Sol** at the airport. At this stage your thoughts may well have turned to Machu Picchu, but also keep in mind the possibility of other diverting side-visits to alternative destinations, such as Paracas, Arequipa and Ayacucho. In any event, before you leave the capital be sure to visit the *Parque de Las Leyendas* in San Miguel, and the *Museo del Banco Central de Reserva del Perú* (carry identification, such as a passport photocopy) in addition to all the other advertised attractions. These include the guard-changing ceremony in front of the Presidential Palace at 1100 on Sundays, Larco Mar with its vista of Horseshoe Bay and the coastline, *Museo* Pedro D.Osma in Barranco, the naval museum at Callao (www.museonaval.com.pe),

---

[45] In more detail: take a 10hr bus from Quito to Coca for $10; then Coca to Nuevo Rocafuerte on the daily 12hr river boat on the Napo for $12; get your Ecuador exit stamp from the police station/immigration office. Take the 2hr boat ride to Pantoja, Peru, variously quoted at $10 to $50, and pass through the military checkpoint. *Lanchas* run from here irregularly to Mazan and on Iquitos, taking 4 or 5 days, price $35; or there is the more expensive *rapido* option; Pantoja itself is a no-frills location.

the fascinating Royal Felipe Fortress also in the port of Callao, and so on – plus cutting through from Ovalo Miraflores to seek treasure in the antique and silver shops of Av. La Paz, stopping off at Restaurant *Rimcon Chami* en route. For those with an eye for curiosities, visit *Puente Piedra* across the River Rimac on the main highway out of Lima to the north, which is also known as the 'Bridge of Eggs' because when it was built in 1608 the masonry was mixed using the whites of 10,000 sea bird eggs, resulting in a highly binding recipe. In January 2012 the first line of the new (and very long awaited) cross-city mass transit urban rail network was opened in Lima (the financial irregularities which caused years of delay having been set aside); on account of the elevation of the track at roof top level, this provides an excellent panoramic overview of the metropolis.

For the flight itself, take a window seat on the right hand side of the aircraft for the 1hr 30min journey to obtain a good view of the snow-capped Andes on the way. Conversely, for your return flight you need to be seated on the left. Once upon a time, Iquitos was an international airport (*Aeropuerto Coronel Francisco Secada Vignetta* - see below) conveniently accepting flights direct from other countries. After a lengthy interregnum, this is once again the case [46], with the possibility of additional airlines/destinations in the pipeline. However, and for the time being, in-bound air services to Iquitos generally originate in Lima, and are operated by the competing domestic airlines of the day (e.g LAN Peru, TANS, Star Perú, Peruvian Airlines, etc – some more transient than others).

If making your own travel arrangements, in olden times it used to be difficult to pre-book Peruvian internal flights from abroad; however, ever more widespread use of the internet has changed all that. Nevertheless, direct on arrival contact with the airline offices in Lima and Iquitos, or with one of the many Iquitos based travel agents (such as *Hurvi Tours,* Jr. Arica 618 telephone (51)-(0)65-243.248 or *Domiruth Travel Service,* just off Plaza de Armas at new premises in *Fitzcarrald* 144 telephone (51)-65-243403, e-mail: iquitos2@domiruth.com) can on occasions be useful, and will generally reduce the cost.

---

[46] The door is once again ajar: on 14 July 2012 international flights to Iquitos resumed, with **Copa Airlines** providing a direct service twice-weekly from its hub in Panama City for around $500 (return) for the 2½hr journey. The Copa office in Iquitos is at Sgto Lores #379 (tel.235395). Next please ...

[The first trial flight from Lima to Iquitos took place on 16th July 1921. The aviation pioneer Elmer Faucett arrived here in 1922, albeit by raft carrying his damaged aeroplane. Those early days were fraught with danger for the pilots: Angel Brusco, friend and flying colleague of previously mentioned José Abelardo Quiñones, died in an aircraft accident on the river Itaya, and Cornejo Portugal, another Peruvian pioneer of flight and chief of the Oriente 'airline' was killed in the same way on the river Ucayali. Hence the Iquitos streets bearing those names. The Armed Forces float plane base was created in 1926 and the first air mail arrived in Iquitos on 6th January 1928, the first passenger service starting just one day later.

The airport runway was un-surfaced until 1943; on 6th September of that year a US B-34 crashed off the runway into adjoining aguaje palms, killing six North American airmen and just 5 days later paving work was commenced. This upgrade was initiated and paid for by the USA, who at the time had an especial interest in the airstrip, serving as it did as an emergency diversion landing point for USAF planes tasked with WWII defence of the Panama Canal.

By 1961 the expanding city of Iquitos threatened to envelop the existing airport and operations were moved to the present less congested area to the south (although now, in its turn, this new site is progressively being swallowed up by un-checked development). The old runway, just behind the new municipal offices, is still used by light aircraft on occasions and by the Peruvian Air Force. Coronel Francisco Secada Vignetta, whose name is borne by the 'new' airport, was an outstanding pilot of the Peruvian front-line Corsair bi-plane squadron during the 1933 conflict with Colombia].

Hotels and Hospedajes

Comprehensive and in-date city accommodation listings used to be maintained in the Iquitos Tourist Office, together with current tariffs for each hotel – as well as the suggestions in all the standard guide books, and at Trip Adviser on-line. Iquitos offers almost as many accommodation options as it does choices of restaurants, and whether you opt for a nominal Five Stars at the highly convenient and comfortable *Hotel El Dorado Plaza* or stay in one of the smaller Iquitos guest houses, the common denominator will be the *Loretano* welcome. However, and as memorably observed in the New York Times not so long ago: 'unless you lost your wallet at the airport, there is no reason to test out the extremely low end of Iquitos lodgings'.

For one of the best vistas of the river Amazon, take a centre room on the fourth floor of the *Reál Hotel* (Malecón Tarapacá, previously *Hotel de Turistas Amazonas* – telephone: 231011) but know in advance that (pending long-awaited redevelopment) some (most, actually) of the hotel facilities are currently closed. To wake up to an even more stunning view overlooking Belén towards the river, take the corner room on the fourth floor of *Hostal Leydy* (Ucayali/Ramírez Hurtado) for a third of the price, although in a rather different ambience – overdue renovation also awaited (ring 223066 and ask for Sr. Rodolfo Mori Bardales). Yet another venue with exceptionally fine river views is the relatively newly re-opened *Hospedaje Shamana* (*Calle* Requena #176, *telf.*065.235293; shamana_iqt@hotmail.com) – go for rooms 105 or 205; refurbishment to an excellent standard was completed in mid-2011: highly recommended in the medium price range ($38-65) (see also www.cumaceba.com). *Hotel el Sol Naciente* (Próspero 1073; telephone 234035) has a *mirador* on the fifth floor that gives one of the most impressive 360 degree panoramic views of the city available, emphasising that Iquitos is but a small 'oasis' in a vast expanse of rain forest. There is a cool breeze at the viewing point and in the evening there is a bar, if required. Likewise, centrally situated *Hotel Doral* (doralinnhotel_iquitos@hotmail.com), at Raymondi 220-222, has a stunning seventh storey 360° *mirador* with a combined vista of the rivers and the city (the *comedor* on the fifth floor also gives a good view whilst catching the breeze perfectly). For handy location and friendliness, *Hotel Marañon* is hard to beat (Fitzcarrald/Nauta 285-289, tel: 242673, hotelmarañon@hotmail.com); a sister hotel, the shiny *Gran Marañon*, has now opened at *Calle* Loreto 446 also with a nice little pool, and rooms with a view on the 5th floor and a *mirador* on the roof, both served by one of the smoothest lifts in town. One of the very newest (2012/2013) well placed hotels in Iquitos is the elegantly presented *Samiria* Jungle at 159 Ricardo Palma (www.samiriajunglehotel.com), whose exterior belies the extent of the beautifully landscaped garden and pool within (don't tell anyone, but *habitacion* 509 is the one with the river view, daily rate around S/.240). Hotel *Victoria Regia* is well recommended, as is *La Rivera Hospedaje*, and finally, for something a little different, go to www.lacasafitzcarraldo.com …

[*Isolated though it is, be aware that Iquitos is not immune from the world-wide syndrome of disappearing bath and basin plugs. And also that other global curse: soap trays that slope the wrong way; to prevent your bar of soap sliding into the bath or shower every few seconds, try sticking a beer top into it.*]

Renting Accommodation

If you are planning to be based in Iquitos for a while, then renting a house or an apartment could well be a less expensive alternative to staying in a hotel. Details of some local letting agents (a relatively rare breed) can be found in the local press, or in the *Telefonica* Yellow Pages under *Corretajes de Propiedades.* Visits to Aura Guzmán at Mad Mick's Trading Post (163 Putumayo – cel.065-9754976) and to *Servicios de Corretaje* (Sra. Eva Antola Bollet) at Ricardo Palma 375 (23-4256/24-1775) are recommended, and a call to Bill Grimes (223730/9939190) in the Dawn on the Amazon office (www.dawnontheamazon.com).

Whilst short lets of under a month are harder to come by, anything over a month is feasible and is not only economic but also has the advantage of greater integration and contact with local life. Talking of which, you can possibly save yourself the odd outing to the market by keeping an ear tuned for the *ambulante* vendors passing your house. '*Hay paltas!*' will call the seller of avocados; *'Hay periodicos!'* calls the newspaper boy; *'Hay helados!'* sings the ice cream man; *'Hay escobas!'*: here are brushes; *'Hay aguajes!'* (see under 'Fruits'), and so forth.

What to Wear

Be cool and comfortable, use cotton rather than synthetics. Long sleeves and long trousers after sundown will help prevent the irritation of insect bites (and subsequent complications, e.g malaria, dengue). Bring your sun hat, obviously – you are only 4 degrees south of the Equator. Handy for muddy trails: an old pair of trainers, but if you suddenly decide that you can't visit the rain forest without a pair of long rubber boots, these can be conveniently hired from Mad Mick's Trading Post (163 Putumayo) – or bought from *Los Chinos* and others in Belén market. The most frequent local comment in respect of visitors to Iquitos is "why are so many tourists so badly dressed?" More directly, the observation goes along the lines of: "*Porque los extranjeros están presentandose en una manera tan sucia, con mal olor y sin peinandose? Fumando y tomando cerveza sin sus camisas en publico – es una falta de respecto.*" No translation needed; not much cause for rejoicing there.

Don't forget to pack .....

If you did forget to pack it, don't worry. The chances are that you will be able to buy one in Iquitos. Apart from remembering your camera and torch, a pair of binoculars and a compass are both worth considering. If you have space in your luggage, insect repellents and sun-protections will probably be cheaper if brought from home but are widely available locally. Hammocks can be bought inexpensively from in the Belen market, or even at the dockside before you embark on your chosen river boat.

River travel by 'lancha'

St Aubin's Bay, Jersey (Channel Isles) – where Próspero was built in 1863

The sugar cane mill at Requena – getting on for a century old

Section IX
A Pinch of Castellano

"Language – the essential key."

This Section does not to attempt to replicate the excellent information already contained in your Pocket Phrase Book. The aim is merely to provide a handy reference list and glossary for some of the words and expressions that may be encountered for the first time during a visit to Iquitos. For more detailed study, "*Vocabulario Regional del Oriente Peruano*" by Luis Castonguay may be bought from CETA (Putumayo 355).

Abas : 'the beans of the Incas' or 'broad beans.' Not grown in *la selva,* but on sale in the markets (also *habas*)

Acerradero : sawmill

Achira : the canna lily; little girls use the petals of the scarlet flowers to 'paint' their nails

Alambre de pua: barbed wire

Albergue : lodge

Ansuelo : fishing rod

Azado : grilled

Barbasco : sometimes described as a 'natural pesticide' because it is 'naturally derived' from a vine of the forest, but hardly 'green' in its effects, which are particularly indiscriminate when it is used illegally in the rivers to fish, killing via asphyxiation

Basura : rubbish

Batan : the wooden trough used for the preparation of *masato* (*aguardiente*), made primarily from pulverised *yuca*, some of which is masticated to promote the two-day fermentation process

Bejuco : creeper or vine (eg *Ayahuasca*), and consequently a nickname for a skinny person

Bijau : the large, dark green leaves in which *tamales/192amale tos/juanes* are wrapped, cooked, sold and served. Likewise fish and some other foods. Not only convenient, dishes cooked whilst tightly wrapped in a *bijau* leaf are protected, thus preserving the goodness and endowing additional flavour

Bola bola : jocularly applied to poorly expressed *Castellano* – also *mola mola* (cf *shegue*)

Bombeando : literally 'bombing' (the offence of fishing with explosives – the equivalent of going on safari with a heavy calibre machine gun)

Brea : black pitch used for caulking the planking of river craft

Bufeo Colorado : 'Pink' dolphin (with legendary powers of fertility – see Section VII)

Calamina : corrugated iron sheeting (CGI – corrugated galvanised iron)

Camote : root vegetable, orange coloured

Cancha : toasted maize

Candela : local word for 'the fire', namely, the concept …

Canela : cinnamon

Carnada : bait for fishing

Carretera : road

Casas de palos y paja o ojas : local houses in traditional styles (literally 'houses of sticks and straw or leaves')

Casas de material noble : cement and stone houses (i.e. as used by the 'nobles')

Cascabel : rattlesnake

Cascabeles : long strings of rattling shells, normally worn on the legs or ankles

Caserio : riverside settlement

Caucheros : the 'rubber barons' of the 19th Century

Caucho : rubber (latex – *jebe, balata, gutapercha*)

Cerdito : little pig

Chacra : small 'farm', smallholding

Chalupa : basic river 'work boat' in metal or fibre glass without even a shading roof

Chambira : palm fibre; used for bags and hammocks

Chamico : a mystical potion that retains the imbiber in the forest for ever

Chancletas : flip flops

Chapaja : a type of palm-thatch roofing, less regular in appearance than *irapay*; also called *shebon*

Charango : Andean musical stringed instrument, favoured by wandering minstrels

Charapas : the hand-sized 'turtles' that live beneath *las huamas* (see below), their favourite food

Charapitas : 'las chicas' of Loreto (*Loretanitas*) – a colloquial derivation from *charapas*

Chatarra : widely used Portuguese importation to indicate that something (usually mechanical) is broken, and is rubbish, of no further value

Chifa : Chinese restaurant

Chifle : fried banana chips, sold in packets everywhere. Handy for travelling.

Chingana : local patois term for a *bodega*, a handy little store for this and that

Chilcano : Culinary style of preparing fish (e.g. *Chilcano de Sabalo, Carachama, Gamitana*), using garlic, onions and coriander

Chonta : tender palm heart (much favoured vegetable of the *selva*); the actual wood of this palm is itself used for the tips of spears and arrows

Chosa/Chosita : humble dwelling or hut

Churo : Water snail, found in still backwaters (can be the size of a tennis ball, with a beautiful, delicately coloured whorled shell). A delicacy, but nowadays only to be found in remote villages – the bigger the snail, the more succulent it is

Cocamera : communal 'round house' of the forest (cf '*maloca*')

Cocha : river tributary, lagoon or ox-bow lake

Colmena : bee-hive

Costa : the coast

Coto : Howler monkey

Cuadra (Cdra) : (street) block

Cucarachas : cockroaches ('Bombay Runner' size)

Cucarda : Hibiscus (hence: *cucardita*)

Curaca : Chief of the tribe (with many wives)

Curandero : the forest 'medicine man' or *Shaman*

Curaré : the poison used for the tips of darts, extracted from frogs

Curuhuinsi : the 'leaf-carrying' ants (they will strip your new hibiscus bare overnight). The column of green particles moving along like little sails can stretch for 100m and more. Amazingly, entire books are devoted to the life style of these highly organised insects, and to the many attendant forest myths involving them

Deslizador : A slender aluminium boat for rapid river travel

Difuntos : The cries, moans and wails of departed souls that may be heard at dead of night in the darkest depths of the forest

Empanada : 'stuffed', in a culinary sense (e.g. *empanada de yuca*)

Estiaje : the time when the rivers are low

Estribor : wheelhouse

Fógata : an open fire

Friaje : a wave of cold air (from the south) resulting from a polar depression

Fundo : a large estate

Ganaderia : a farm dedicated to oxen and cattle

Glorieta : a summer house, strictly speaking, but in the context used, a bandstand

Grama : a form of riverside 'grass or reed', which when dried and coloured is used to make flowers for *El Día de la Madre*

Grifo : filling station

Gringo : me – and quite possibly, you

Habas : Broads beans, as in ***abas***, sun-dried and fried lightly (thus retaining the abundant vitamins and proteins) on sale in little packets on every corner

Hospedaje : lodging house, hostel

Huamas : the blue/lilac water hyacinth, especially prevalent when the river is high

Huanchaka : Parrot-sized bird of the forest, red breast and forehead, black body, white stripes

Huatchiman : commonly used *Spanglish* term for (night) watchman

Irapay : traditional palm-frond roofing for dwellings

Isangos : grass mites, with a predilection for the tender parts; they needed to be tracked down and dealt with individually

Jerga : local slang (generally vulgar)

Jergón : the Fer-de-Lance snake, relatively small but the bite can be fatal

Jugo : liquidised blended fruit drink

Lagarto : alligator

Llevo-llevo : a generally extinct species of informal hop-on, pack-in, hop-off transportation that preceded the advent of regular buses and the abundance of motor-taxis

Lluvia warme : prolonged rain (*warme* = Quechwa for 'woman'; the link is oblique)

Makisapa : spider monkey (hence applied to a 'long-armed person')

Malecón : embankment or 'seafront' – promenade

Maloca : traditional native 'round house' of the forest for communal use

Manguare : cylindrical wooden 'drum' used for sending messages in the forest

Maracuya : Passion fruit

Masho : local name for bats (normally *murciélago*); the diminutive sack-winged bats of the forest are to be found hanging in line on the underside of boughs

Maso : name for a domestic 'pulverising' implement used in conjunction with the ***pilon*** (below)

Matriz : 'Mother church'

Mijano : shoal of fish

Minga : any community activity where the villagers unite to clear, repair, clean, construct etc

Monte : the whole concept of *la selva* – the 'woodland' (e.g. *carne del monte*)

Mosquitero : mosquito net

Motelo : tortoise

Motocarro : (noisey) 3-wheeled 'motor-bike taxi.'

Musmuki : Owl monkey

(New Year's Day : folklore has it that rain on New Year's Day will be followed by 15 days rain)

Pakucho : jocular appellation for an indigenous native (*pakucha* – female) who happens to look like a *gringo/gringa.* Also *pacucho/pacucha.*

Pamacari : the slender, ubiquitous river boats of varying lengths, conspicuous by their vee-shaped roofs of *irapay* palm-fronds

Papagayo/a : parrot (male/female)

Peque peque : outboard motor, normally using a long shaft trailing astern; onomatopoeic, also *pecka pecka*

Pichona : young bird (also *pichon*), and accordingly a term of flattery or endearment

Pihuichos : little green birds kept as family pets, their singing gives advance notice of coming rain. Forest people know from the language of the songbirds in general when rain may be expected.

Píjuayo : a tall, slender and graceful palm-like tree with clusters of little green fruits which turn yellow and red when ripe, and are used in ices, chupetes and drinks (harvesting is impeded by the thorns on the trunk, making it impossible to climb)

Pilon : the upright wooden 'bowl' wherein the newly harvested rice is pounded to remove the husk (using the ***maso***)

Pinsha : Toucan (who makes himself heard just before dawn, anxiously calling for the light). Also the jocular name for anyone with a long nose …

Pueblo : town

Pueblito : small town or village

Quipu de Algodon : an Inca calculator comprising a bundle of knotted strings of varying lengths that thus far has defied modern interpretation

Refresco : fruit drink based on water and natural fruit juice

Remolino : whirlpool – frequently encountered on the rivers

Remomocho : a broken or incomplete paddle

Ribera(s) : the river bank(s)

Ribereños : those who live along the river banks

Ronsoco : Capybara – shy, gentle rodent related to the guinea pig, expert swimmer and diver; can grow up to 4 feet in length, families can be found at the riverside

Sable : machete

Sábila : Aloe vera, originally from North Africa

Sajíno : a 'furry pig' (wild hog), from *la selva alta;* also *pecari* (peccary)

Salpicon : literally 'mixed' (much encountered on menus, e.g. salads)

Sapa : 'big' in Quechwa, leading to endless applications and permutations (e.g. *sikisapa* – big bottom; *singasapa* – big nose; *rinrisapa* – big ears; *umasapa* – big head; *buchisapa* – big stomach;

Selva : the forest

Selva alta : literally the 'high forest', i.e. the area around Tarapota

Serenazgo : the municipal security service

Shaman : *el curandero* or forest 'medicine man', widely believed to be endowed with extra-sensory powers, amongst which are the ability to bestow protective auras and the solving of disappearances, robberies and murders

Shambo : a term applied to *aguajes* of the ultimate quality, optimally ready to eat – thereby on occasions a word applied to other enviable objects

Shegue : exactly that – shakey, dubious, of doubtful worth

Shihuanga : local name for the yellow-headed *caracara* bird

Shushupe : Bushmaster snake, much feared for its aggressive and repeated strikes

Sierra : the mountain region

Tamales : ground sweet corn, peanuts, meat and olives cooked in *bijau* leaves

Tambo : simple dwelling (or ***chosita***), often associated with a ***chacra***

Tahuampas : creeks and backwaters, ideal for fishing – the areas that flood when the river is high (marsh and swamp land)

Tibe mama : Osprey

Timbuche : cf *Chilcano* above – indigenous term for this method of presentation, which results in a concentrated fish soup/broth

Tizón : a glowing ember borrowed from your neighbour's fire, with which to re-ignite your own

Tortuga : turtle

Tuchpa : the cooking area – the fire and stove (i.e. the hearth) (sometimes *tushpa*)

Umisha : (pronounced *Umbisha* in some locales) the specially selected stately palm which is ceremoniously carried to each village/township and erected with much festivity, around which the culminating dance of Carnival (i.e. before the start of Lent) is conducted and gifts for the children are suspended from the plaited fronds for distribution when the tree is finally felled with axes (it is the self-same *umisha* palm that provides the edible *chonta* 'salad' and which is in consequence in danger of extinction)

Uraño : a 'mystical' person, living apart in their own world

Ventaron : a gust of strong wind that on occasions disturbs the calm of the forest

Victoria Regia : the giant water lily named in honour of Queen Victoria; the white flowers finish the day flushed pink and perfumed – the sole beetle-pollinator is attracted by the scent in the afternoon, the flower closes, trapping the beetle for 24 hours and immersing it in pollen; the flower dies, the beetle flies, job done (VR may also be seen at Kew Gardens and at Ventnor, Isle of Wight!)

Yagé : the name for Ayahuasca in Colombia

Yapa/Yapita : Loretana word to plead a little 'top-up' for your *jugo*

Yuca : Root vegetable, also known as cassava and manioc in other parts of the world. Grown extensively, identifiable by the dark green, feathery, waist-high foliage. When heated/cooked and ground, the resultant farinaceous mealy-powder becomes tapioca/sago.

Yute : 'jungle rope' – jute, formerly exported

Tranquilidad de la Selva

'Tarrafiando' – casting the circular net upon the river, difficult enough in itself, quite aside from executing the skill from an unstable canoe.

Faces of the Forest

Section X
Conclusión

"La fiesta acabó. La luz se apagó. Y ahora, José?"

Conservation: Save the Rainforest

The eco-system of Amazonia is not only of great fragility but also of great complexity. The bio-diversity of plants and animals in the tropical rain forests is vastly greater than in any other habitat of planet earth (for example, one hectare of *selva* contains more species of trees than all of Europe). At the current rate of destruction (in common with other countries in the region – and dare we say it, Brazil in particular – Peru has yet to be blessed with an Administration with the vision to see beyond the short-term financial returns accruing from the forest) it is estimated that the rain forests could be gone by the end of this century – or even sooner – not only with the consequent loss of countless species of wild life but also with catastrophic effect on global climatic patterns. For example, the Amazon rain forest (the 'lung of the world' – an area around three million square miles, about the size of the whole continent of Europe) is variously estimated to produce between 20% and 50% of the globe's oxygen supply. Hence, when we have finished cutting it down, the corollary will become obvious to all of planet Earth's nine billion inhabitants.

More pressingly and immediately, if the present oblation rate of the glaciers of the Peruvian Andes as a result of global warming continues unabated, it could lead to their disappearance within the next twenty years. The annual rhythm of the rivers, the cyclical rise and fall, so vital to the preservation of the humidity of the forest, not to mention the feeding pattern of the fructiferous fish, will then be irrevocably disturbed, along with the rainfall sequence, leading to a doomsday spiral of drought, forest fires and devastation. Indeed, the cycle has already started, as evidenced by the recent unprecedented high levels of annual flooding, occasioned not so much by distorted rainfall patterns but by the globally warmed and accelerated melt-rates of the ice fields in the mountains far to the south.

Our aim should not be the domination of these regions but the development of a greater understanding of their unique characteristics, so that we may learn how to maintain and how to live in harmony with these miracles of nature, in the same way that the native population of the forests have done for countless centuries, with the philosophy that "in the rain forest, no one dominates". As the poet César Calvo wrote: "When the last tree has been cut down, when the last river has been contaminated, when the last fish has been caught, only then will mankind learn that it cannot eat money."

Controlled eco-tourism to the rain forests can lead to a greater world-wide awareness of the immense importance of these regions and to an increasingly well-informed lobby for their preservation. Revenue from tourism assists local economies, leads to a diversification of activities and can be channelled towards the protection of the forests.

"Kill nothing but time
Shoot nothing but film
Leave nothing but footprints
Take nothing but fond memories"

(Author undetermined ...)

In June 2007 the findings of an expedition of Brazilian scientists extended the Amazon's length by 176 miles (284 kms), thus making it 65 miles (105 kms) longer than the Nile. The rivalry between the two rivers continues: Amazon now 4,225 miles (6,800 kms); Nile 4,160 miles (6,695 kms). The difficulty and controversy stems from determining the precise beginning and end of the rivers. For example, a multinational expedition in 1996 placed the origin of the Amazon River as the Apacheta stream in the Quehuisha mountains (Dept. of Arequipa), this finding being endorsed by the Geographic Society of Lima (sic), and thereby extending the length of the Amazon to 4,388 miles...

"Destroying rainforest for economic gain is like burning a Renaissance painting to cook a meal"

Professor Edward Wilson, Harvard Biologist (October 2007)

"Be sure to take the road less travelled."

Derived from Robert Frost's poem (1920)

In conclusion, and once again: welcome to the Amazon rain forest, where the rivers run through people's lives and where time stands still.

The First Edition (2001, price S/.25.00) of this alternative travel guide totalled just 82 pages; the Second Edition (2006, still priced S/.25.00) contained 126 pages). The Third Edition (2010, price S/.40.00 - $15 - £10) somehow grew to 187 pages, with overall sales to visitors to Iquitos running into thousands. As further historical, cultural and social, and natural history information became available, it was captured for posterity and included in the amplified Fourth Edition (July 2012), using a slightly smaller paper-saving font. Equally, changes occasioned by developments, new services or closures were reflected as far as possible, notwithstanding that some aspects of the Iquitos scene are perennially highly fluid and forever on the move. Two years later these processes have been repeated in the production of this Fifth Edition. Any inadvertent errors and omissions (which, as they say in the trade, are mine and mine alone) are regretted, and Web site ***www.johnlanebooks.com*** *is available for the receipt of any contributions or suggestions that readers may have. The site also provides details of how to purchase additional copies of* ***Iquitos – Gateway to Amazonia.***

John Lane London, England and Iquitos, Perú, 31st October, 2014

❖ ❖ ❖

The motocarro – symbol of Iquitos (all 25,000 of them)

Amazon Sunset

Index – Iquitos: Gateway to Amazonia

BRIG PROSPERO
1862

General overview of the river network – artistic impression

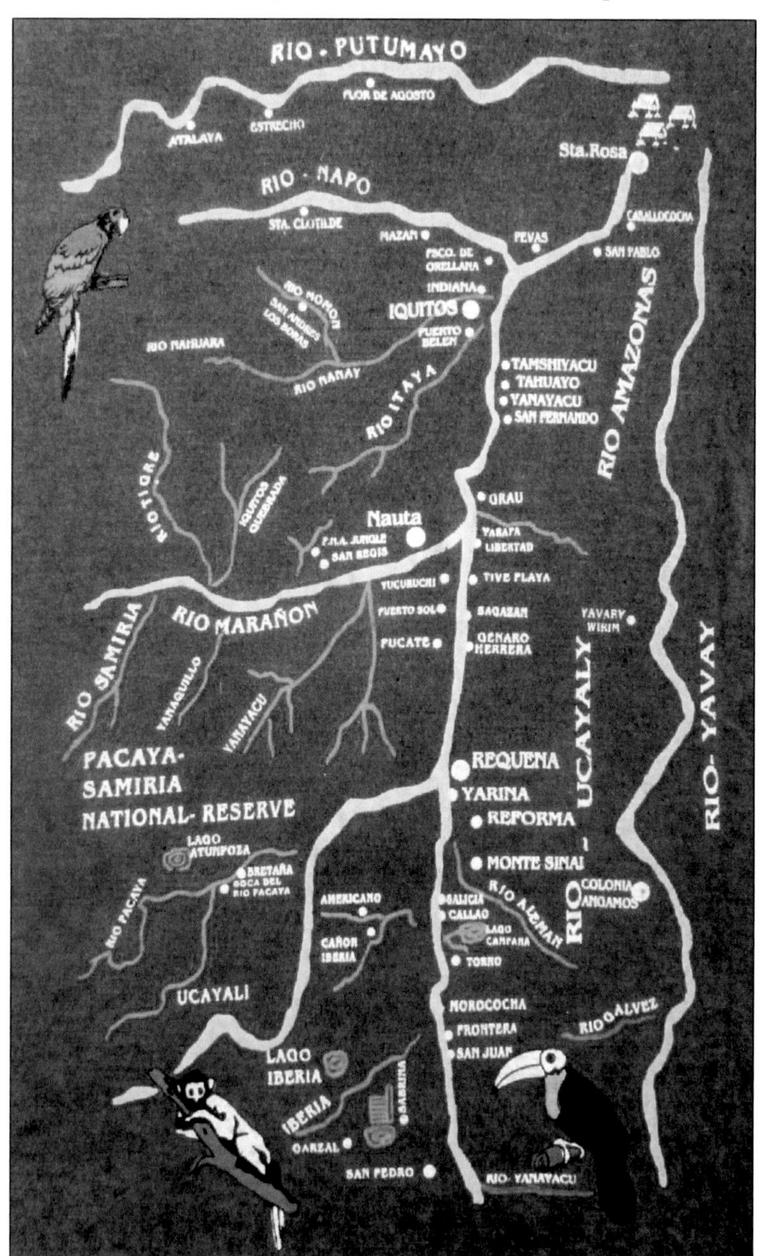